D0146075

The Origins of Walter Rauschenbusch's
Social Ethics

Walter Rauschenbusch, theologian of the social gospel (American Baptist Historical Society, Rochester, N.Y.)

The Origins
of Walter
Rauschenbusch's
Social Ethics

DONOVAN E. SMUCKER

McGill-Queen's University Press
Montreal & Kingston • London • Buffalo

© McGill-Queen's University Press 1994
ISBN 0-7735-1163-6

Legal deposit second quarter 1994
Bibliothèque nationale du Québec

Printed in the u.s. on acid-free paper

This book has been published with the help of a grant
from the Social Science Federation of Canada, using
funds provided by the Social Sciences and Humanities
Research Council of Canada. Funding has also been
received from Conrad Grebel College, University of
Waterloo.

Canadian Cataloguing in Publication Data

Smucker, Donovan E., 1915–
    The origins of Walter Rauschenbusch's social ethics
    Includes bibliographical references and index.
    ISBN 0-7735-1163-6
    1. Rauschenbusch, Walter, 1861–1918. 2. Social ethics.
    3. Church and social problems. I. Title.
    BX6495.R3558 1994   261.8'092   C94-900060-4

Typeset in Palatino 10/12
by Caractéra production graphique inc., Quebec City

To James Luther Adams
at Chicago and Harvard
Eminent Scholar of Dissent
Great Teacher
Encyclopaedic Bibliophile

Contents

Preface

James Luther Adams of Chicago and Harvard was my initial guide in researching the new paradigm for innovative social ethics in the analytic of Walter Rauschenbusch. It is surprising that three decades later, studies of the Rochester social prophet continue, starting with a new biography in 1988.

My own research was enhanced by the definitive collection of materials in the Rauschenbusch Family Papers at Colgate-Rochester Divinity School, Rochester, New York. The monumental library of D.R. Sharpe, Rauschenbusch's first secretary and first biographer, finally came to Rochester from California. Conrad Moehlman, Rauschenbusch's successor in church history, placed his *Walter Rauschenbusch Scrapbook with Commentary* in the Colgate-Rochester Divinity School library.

I also had access to the Leuschner papers, now in the archives of the Kaiser-Ramaker library of Sioux Falls College and Seminary in South Dakota. The Eden Theological Seminary of St Louis permitted me access to letters that August Rauschenbusch wrote to friends and colleagues in Germany and North America. Help was generously given by Rudolph Schaade of Elmhurst (Illinois) College, who served the German Baptist Church in New York City's Hell's Kitchen area, where Rauschenbusch was minister for eleven years.

The University of Chicago library, one of the great university libraries of North America, was a source of great assistance. More recently, the libraries of the University of Waterloo and Wilfrid Laurier University in Waterloo, Ontario ably assisted me in updating my research.

Along with my literary research I have had direct experience with modern urban industrialism. During university summers the American Friends Service Committee placed me in the Philadelphia textile area and the Pittsburgh coalfields to work with unemployed coal miners. While studying at Yale Divinity and Yale Graduate schools I was secretary of the New Haven Committee for the Unemployed. The next summer I was secretary of Yale Industrial Research in the Ford Motor Company's gigantic Dearborn, Michigan factory. This was followed by a trip in 1938 to the Stalinist Soviet Union to observe totalitarian communism attempting to solve the urban industrial problem. For nearly twenty years our family lived in Chicago, where racial and ethnic conflict and political corruption tested the social order to the breaking point.

After seven years of teaching in a church-related liberal arts college in an upper-class community, I was elected president of a black college in Mississippi during a clash of wills in a rigidly segregated society where the Ku Klux Klan was the *de facto* ruler. In recent decades in moderate Canada, I learned to adjust to outbursts of ethnic, linguistic, and cultural conflict between Quebec separatists and Anglo-federalists, the outcome of which is still being decided. Rauschenbusch's synthesis of realism and idealism, pessimism and optimism under Christian teaching seemed relevant.

My long series of experiences with urban industrialism is analogous to Rauschenbusch's encounter with the social pathology of New York City before the safety net of the welfare state was available. The lively development of social policy in New York by Henry George and Edward Bellamy persuaded Rauschenbusch to visit the United Kingdom and continental Europe. His move to Rochester took him to a city throbbing with social change. A new paradigm provided a new theory to interpret new social facts.

Walter Rauschenbusch was a bilingual, cross-cultural scholar always in touch with both Europe and North America. His *Theology of the Social Gospel* is still in print and his inspiration continues to this day.

I am grateful to David Kroeker for editorial assistance, Tryntje Miller of the Conrad Grebel College library for bibliographic help, David Switzer of Conrad Grebel and Arthur Shelly of Bluffton College for word processing, Joan Harcourt, Joan McGilvray, and Claire Gigantes of McGill-Queen's University Press for editorial assistance and encouragement, and the Social Science Federation of Canada for giving me a third grant with funds provided by the Social Science Research Council of Canada.

The Origins of Walter Rauschenbusch's Social Ethics

CHAPTER ONE

Introduction

It was Walter Rauschenbusch's destiny to be in places where vigorous historical forces had their origins. His family was sympathetic to the German liberal revolution of 1848. Walter and his father were the first American historians to encounter the left wing of the Reformation. The theological revolution led by Albrecht Ritschl in Europe and North America fuelled a rejection the School of traditional orthodoxy. In 1886, at the age of twenty-five, Walter felt ready for a pastorate in the tough immigrant working-class neighbourhood of New York City bearing the ominous name of Hell's Kitchen. He was ready to face the acids of industrialism and massive urbanism.

After plunging into his pastorate, however, he discovered that he was not prepared for the shock of nineteenth-century living conditions among the lower classes. Immediately he was called upon to conduct an unceasing number of funerals, a high proportion of which were for small children, the victims of poverty with its harvest of malnutrition, limited medical care, poor clothing, and inadequate housing. He encountered ghastly sanitary facilities, tainted food, dishonest labels on consumer goods, postponed marriages and prostitution, lack of compensation for industrial accidents, political corruption, gambling, and a feeling of "lostness" among European immigrants.

Although his education, travel, and reading gave him an unhackneyed outlook on matters of faith, Rauschenbusch was still a pietist. His religious orientation remained essentially inner, emotional, subjective, and individualist. Under his pastoral compassion and persuasive preaching, the people of Hell's Kitchen made decisions to accept Christ and to join the fellowship of the Church. The little Baptist congregation was a colony of heaven, a fellowship of love.

Nevertheless, the tough, intractable evil in their daily lives continued to crush even those who found new life in his parish.

Walter Rauschenbusch soon began to protest against specific acts of injustice. When an elderly lady in the parish was killed by a street car, his representations resulted in the reluctant payment of a few dollars in compensation to the family. When the need for such interventions multiplied, he soon developed a powerful conviction that the powers of darkness were not only organized but also institutionalized, legalized, and domesticated. He began to see that while deliverance starts with individuals, it cannot and must not end there. He saw that many leaders of unjust institutions were morally pure and personally pious. Yet the message of Amos and Jeremiah suggested to him that there was something bigger and more fundamental in the wrongdoing of a whole city and society.

Stimulated by Henry George's adoption of a reform platform in his campaign for mayor, the young Rauschenbusch wrote his first paper on social issues. Not for publication, the study was meant for his own personal clarity about the thrust of the world upon the people of his parish. He wrote in part, "Dear friends, there is a social question. No one can doubt it whose ears are ringing the wails of the mangled and the crushed, who are borne along on the pent-up torrent of human life. Woe to the man who stands afar and says: Peace, peace when there is no peace."

In this same pioneering paper he anticipated the objection of those who would point to New York as an exception. To this criticism he replied, "All the country is getting to be New York. Conditions in a great city are not abnormal, governed by different laws of development than the rest of the country. New York is only the most striking manifestation of laws operative elsewhere; it is the vortex of the whirlpool, but every drop of water in the circling mass is swung by the same forces that crowd resistless at the center. The question is not, where are we, but where are we going?"

Desperate for further light in the midst of Hell's Kitchen, Rauschenbusch sailed for Europe in 1891, a trip that would prove to be decisive in his spiritual development. In Berlin he studied New Testament and social policy, probing like a scientist on the trail of a new discovery. Was the Bible's message limited to people's inner life? Was Christianity only a preparation for heaven? It was questions such as these that he asked of European Bible scholars who were setting the pace for that era.

Moving on to England, his inquiry became more practical. He investigated the Salvation Army, the cooperative movement, the Fabian socialism of Beatrice and Sidney Webb. His discoveries convinced him that welfare and social service were not enough. The larger need was for far-reaching social change and reconstruction. He began to formulate the issues with a prophetic insight.

It was during this "sabbatical" year that the integrating centre of his social theology began to emerge. He described his discovery in these words: "In the Alps I have seen the summit of some great mountain come out of the clouds in the early morn and stand revealed in blazing purity. Its foot was still swathed in drifting mists, but I knew the mountain was there and my soul rejoiced in it. So Christ's conception of the Kingdom of God came to me as a new revelation. Here was the idea and purpose that had dominated the mind of the Master himself. All his teachings center about it. His life was given to it. His death was suffered for it. When a man has once seen that in the Gospels, he can never unsee it again."

Based on the insights of field trips and fresh biblical study leading to an orientation around the Kingdom of God, Rauschenbusch started the first draft of his book *Christianity and the Social Crisis* during his European sabbatical. Although it was sixteen years before the book was completed and published, its basic foundations were already clear. Before he had finished writing, Rauschenbusch left the New York pastorate after eleven fruitful years to teach at the Rochester Theological Seminary. Three times the blazing passion that moved his pen burned out in the middle of the manuscript. New convictions dawned so rapidly that each of the partly completed books was discarded as outmoded.

When the ink was dry on the final draft, the author was convinced of both its truth and its explosive power. Fully expecting to lose his job at the seminary, he mailed the manuscript to his publisher. D.R. Sharpe, his biographer, wrote that the appearance of *Christianity and the Social Crisis* "was like lightning striking a haystack." The book became the publishing sensation of 1907. Far from causing his dismissal, it established Walter Rauschenbusch as a national figure.

As a work of social protest, *Christianity and the Social Crisis* can be compared with such classics as Harriet Beecher Stowe's *Uncle Tom's Cabin*, Henry George's *Progress and Poverty*, and Edward Bellamy's *Looking Backward*. In the more formal religious field, its impact can be compared with Reinhold Niebuhr's *Moral Man and Immoral Society* and Martin Luther King's *Stride Toward Freedom*.

His first book was followed by a sequel in 1912, titled *Christianizing the Social Order*. A small volume that he called *Prayers of the Social Awakening* had an enormous effect on Protestant piety of the day by introducing social passion into the prayers and litanies of the Church. *Dare we be Christians?*, his commentary on 1 Corinthians 13, provides a sample of his own lyrical gifts, which approached St Paul's in eloquence. The contents of *The Freedom of Spiritual Religion* is typical of Rauschenbusch's work as a pamphleteer.

For the Right was the name of a Christian socialist paper founded by Rauschenbusch and two co-workers in 1889 during the former's pastorate at Hell's Kitchen. Although the periodical survived only two years, its editorials and fictionalized sketches provide excellent insight into the earliest days of his witness against the evils of society. Of particular interest today is his criticism of the unjust Czarist dictatorship in Russia along with a positive platform for overdue changes in Russian politics and economics. What a tragedy that his warning was not heeded! These early writings are sprightly and full of pathos, although less mature in theological understanding than his books. Nevertheless, the Rauschenbusch of *For the Right* was a prophet crying out in the wilderness of New York City, one who was only twenty years away from a real hearing when his first book was acclaimed and applauded[1].

More than eighty years after the publication of Rauschenbusch's first book, his writings are still being read, debated, and published. For many years the major line of interpretation was this: that he was a prophetic spirit of unquestionable moral integrity and catholicity of spirit. In the context of a burgeoning industrialism he awakened the Church to the evils of his day.

Removed from this context, his viewpoint is uncritically saturated in the thought forms of liberalism. For example, he declared that the more scientific life becomes, the closer it comes to Jesus. He stressed experience rather than dogma, reason rather than miracle, the historical Jesus rather than the mystical Christ, the Kingdom of God as a moral rather than a redemptive reality, the cross as vicarious suffering rather than as forensic atonement.

Moreover, he identified the Kingdom of God with the specific social hopes of his day in the Bull Moose politics of Teddy Roosevelt and the struggles of the working classes generally. Yet Martin Luther King is one of many who frankly confess that they "came early to Walter Rauschenbusch's *Christianity and the Social Crisis*, which left an indelible imprint on my thinking by giving me a theological basis for the social concern which had already grown up in me as a result of my early experience."[2] After this tribute King indicates some disagreement with Rauschenbusch, but always there is an endless procession of witnesses from 1907 to the present who find something vital in this remarkable man. What is it that makes his witness vital almost a century later? Consider three discoveries that are as relevant for our day as for his.

First, he discovered the social dimension of the Christian faith through the reality of the Kingdom of God. Christianity had been viewed as the sum total of individual decision. He rejected this unbiblical view by affirming the corporate emphasis of the Old Testament prophets, noting that they "conceived of their people as a gigantic personality which sinned as one and ought to repent as one."[3] The sins they denounced were national sins; the covenant was a national agreement. The New Testament also set forth the coming of the kingdom, something far greater than a loose association of individuals. It was nothing less than the thrust of God's will into the totality of human life.

While Rauschenbusch overestimated the role of human decision in the advancement of the Kingdom of God, he was essentially in line with the latest findings of biblical studies, which said God's basic intention was to find a people. The Old and then the New Covenant set forth the rise and fall and re-emergence of the people of God. This truth and its implications for the total life of humanity are Rauschenbusch's permanent contributions.

Second, Rauschenbusch discovered the social dimension of sin and evil. In his Yale lectures he boldly announced his intention to defend the doctrine of original sin as "one of the few attempts of individualistic theology to get a solidaristic view of its work." He proceeded to reconstruct his view of original sin in terms of social tradition. Borrowing from medicine, the Rochester prophet drew an analogy between syphilis, which is forced on the helpless foetus in the mother's womb, and "these hereditary social evils forced on the individual embedded in the womb of society and drawing ideas, moral standards, and spiritual ideals from the general life of the social body."[4]

Rauschenbusch elaborated these discoveries into an impressive social doctrine informed by religious insight. Human solidarity takes wrongdoing and builds it into injustice, which gains momentum with each generation. The danger is not from a mere accumulation of wrongdoing. Poisoned institutions develop a superpersonal quality. The ugly devils of injustice demand allegiance, an idea that is similar to Paul Tillich's emphasis on the demonic element in history. These devilish superpersonal institutions project ideology for their defence, justification, and idealization. Rauschenbusch's writings were a generation ahead of their time in pointing to the totalitarianism inherent in large segments of Western culture.

Third, the Hell's Kitchen pastor restored the element of creative conflict within history because he observed the fundamental struggle between the Kingdom of God and the kingdom of evil. The struggle for human life does not take place in the hush of the cathedral with dimly lit tapers and wisps of smoke rising from the altars; nor is it found in the glowing individual heart of a happy Christian singing in a barren chapel. The showdown comes within society, where the kingdom of evil fights for victory over human organizations that have an idolatrous image of personal beings demanding affection and obedience. Even though he never caught up with Albert Schweitzer's exciting new insights into Christ's teaching on the Kingdom of God, Rauschenbusch recovered a rugged view of history that was superior to a rosy romanticism and a soft pietism.

Against this background the Church faces a crucial decision. Its vocation was to be the medium through which the kingdom comes and to face the living God working through dynamic social movements, regardless of any explicit denial of the Christian faith in those movements. Yet Rauschenbusch loved the Church and longed to see it become the main seedplot for democratic institutions. When the Church is a disciplined, democratic, voluntary fellowship it creates similar institutions in society at large. Likewise, when it is autocratic and repressive it spawns autocratic cultural patterns that frustrate the kingdom. Indeed, the social-gospel movement was quick to label the Church as anti-Christian when it was not heralding this socially defined Kingdom of God. Rauschenbusch was frank in drawing the Church's line of development from the apostolic fellowship to the medieval sectarians to the Anabaptists of the Reformation and, finally, to the Church envisaged by the social gospel.

These insights stand as a challenge to twentieth and twenty-first-century Christians. Many of Rauschenbusch's affirmations have survived merciless criticism. The blend of realism and hope, social insight and faith, divine intention and human decision is worthy of study in the perennial quest for the Christian answer to the challenge of the world and its culture.

Rauschenbusch's pilgrimage from pietism to Hell's Kitchen to social activism in Rochester remains an enigma until one understands the complexity of his mature social ethic. To understand his definitive formulation of the social gospel, it is necessary to inquire into his appropriation and selection of materials from four basic influences: pietism, sectarianism, liberalism, and transformationism – the tributaries that poured into the mainstream of Christian social ethics. The development of the social gospel will be presented here in its rich historical context in order to account for the fruition and subsequent regrowth of the social gospel in our own day.

The investigation of Rauschenbusch's milieu will reveal the hitherto neglected role of sectarianism in his ethics. The interaction of this motif with the others explains the true role of liberalism. With this in mind, we will discover why there were tensions and contradictions in the system. An examination of the books, thinkers, leaders, movements, and forces that moulded him will help broaden our knowledge of the background and actual character of social Christianity as it gained maximum influence in the United States.

The term pietism is used here to mean the Protestant reaction against orthodox intellectualism and formalism in favour of a personal, devotional, subjective, individualist, conversionist evangelicalism that stresses vital religious experience. The pietist movement as understood here stems from the seventeenth century.

Sectarianism is used to signify a particular view of the Church as a voluntary, intentional, committed, suffering, laity-centred fellowship living in tension with contemporary culture. Sectarian Christianity also stresses discipleship, love, and ethical reality rather than polity, the sacraments, or theological formulation. In addition, sectarianism implies the separation of church and state and affirms the demand for religious liberty.

By liberalism I mean the rationalistic movement of the eighteenth century that led to a revolt against authoritarianism in both religion and secular culture. The term has two connotations, one theological and the other cultural. Theological liberalism seeks to minimize the supernatural and sacramental elements of Christianity; cultural liberalism seeks to curb unethical forces in society.

Transformationism, a term borrowed from H. Richard Niebuhr, is meant to convey a positive and hopeful attitude towards culture, based upon the oneness of creation and atonement. Originally, it emphasized the earthly hope of transforming ruthless economic and social systems through the development of Christian socialism as a manifestation of the Kingdom of God.

These four influences provide the interpretive framework for Rauschenbusch's creative response to modern industrialism prior to the rise of the welfare state.

CHAPTER TWO

Chronological Development

In order to understand the chronological development of Walter Rauschenbusch's thought, one must keep in mind the four influences already defined: pietism, sectarianism, liberalism, and transformationism. All four were operative almost from the beginning of his life, however unevenly. Pietism and Anabaptism exerted a strong influence in the early days, while liberalism and transformationism gained later. All four influences were present also, in varying degrees, in the background of his father, August Rauschenbusch. The interaction of these factors is germane to the American careers of both father and son, for it played a vital role in each period of the son's life: his childhood, youth, the New York pastorate, and his Rochester teaching ministry. In each period there were major experiences that shaped his outlook on Christian social ethics.

I consider first the life and works of the father, August. In his 1954 presidential address to the American Society of Church History, Carl E. Schneider described the elder Rauschenbusch as an unusually vital and dynamic man who reflected religious and cultural tensions within and between German and American movements of the day.[1] What emerges most clearly from Schneider's study of August Rauschenbusch is the man's complexity. With five generations of Lutheran pastors behind him, one is tempted to see in August a simple continuation of Augsburg confessionalism, or a singular thrust of the powerful movement that affected Europe, Great Britain, and America. Yet this tendency to oversimplify must be set aside, as Schneider does convincingly even while omitting one major factor in the development of the elder Rauschenbusch, namely, his encounter with the Anabaptists and the Mennonites.

This factor complicates the story considerably, adding a whole new dimension. In a biography of his father, Walter Rauschenbusch documents his deep interest in sectarian research.[2] The most revealing indication of this interest was a trip to Germany made in 1868–69 after August's appointment to the faculty of the German Baptist seminary in Rochester. During this trip, whose chief purpose was to gather material for a history of the Anabaptist movement, August Rauschenbusch visited Waldshut, a town in lower Austria where Balthasar Hubmaier had preached and where the Peasants' Revolt of 1524–25 had broken out. He also visited the key universities of Freiburg, Zurich, and Basel, searching for Waldensian and Anabaptist literature. With true scholarly concern for primary sources, he made copies of original documents and other rare publications. Furthermore, August sought out scholars who could help him to understand the left wing of the Reformation: a learned Greek priest in Waldshut, several Catholic professors at Ulm, Otto Schreiber, professor at Freiburg, and, above all, C.A. Cornelius of Munich, the leading scholar of radical Protestantism.

Cornelius had already published (during the years 1855–60) a sourcebook on the Anabaptists titled *Geschichte des Münsterischen Aufruhrs in drei Büchern*. It was from this work that the younger Rauschenbusch would later translate a letter written by Conrad Grebel, pioneer of the Swiss left wing of the sixteenth-century Reformation, to his friends at Zurich.[3]

The elder Rauschenbusch's efforts in social research were so well known that the definitive encyclopaedia of German sectarianism, *Mennonitisches Lexikon*, published a biographical essay on his work.[4]

It is for these reasons that Carl Schneider might have added another dimension to the already complex list of influences operating on the elder Rauschenbusch as a representative type. That dimension is sectarianism. Son Walter thus represented a second-generation orientation in sectarian research and outlook, a factor that constituted one of the foundations for his career as an ethical prophet and church historian. Chapter 3 documents the role of radical Protestantism in his outlook.

FAMILY HERITAGE

In addition to the cultural and theological impact of the father on the son, one must consider the rich family heritage of educational excellence and intellectual distinction. That the father attended the universities of Berlin and Bonn was typical of this keen German *Freundschaft*. The continental emphasis on languages led to his mastery of Latin at age six, French at seven, and Greek at eight. At the beginning of his teens he added English and Hebrew to the list of languages a prospective candidate had to master before being admitted to the great universities of nineteenth-century Germany. When August Rauschenbusch left home at eighteen to attend university in Berlin, he was soundly prepared in the grand tradition of cultured middle-class families in Europe.

This cultural legacy from his father made it impossible for Walter Rauschenbusch to fall into the pattern of anti-intellectualism that captured the citadels of pietism. What is more, the solid classical education that permitted young Walter to spend ten years in Europe – mainly in German educational institutions – also opened the doors to the rationalism of the nineteenth century.

A final family contribution was political liberalism. August Rauschenbusch came to America in 1846, just two years before the ill-fated German revolution of 1848. He was deeply moved by the democratic fervour of the university students of his native Germany. His brother Wilhelm sacrificed professional status to defend a hundred students arrested for political zeal.

Walter Rauschenbusch inherited the moral earnestness of pietism, the ethical radicalism of sectarianism, the political ethics of the democratic enthusiasm of 1848, and the rationalistic idealism and culture of the Enlightenment as it influenced a family of gifted, learned ministers endowed with linguistic facility and accustomed to reflective thought, extensive travel, and literary expression. Few notable figures come to their moment of historical destiny so richly prepared. Walter Rauschenbusch was not a mutation. His life was the climax and fruition of forces that had already germinated in his father and were at work in his forebears over four generations.

A simple outline will help to show the parallel development of Walter Rauschenbusch and the social gospel.[5]

Rauschenbusch	Christian Social Ethics
1 Childhood: 1861–79 Education up to gymnasium	1 Birth of social Christianity 1865–80
2 Youth: 1879–86 Gymnasium through seminary	2 A youthful movement: 1880–90
3 New York pastorate: 1886–97, interrupted by European trip, 1891–92	3 The social gospel comes of age: 1890–1900
4 Rochester teaching and intensive social-ethics leadership: 1897–1918	4 Maturity and recognition: 1900–18

In using Hopkins's outline, it is not necessary to accept his assumption that social concern arose in the latter half of the nineteenth century. This approach obviously ignores the vigorous social concern of the Puritans as early as the seventeenth century. Yet his book reveals the remarkable relationship between Rauschenbusch's career and the general development of the social message of the Protestant churches in the nineteenth and early twentieth centuries. At the same time, it also makes clear that his real impact came during the years of "maturity and recognition" (1900–15). Indeed, in his *Christianizing the Social Order*, Rauschenbusch pays tribute to Washington Gladden, Josiah Strong, and Richard T. Ely as the pioneers of social thought, all of whom preceded him by a quarter of a century. It is significant that Rauschenbusch's three greatest books were written in 1907 (*Christianity and the Social Crisis*), 1912 (*Christianizing the Social Order*), and 1917 (*A Theology for the Social Gospel*). I turn now to examine crucial developments in the four phases of the life of Walter Rauschenbusch.

CHILDHOOD

The birth of Walter Rauschenbusch was interpreted by his family in pietistic terms. The new baby was under damnation but was a candidate for grace. The family conducted regular worship and Bible study. The children were prepared for a crisis conversion experience, which came to Walter at the age of seventeen. Even after he had passed beyond the theological framework in which his conversion took place, he cherished it as a deeply moving experience. Pietism came to him through both the American and German streams. In America the family of August Rauschenbusch was initially part of the German Baptist fellowship and the wider fellowship of German pietists, including the *Kirchenverein des Westens*, in which the Niebuhrs were nurtured. The latter group represented the impact of the Basel mission, the outreach of European pietism to German immigrants in the United States of America.

In 1865 Walter Rauschenbusch, a child of three, went with his mother and siblings to Germany for four years. His childhood experiences in Germany not only confirmed the American pietism he knew but also laid the foundation (in travel, education, and aesthetics) for his cultural sophistication, which was essentially unpietistic. In his most impressionable years, young Walter had a delightful experience of European travel and study.

Towards the latter part of this visit to Germany, Walter's father joined the family in order to complete some projects of his own and return to America with his wife and children. Walter was aware that his father was doing research on the sectarians; he recorded the following when he was only seven years old:

In July Father went to South Germany and Switzerland partly to study up the history of the Baptists, which he then meant to write some time ... When our vacation came, in August, we joined Father in the Black Forest. We stayed at a simple bathing beach called Freiers Beach, and had a happy time there. We made excursions, climbed the mountains, played by the brooks, and I hunted butterflies with a net, after the fashion of little German boys. I caught my first fish in the brook with my hand. Later we made a tour on foot with Father to the Donau Springs beyond Donau-Eachingen.[6]

Once back in the United States, Walter entered Pfafflin's private school in Rochester. He took the classical curriculum, soon showing unusual linguistic gifts. His two closest friends were not pietists; in fact, one of them, Ed Hanna, later became the Roman Catholic archbishop of San Francisco. During these years, August Rauschenbusch observed liberal tendencies in his son and threatened to expel him from Sunday school because he tended to exercise independent judgment in religious thought.[7]

YOUTH AND TRAINING

Throughout young Rauschenbusch's high-school years the influence of pietism, sectarianism, and idealism was strong, pietism being the dominant force. With regard to liberal idealism, the beginning of his life followed the pattern of an old-line, upper-class American family of the eastern seaboard, with stress on classical education, travel, and cultural pleasures. Sheer delight in the phenomena of nature, the study of languages, and the stimulus of travel with a circle of friends well outside the strictly pietist conventicle – all of these helped to lay the foundation for a liberal outlook on life, an outlook quite in contrast to the constricted cultural viewpoint of pietism.

The only element missing from Walter's youth was the Calvinist and Catholic transformationist vision. Implicit in some of these other experiences were convictions essential to this outlook: the quest for religious reality in pietism, the awareness of his father's search for Anabaptist materials, the liberal cultural development with its love of beauty (during his New York pastorate he would express shock at the ugliness and bleak emptiness of industrial capitalism). Explicit transformationist influences were to come later.

Upon completing classical grade school and high school in outstanding private schools and one year of public school, Walter went to Germany for what was essentially his college education. Any serious analysis of his development must take cognizance of the fact that his liberal-arts training was fundamentally in the context of late nineteenth century German university life. In 1879 he entered the Evangelical Gymnasium at Gütersloh in Westphalia, where the major offering was immersion in classical, biblical, and modern languages. He mastered these, writing many letters to his parents in English, German (script), Greek, and Latin. He showed early distinction in scholarship, rising to the top of his class: *Primus Omnium*.

At the same time the young lad had many stimulating travel experiences and contacts of the most sophisticated kind with artists, poets, writers, and scholars. He father considered travel one of the chief sources of his son's education and kept him supplied with money for this purpose. The young student visited Leipzig, Jena, Berlin, Bonn, Cologne, and many other cities. He read Plato, Sophocles, and Norse mythology. All in all, it proved to be a tremendous awakening.

After finishing his studies in Gütersloh in 1883, Walter entered the University of Berlin, where he studied under Mommsen, Curtius, and other leading figures of the time. He was moved by the art treasures in Berlin and Dresden. Indeed, his interest in art was serious and highly developed. His letters during this phase breathe the spirit of the Renaissance and the Enlightenment. He bubbled over with the hedonistic pleasures of art, travel, study, and conversation.

Walter returned home by way of England, stopping at London, Oxford, and Liverpool. Soon after his return he registered simultaneously for the senior year at the University of Rochester and the junior year at the seminary. In addition, he signed up for extra courses in everything from Septuagint Greek to zoology. With his brilliant educational background, this double or even triple assignment was quite possible. In due time he received his bachelor-of-arts degree from Rochester (1884), a diploma from the German department (1885), and his bachelor of divinity from the English seminary, later Colgate-Rochester (1886).

At the seminary, Walter Rauschenbusch studied under his father, doing systematic research in the left-wing groups of the Reformation. It was during his seminary career that he experienced his second major religious development. While in Germany in 1882, he underwent his conversion and decided to enter the ministry. What may be called his discipleship began in 1886. After his conversion he had resolved to "preach and save souls." With the experience of discipleship, he saw life in a new dimension.

"I wanted to do hard work for God," he said later about his seminary experience. "Indeed, one of the great thoughts that came upon me was that I ought to follow Jesus Christ in my personal life and die over again his death. I felt that every Christian ought to participate in the dying of the Lord Jesus Christ, and in that way help to redeem humanity, and it was that thought that gave my life its fundamental direction in the doing of Christian work."[8]

Both Walter Rauschenbusch and his biographer, Dores Sharpe, believed that this experience pointed him towards larger social concerns. It moved him out from the soul-massaging subjectivism of pietism into the more historical, more objective, more radical aspects of discipleship – a discipleship integrated with liberalism and transformationism. It was the Rauschenbusch formula for the social gospel.

During the American phase of his education, Rauschenbusch had an important summer pastorate in Louisville, Kentucky (1884–85). It was during these two summer pastorates that pietism, sectarian discipleship, and liberalism were thoroughly integrated in his mind. And it was this basic trilogy that he was to take to New York's Hell's Kitchen, where he would discover the need for transformation as well as for some of the more radical aspects of sectarianism.

After his first summer in Louisville, he was ready to abandon his hopes of becoming an effective literary theologian and concentrate on being a pastor "powerful with men, preaching to them Christ as the man in whom their affections and energies can find the satisfaction for which mankind is groaning."[9] By the end of the second summer he displayed an interesting combination of sobriety, discipleship, and liberal independence:

Unselfishness and self-sacrifice seem to me the idea of Christ's life and therefore the expression of God's character. In proportion as they become dominant facts of our own life, we are conformed to his image. I tell you I am just beginning to believe in the Gospel of the Lord Jesus Christ, not exactly in the shape in which the average person proclaims it as the infallible truth of the Most High, but in a shape that suits my needs, that I have gradually constructed for myself in studying the person and teaching of Christ, and which is still in rapid progress of construction. I don't believe that believing any doctrine will do a man any good except so far as it is translated into life. I don't believe that if a man believes in the vicarious death of Christ that death will be imputed to him; how can it? But if he begins to live a Christ-like life, he will find that though there is no Cross for him to be nailed to, he will die piecemeal by self-sacrifice just as Christ did even before his crucifixion, and then he is at one with Christ and placed by God into the same category.[10]

NEW YORK PASTORATE

It was precisely this outlook that caused Walter Rauschenbusch to reject an offer to become head of a seminary in India under the

American Baptist Foreign Mission Society. His own professor of Old Testament studies objected to his views on the Bible. He was refused a prominent pulpit in Springfield, Illinois. It was because of these repudiations that he went to Hell's Kitchen in New York City. Here he found the anvil on which he hammered out his ultimate faith.

The pathologies of the American industrial-urban capitalism of the nineteenth century would have tested the resilience of any position. No one could speak glibly in the face of the evil inherent in the city's complex institutional patterns. This was particularly so for a sensitive, honest man like Walter Rauschenbusch. Yet it is false to assume that the human scene in Hell's Kitchen in 1886 automatically brought about changes in his patterns of thought and behaviour. There were other pietists in New York. Most of them were not fundamentally changed. The fact is that Rauschenbusch had been changed before coming to New York by the unique trilogy of influences already traced.

The historical situation during his pastorate added fuel to the fires of change. The major interpretive responses to this historical situation were liberalized transformationism as exemplified by Henry George and Edward Bellamy and the liberalized sectarianism of Richard Heath. It is debatable whether Henry George was more a child of the Enlightenment than of American Puritan evangelicalism. The content of what he said was strongly liberal, and its dynamic stemmed from distinctly religious roots. Richard Heath was an English Baptist in touch with European sectarianism in both scholarly and functional terms. Rauschenbusch's background permitted him to accept much of the teaching of George and Heath as a proper interpretation of the radical reality of the Kingdom of God.

In 1891 the young pastor of Hell's Kitchen did a very characteristic and understandable thing. After trying desperately to put the pieces together in the midst of the New York situation, he dropped everything and went to Europe for nine months. As a pietist he might have relied solely on prayer for guidance. As a multicultural German-American, a child of Continental sectarianism and the Enlightenment, and a stepchild of transformationism, he needed to probe further into the meaning of capitalism and industrialism. This rich array of basic forces in Western culture called for an encounter with the European mind. Thus, on 14 March 1891 he sailed for Europe on his third trip abroad. He was thirty years old and approaching the final synthesis of his intellectual development.

On the Continent he took some time to study the New Testament and sociology in Berlin. It was during this time that the Kingdom of God concept dawned on him with powerful and decisive effect, integrating what was already in his experience. It was here that

Rauschenbusch acquired an organizing principle for his total orientation. In addition, he investigated the Salvation Army, the cooperative movement, and Fabian socialism in England. The English
investigation under the tutelage of Beatrice and Sidney Webb convinced him that the welfare-relief service approach was not enough.
His study of Fabian socialism pointed him in the direction of far-
reaching social change and reconstruction.

It is difficult to tell exactly to what extent he encountered Christian
socialism, either British or Continental, on this trip. There is some
circumstantial evidence indicating that he may have discovered the
writings of F.D. Maurice and Charles Kingsley, since both are mentioned in his book *Christianity and the Social Crisis*, the first draft of
which was prepared during this trip. However, since the two British
authors antedated Rauschenbusch by roughly fifty years, and since
Leonhard Ragaz and Herman Kutter of Switzerland were essentially
contemporaries, it appears more likely that he discovered continental
Christian socialism on his last trip to Europe in 1907–08.

Walter Rauschenbusch returned to his New York parish on 24
December 1891 and stayed for six more years. During this time,
Leighton Williams and Nathaniel Schmidt replaced Munson Ford
and Ed Hanna as his closest friends. These exponents of the social
gospel collaborated with him on the provocative publication "For the
Right" and helped him organize a conventicle of social concern, the
Brotherhood of the Kingdom. The Brotherhood was sectarian in that
each member was to "exemplify obedience to the ethics of Jesus in
his personal life" and to "propagate the thought of Jesus to the limits
of his ability in private conversation, by correspondence, and through
pulpit, platform and press."[11] Rauschenbusch publicly defended
Nathaniel Schmidt when the latter was rejected from Hamilton Seminary on the Colgate University campus on charges of heresy. He
argued that a creedless denomination devoted to the Bible must grant
the new liberal wing of the Baptist church the same right to speak
as the conservatives.

The significant point in this chronicle is that the Walter Rauschenbusch who went to Rochester as a seminary teacher in 1897 had
reached final ground in his position. During his Manhattan pastorate
he had seen the necessity of transforming the entire social order
along the Christian pattern – a mixture of Puritan and sectarian ideas
– and of moving into a more aggressive mode. In ten years he had
fully prepared himself for his definitive formulation of the social
gospel. Pietism, sectarianism, liberalism, and transformationist Calvinism and Catholicism were all present in his experience. Teaching,
writing, and extensive involvement in the social life of Rochester and
social movements outside the city would be his next frontier.

ROCHESTER YEARS

From one vantage point the loss of a rugged activist context with his removal from New York was a great handicap for Walter Rauschenbusch. But while Rochester was less challenging than New York City, it was a stimulating community where the social gospel had been welcomed quite early, providing a ready outlet for his concerns. There were liberal movements, labour forums, socialist groups, reform organizations, and institutional churches. Above all, he had many outlets for lecturing, which contributed to the refinement and clarification of his social ethics. Genuine freedom prevailed; newspapers gave generous coverage to his speeches.

Rauschenbusch's career in Rochester was divided into two parts. From 1897–1902, he was connected with the German department of the seminary, teaching the New Testament as well as government, zoology, English, and natural sciences. This led to the publication of *Die politische Verfassung unseres Landes*, a handbook on American government for German-Americans. The second phase began in 1902 when he became professor of church history at Rochester Theological Seminary, where all courses were taught in English.

During his teaching career, Rauschenbusch achieved great distinction and effectiveness. It was during this phase of his life that he delineated the role of the Anabaptists and, to some extent, the Puritans. He made frequent reference to left-wing Protestantism in his lectures, according to former students. His knowledge of left-wing materials seemed to go well beyond that found in professional historical circles, since a working knowledge of the Anabaptists was not available to most American historians until considerably later.

Moreover, he travelled widely, filling four major lectureships and accepting many lesser engagements. He worked actively in the Baptist congresses and in the Federal Council of Churches, which he had helped to found in 1908. However, it was his books that catapulted Walter Rauschenbusch to fame. Upon publication of his first book, he went to Europe – good, familiar, hospitable Europe – to await with trepidation the expected attack. But the response was friendly, if not highly enthusiastic.

Rauschenbusch was an excellent stylist in both German and English. Among modern English-language writers on ethics, only John Bennett can be compared to him. Vida Scudder noted his exceptional command of sardonic speech. D.R. Sharpe lauded his mastery of the short sentence and his whimsical use of metaphor. Of course, his education was far superior to that of most Americans. Out of this background came well-documented books,[12] a feeling for history, a fearless desire to know the truth, and a general thoroughness. In the spirit of the Enlightenment, he had a tendency towards syncretism and a loose way with theological language, something that made it easy for him to telescope highly dissimilar concepts.

The latter part of Walter Rauschenbusch's life was tragic and sombre. He died in 1918, just as World War I ended. These years were difficult for many reasons. In the anti-German hysteria that swept over America, everything from Wagnerian opera to German ancestry was suspect. A man named Rauschenbusch who had spent ten years of his life in Germany and was known to be deeply attached to German culture was a natural target for superpatriots. To make matters worse, he had pacifist tendencies that led to his joining the Fellowship of Reconciliation, a Christian pacifist organization. Furthermore, he was an internationalist, hardly capable of chauvinistic hysteria.

With his friends rejecting him and with history working against him, he fell from widespread popularity. In grim Lincolnesque style he remarked, "Since 1914 the world is full of hate, and I cannot expect to be happy in my lifetime." All of this culminated in the discovery that he had terminal cancer. He died at Johns Hopkins Hospital in Baltimore in May 1918 at the age of fifty-seven.

Had he lived longer, Walter Rauschenbusch would undoubtedly have played an important role in the chastened post-war era. It was his lot to live between the Civil War and World War I, and in this parenthesis of wars there was more suffering than he could have anticipated. In spite of the forces of history, he made a major contribution to the quest for a profound social ethic. Posthumously, W. Rauschenbusch became a major mentor of Martin Luther King.

CHAPTER THREE

The Influence of Pietism

The emphasis on Walter Rauschenbusch's role as an evangelical has obscured the more clear-cut and identifiable influence of pietism upon his character and work. It was through his father that he was influenced by pietism, one of the most powerful post-Reformation Christian movements. In one way evangelicalism and pietism are synonymous: in both, the emphasis is on regeneration, devotional exercises, and evangelism. In a number of countries, however, the term "evangelical" is used to distinguish Protestants from Catholics. In England it tends to be synonymous with Low Church. In North America, many fundamentalists use it as a less pejorative term for fundamentalism. Others equate it with the Great Awakening in eighteenth-century America.

It seems less confusing, therefore, to use the term "pietism" in connection with the origins of Rauschenbusch's social ethics. As noted above, pietism was a distinct movement, starting in Germany in the seventeenth century and subsequently exerting great power in England and America. It rejected orthodox Lutheran formalism in favour of a personal, devotional, subjective, individualistic, conversionist pattern of Christianity. Its aims were vital religious experience and upright conduct.

Because Rauschenbusch's pietism was moderated during his New York City pastorate, one is tempted to write it off as being of little consequence to his work. While this might be the case in terms of theological and ethical content, the picture changes when his attitudes and perspectives are taken into account. Some of the basic origins of Rauschenbusch's ethics are to be found in this legacy of pietism; there is a close affinity between pietism and liberalism, and between pietism and sectarianism. Out of his Anabaptist research grew his pluralism, discipleship, and emphasis on experiential Christianity. His interest in welfare work and his passion for political liberty are pietism's immediate products, as Ritschl points out in his *Geschichte des Pietismus*, where he discusses the peculiar qualities of the Württemberg pietism that nurtured August Rauschenbusch.

Of the four methods of demonstrating origins – family, *Zeitgeist*, self-image, and books – it is clear that the family and *Zeitgeist* are the most influential. The pietist pilgrimage of Rauschenbusch's father climaxed in his migration to America in 1846 at the age of thirty and his entrance into the Baptist church ten years later. This journey of faith reflects the phase of German *Zeitgeist* in which Enlightenment rationalism was in serious conflict with both the old orthodoxy and the new pietism. After a long struggle with orthodoxy and rationalism, the elder Rauschenbusch emerged a convinced pietist. A considerable part of the son's ethics thus stemmed from the theological and cultural milieu of nineteenth-century Germany.

Walter Rauschenbusch was particularly conscious of himself as a pietist in his earlier years. He regarded his own conversion in pietistic terms, and through membership in the German Baptist church, his pietism was sustained at its height up to the days of his shift to the English-speaking Rochester seminary. Some of his feel for the kingdom motif emerged from this background.

Evidence for pietist influence is very sparse in Rauschenbusch's writings. His early education was classical and sophisticated rather than devotional. His early German Baptist writings in the *Jugend Herold* were simple biblical expositions without footnotes. As a mature writer he no longer operated within the literary context of pietism. The demonstration of origins, therefore, rests primarily in the impact of his family as it reflected an aspect of the German *Zeitgeist*.

The most authoritative study on the subject is that of Carl E. Schneider of the Eden Theological Seminary. In his 1954 presidential paper to the American Church History Society entitled "The Americanization of August Rauschenbusch," he outlines the role of pietism in relation to the other powerful movements that influenced the elder Rauschenbusch. Schneider based his paper on twenty-two hitherto unavailable letters written by August Rauschenbusch during the crucial American years from 1845–54. Now housed in the Eden Theological Seminary archives, the letters were discovered by Schneider in the archives of the Rhenish Missionary Institute in Wuppertal-Barmen, Germany.

Schneider describes the elder Rauschenbusch as a representative type, "a person who in an unusually vital and dynamic way reflected religious and cultural tensions within and between German and

American movements of the day. We begin with a Rauschenbusch struggling through the phenomenal gamut of nineteenth-century German rationalism, romanticism, orthodoxy, confessionalism, ecclesiasticism, and emerging from this conflict, a radical Pietist."[1] He continues the story with "a Rauschenbusch projected into the maze of nineteenth-century American Christianity bearing on it the earmarks of the Puritan heritage." His subject emerges "from this interpretation of German and American traditions with a sense of freedom and emancipation," which Schneider refers to as August Rauschenbusch's "Americanization."

Here is a well-documented picture of August Rauschenbusch through four phases: rationalist, pietist, pietist-Puritan, and Baptist. His emergence into a radical pietism took place in 1834 towards the end of his theological studies at the University of Berlin. The usual stereotypes of pietism were present: a black and white world, a sharp sense of being lost, the rejection of worldly institutions such as art and the theatre, a demand for conscious conversion, and high standards for church membership beyond catechism and confirmation. All this, of course, took place in a subjectivist experiential context. For example, an early expression of social concern was the father's part in establishing a temperance society in Altena, in the Prussian province of Westphalia, where he was the sixth in a direct line of Lutheran pastors with pietist leanings.

MISSION TO AMERICA

August Rauschenbusch regarded his decision to emigrate to America as the result of a revelation of God's will. Moreover, he insisted that the Kingdom of God took primacy over any ecclesiastical loyalties. This posed the question who would sponsor his trip. Once again the pietist context of his outlook on life became evident. He applied to the Langenberg Society, a product of Württemberg pietism. It may be recalled that this centre of pietism was developed by Philipp Spener into a movement that had very little political or ecclesiastical opposition; in addition, the Württemberger pietists were friendly to the Moravians. Thus, it was a biblicist and interconfessional pietism that sent him to America.

August Rauschenbusch arrived in the United States of America in 1846, just two years before the immigration of the famous band of politically liberal German refugees headed by Carl Schurz, the so-called Forty-Eighters. The spectre of American sectarianism greeted him upon arrival. After an unhappy encounter with the Methodists, he discovered the American Home Missionary Society, a semi-

Presbyterian/Congregational society for reaching Germans in the West. He also worked with the American Tract Society.

American activism was tested from the beginning. In January of 1846 he wrote to W. Coleman in Langenberg, "You know that in America all activity including the spiritual proceeds as though driven by steam ... Here is no place for solitary life or studies."[2] His inter-denominational spirit is revealed in a letter to Germany of 22 October 1846: "God has given me a free evangelical spirit to seek and to find his children under all sorts of names and forms. I've brought them with me from Germany and propose to maintain it here to do my part to reduce the walls of division between the various denominations or parties that may finally break down."[3]

A Son is Born

After itinerating for the American Home Missionary Society, Rauschenbusch went to Mt Sterling, Missouri. There he ministered in the Baptist church, which he believed had a deeper comprehension than other denominations of the Kingdom of God. His first son was born there on 24 April 1857, and he wrote this pietistic description of the event:

I know you will be happy to hear the news on April 24th that there was born to my wife a strong boy. Mother and child are thus far getting along very well.

You may well imagine that we look upon this son as a welcome and worthy gift from God. If you would show me a kindness, then pray (not often, not daily, not ceaselessly, no, pray) only once that God might bless my son, who has inherited nothing from me but sin, death and damnation, and allow him to inherit life and salvation in Christ; so that he might become a firebrand, toward which he already has all the tendencies, thanks to his parents, but a child of grace and an heir of heaven, and if it pleases God, may he in his day become a fruitful representative of truth in this false and untruthful world.[4]

The emphasis upon conversion was already present, together with an ecumenical spirit and a practical ethical concern. The first record book at Mt Sterling affirms a decision by the congregation and its pastor that "No slaveholder can ever be a member or be a Communicant of this church."[5]

According to this ruling, being against slavery became a test of membership. The Baptist minister became eloquent in his opposition to slavery, urging Germans to come to Missouri because this would lessen the possibility of slavery. His pietism thus did not deter him from entering into the greatest moral and political controversy of nineteenth-century America. Perhaps this objective ethical dimension of the family background was a latent factor in the eclipse of the simple subjective Christianity after Walter Rauschenbusch's move to New York.

Speaking of August Rauschenbusch, President A.H. Strong of the Rochester Theological Seminary said he was "a pietist of the biblical sort" who "would have become a Puritan of the most rigid kind had he lived in those days. What he did he did well. It was of the utmost importance that the German Baptist churches came under the influence of such a man. He was a great man of God."[6]

Walter Rauschenbusch's pietist legacy from his father included at least the following elements: a rejection of the ecclesiastical *status quo* in the state churches of Germany as well as a rejection of rationalism in favour of a pietism that led to a missionary assignment in America under interdenominational, pietist auspices (eventually leading August Rauschenbusch into a fully pietistic denomination – the German Baptists of North America); partial rejection of confessional dogmatism in favour of religious experience through conscious conversion; criticism of the world expressed through a life of personal purity, a network of welfare institutions and schools, and selected social issues (such as temperance and slavery); and an interdenominational, interconfessional missionary spirit.

The younger Rauschenbusch was born to this legacy, started his life pilgrimage with it, then found that it broke down in his New York parish. Yet some of the elements of his new position remained rooted in this legacy, despite his later rejection of the overall pattern.

Walter Rauschenbusch's climactic conversion at age seventeen followed the normative pietist pattern – an experience that he interpreted later as the Prodigal Son returning from a far country where he had wasted his inheritance.[7]

After completing his education, he became pastor of the Second German Baptist Church of New York City, which was affiliated not with the Northern Baptist Convention but rather with the distinctly German group now known as the North American Baptist Church. This pastorate lasted from 1886–97. For four of those years, Walter was editor of the *Jugend Herold*, a denominational German-language periodical. In addition, his earlier pietism found an outlet in the translation, with Ira Sankey, of 137 hymns into German – most of them in the gospel-song tradition exemplified by the works of Fanny Crosby.[8] The bulk of this material appeared in 1897, during the final year of Rauschenbusch's New York pastorate.

Walter Rauschenbusch's career as hymnologist indicates that he was not limited to the American gospel song. While it is true that his translations conveyed the American pietist hymnology to the German Protestant immigrants in its most superficial form, his radical shift away from pietism is seen in the list of favourite hymns recorded in the Rauschenbusch memorial issue of the *Rochester Theological Seminary Bulletin* of 1918, which gives the full transcript of his funeral and memorial services. Seven of his favourite hymns in the post-pietist phase of his career were Paul Gerhardt's "Befiehl du deine Wege"; Bates's "O Beautiful for Spacious Skies"; Ebenezer Elliott's "When Wilt Thou Save the People?"; G.K. Chesterton's "O God of earth and altar, Bow down and hear our cry"; John Haynes Holmes's "God of the Nations, near and far"; and William Ballantine's "God Save America."

Ballantine dedicated his hymn to the Rochester social prophet. The distance between this hymn of praise to America and the American gospel song is great; this is the distance Rauschenbusch travelled. At the end of his essay on hymnology he says, "If the church has old hymns of social redemption stored away, let us have them. But social redemption wants hymns."[9]

FROM PIETISM TO SOCIAL AWARENESS

Walter Rauschenbusch's career as a hymnologist in New York was the last formally pietistic responsibility he discharged. If the *Zweite Deutsche Baptisten Gemeinde* in New York was a *Collegie pietatis* surrounded by walls, these walls were now crumbling. The basic thrust of pietism is to offer spiritual rebirth through the cross of Christ and then to gather the converts into cells or churches. A limited amount of welfare work may be done for the victims of social tragedy, but it is considered of secondary importance to saving people's souls. Rauschenbusch had crossed over the line.

In seeking the origins of Rauschenbusch's ethics in New York, one observes first the negative breakdown of an individualistic approach, then the emergence of a prophetic, sectarian feeling of righteous indignation with the suffering that seemed to be imposed on the people, and finally the encounter with liberalism in social and political movements and in the literature of protest. Interposed among all this is a trip Rauschenbusch took to Europe in search of a deeper insight into social questions and Baptist colleagues who were not pietists.

I shall now outline some of the details of these developments in New York between 1886 and 1897. The introduction to Rauschenbusch's first book contains this moving paragraph:

I have written this book to discharge a debt. For eleven years I was pastor among the working people on the West side of New York City. I shared their life as well as I knew then, and used up the early strength of my life in their service. In recent years my work has been turned into other channels, but I have never ceased to feel that I owe help to the plain people who were my friends. If this book in some far-off way helps to ease the pressure that bears them down and increases the forces that bear them up, I shall meet the Master of my life with better confidence.[10]

His literary activities on behalf of the social gospel apparently fulfilled a solemn covenant made during the New York pastorate. Chapter 5 of *Christianity and the Social Crisis*, entitled "The Present Crisis," is in effect a systematic commentary on his New York sojourn. It contains dozens of comments that come directly out of the shocking experiences of a sensitive young pastor confronted by the callous industrialism of a hundred years ago. He speaks of overworked men and women raising their families in utter poverty, and of young children forced to work in factories "during the crucial period of adolescence ... to make goods a little cheaper, or what is more likely, merely to make profits a little larger."[11] He describes the death and funerals of many small children, the ghastly facilities, the exploitation of clerks in department stores, the suppression of news about liberal and radical political parties, the tainting of food, gambling for little men, gambling on the stock market for big men, dishonest labels on consumer goods, vicious competition, postponed marriages and prostitution, lack of home ownership, exploitation of women in commerce and industry, dirt, ugliness, injustice, disorganization, class, caste, decay, and poison. Such was the impression of a grinding, abrasive social system on a young pastor who had been sensitized by Christian nurture, a good family background, and a brilliant cultural training in Europe and America.

In his very first paper on social issues, Rauschenbusch called on his "friends" to heed the plight of the poor – those who are "mangled and crushed" – and to work for positive change in society.[12] This paper was written in 1887, one year after Rauschenbusch came to New York. While he was aware that the crisis he found there might be regarded as peculiar to that one vast, teeming metropolitan area, he believed that "all the country is getting to be New York" and that

"New York is only the most striking manifestation of laws operative everywhere."[13]

Rauschenbusch found pietism at odds with the immediate context in which he lived and worked. But there are also inherent weaknesses in pietism that no doubt contributed to his rejection of it. James Nichols points to the pietist insistence on maintaining the character of the Church as an effective historical community, and its tendency to reach for the gnat of personal morality while swallowing the camel of social and political reaction. Moreover, in being anticultural, pietism is "cutting off its head."[14]

There is also a strange affinity between pietism and the Enlightenment. According to Carl Mirbt, some see the Enlightenment and pietism as antithetical while others view the Enlightenment as the product of pietism. "In reality," he says, "the relation between these two trends was neither one of mere antithesis nor yet one of cause and effect."[15] He proceeds to show that there were points of deviation regarding revelation, piety, and the Bible, and points of agreement on opposition to Lutheran orthodoxy, the religious rights of individuals, and practical Christianity. The common goal was the destruction of clericalism.

"At the same time," warns Mirbt, "the sincerest pietism indirectly cited the rapid growth of the Enlightenment in Germany not only for its contempt of culture by giving the younger generation no training to cope with the Enlightenment, but also, through its neglect of such education, by depriving those of scholarly inclinations into the rationalistic camp."[16]

The anticultural variety of pietism is thus vulnerable to attack. But Walter and August Rauschenbusch were not anticultural in any sense. With typical European thoroughness, both were superbly educated in languages, travel, the fine arts, history, and literature. Walter Rauschenbusch rejected confessionalism in favour of religious experience and then spelled out this experience-centred faith in pragmatic terms. Once confessionalism had been rejected, the field was wide open to various liberal theologies. The American *Zeitgeist*, particularly in New York, permitted the inclusion of a liberal social ethic as well as theology. But for Rauschenbusch, the chain reaction was started by pietism.

The affinity between pietism and sectarianism is no less than that between pietism and liberalism. In a definitive study of the relation between pietism and sectarianism, Robert Friedmann, formerly of the University of Vienna, quotes nine different authorities, from Ritschl to Müller, who believed that pietism had its genesis in the Anabaptist-sectarian milieu. While Friedmann rejects this theory of origins in terms of Anabaptist sectarianism, he nevertheless sadly concludes that sectarianism is constantly plagued by pietism, which leads to the dissolution of sectarian discipleship and community into individualistic subjectivism.[17]

Against this background it is easy to see how August and Walter Rauschenbusch operated both in pietist and sectarian contexts. This is particularly true of Baptist pietism, which led August to a vigorous scholarly pursuit of these sectarian backgrounds. The origins of Walter Rauschenbusch's social ethics were thus partially derived from pietism as mediated through his father and the German *Zeitgeist*. The quest for religious reality and a warm compassion for people, both fundamental to Walter Rauschenbusch, must be attributed to the pietist influence.[18]

CHAPTER FOUR

The Influence of
Anabaptist Sectarianism

The effort to discover how the sectarian motif moulded and shaped the ethics of Walter Rauschenbusch is divided here into two parts. The first part documents in great detail the indoctrination of both father and son in the literature and outlook of sixteenth-century sectarian thought. A number of Walter Rauschenbusch's lectures, essays, and addresses reveal that sectarianism was one of the major influences that shaped his own thinking as well as his father's.

The second part, more complex and difficult to analyze, reveals that the son's Kingdom of God ethics originated in a very free and original appropriation of sectarian motifs. He did not have a compact typology of sectarian parties; he borrowed his sociology from the aggressive sects and his love ethic – without modification or qualification – from the peaceful Anabaptists. At times he lumped the Puritans together with the Anabaptists as belonging to the same general family of Christians. He accepted the imitation of Christ, discipleship, and Jesus literalism. While he made love primary (although at times synonymous with justice), placed the kingdom in history (as the sectarians do), and stressed the analogous effect of the Church on cultural institutions, he rejected any tendency towards withdrawal, emphasizing the transformation and Christianization of culture.

Walter Rauschenbusch exchanged the sectarians' emphasis on redemption for the teleology of the kingdom; he set aside their tragic view of history but accepted a kind of periodization in which the present is an unusually pregnant moment of insight and social concern. He rejected the Fall but affirmed Original Sin. Generally, he cast his ethics in the mould of sectarianism, deriving much of his content from the new liberalism of the day.

In considering the development of sectarianism in Rauschenbusch's thinking, family background is once again basic. In 1868, when Walter was seven years old, his father went to Europe to do research for a book on Anabaptist origins. From his earliest days, Walter was made aware of sectarianism through his father. It is false to assume that he used the left-wing motif only to please and placate his Baptist contemporaries. This interest was clearly a legacy from his parent.

The sectarian development was definitely not drawn from the spirit of the times. Indeed, the pursuit of reliable materials by the elder Rauschenbusch went against the grain of contemporary scholarship and popular religion. The left wing of the Reformation was commonly ignored or caricatured as *Schwärmer*.[1] In many ways August Rauschenbusch was one of the genuine pioneers of left-wing research in America. Even his son's essay on Conrad Grebel, published in 1905, placed him in the category of a trail-blazer, because so little was available in English at the turn of the century. Therefore, the *Zeitgeist* provides no explanation for sectarian motifs.

The self-image of the son was replete with sectarian consciousness. Anabaptist prophetism suggested to him the revolutionary impact of the Kingdom of God in attacking both church and society. The twentieth-century meaning of this attack was a bold critique of Mennonite industrialism. The interaction of Rauschenbusch's sectarian consciousness with liberalism and transformationism provides us with a basic clue to the underpinnings of his Kingdom of God ethics.

As for books, father August bequeathed his son some of the key primary sectarian sources available in the German language. These sources were used throughout Walter's career, with special emphasis on the writings of an English Baptist, Richard Heath, a serious Anabaptist scholar of his time as well as a bold pamphleteer against the tragic movement of the working classes away from the Church. Other relevant books permit us to see how the writings of others entered into his thinking.

I shall look first at the Anabaptist-sectarian materials known to Walter Rauschenbusch, and then at his highly original appropriation of these materials in building his master truth of the Kingdom of God – the key to his theology as well as his ethics.

ANABAPTIST SOURCE
MATERIALS

Studies in the left wing of the Reformation have reached an all-time peak both in quality and quantity. The Continent has been studied by German, Swiss, English, and American scholars. The Anglo-Saxon left wing has received even wider attention in North America because of linguistic and cultural ties with Great Britain. Walter Rauschenbusch stood in closest relation to the Continent, but the evidence shows that he related himself to English nonconformists as well. I have shown that his spiritual and scholarly understanding of the European left wing was a gift from his father. Unfortunately, August's orientation in left-wing research never culminated in the book he hoped to write, a book that the American public badly needed. He did write three articles for the German encyclopaedia, edited by a Professor Schem in New York, on the Baptists, Mennonites, and Dunkers (now known as Church of the Brethren).[2]

In general, August Rauschenbusch stressed the continuity of the sectarian-pietist motif from modern times to the apostolic era through the Anabaptists. He believed that true Christian congregations always existed, sometimes secretly. In writing his father's biography, the younger Rauschenbusch suggested that the Baptists overstressed external continuity. He made a counterproposal that *Ubi Spiritus Sanctus, ibi ecclesia* (Where the Holy Spirit is, there is the Church) would convey the true state of affairs.

As for Walter Rauschenbusch himself, it is clear that he considered himself explicitly related to the mainstream of Anabaptist scholarship. One vivid indication is his translation of and commentary on Conrad Grebel's letter to Thomas Muenzer (Müntzer), published originally in C.A. Cornelius's *Geschichte des Münsterischen Aufruhrs*, the book discovered by his father in 1868.[3] Here is proof that the father's scholarly concerns had been instilled in the son. The opening paragraph gives an interesting picture of the bilingual, left-leaning Rauschenbusch:

The letter of Conrad Grebel and his friends at Zurich to Thomas Muenzer of which a translation is here presented was published by Professor C.A. Cornelius in his *Geschichte des Münsterischen Aufruhrs*, Book II (Appendix I), 1860. It is often referred to as one of the most important sources of information about the Swiss Anabaptists in their earlier stage, but, so far as I have seen, no really adequate use has been made of it. For English and American students of Anabaptist history its use is hedged about with several difficulties. The book of Cornelius is becoming rare. The German text not only presents the usual difficulties of literal reprints from the first quarter of the sixteenth century, but it is filled with Swiss idioms, so that even those who read German fluently might find it hard to get more than general thought.[4]

Thus, to make this rare document available to English and American students of Anabaptism, Rauschenbusch undertook its translation and commentary.

It is significant that nearly ninety years after its publication, this material still appears in most standard bibliographies on the Reformation radicals. It is the first quotation in the chapter on "The Quest for the Essence of Anabaptism" in Franklin H. Littell's *The Anabaptist View of the Church*.[5] Obviously, Walter Rauschenbusch not only pioneered in the use of Anabaptist materials but displayed the kind of sound scholarship that has survived for nearly a century.

It is noteworthy that Rauschenbusch's paper on Grebel appeared in the *American Journal of Theology*, which was published by the University of Chicago from 1897–1920. This suggests his close relationship with another essentially Baptist faculty.

At his funeral service in Rochester on 27 July 1918, Henry B. Robins, a colleague, referred to Rauschenbusch's basic approach to church history as the study of real people and the world that conditioned them, of the ideals that controlled them and the passions that either made them great or covered them with shame.[6]

Total Change or Futile Irrelevance

Rauschenbusch affirmed the normative character and then the fall of both the early church and the Anabaptists as the key to the Reformation; he set both against the background of church history as dynamic aspects of the total interaction of state, church, and society. The end result of that interaction had to be either total change or futile irrelevance. His views on the basic role of the Reformation sectarians were contained in a sermon titled "The Freedom of Spiritual Religion," which he preached at the Northern Baptist Convention in Chicago on 8 May 1910:

The organization of our denomination began in the last grand transitional age, in the Protestant Reformation. In that transition we were far to the front, on the skirmish line. We were the radicals. Of the three great reformers – Luther, Calvin, and Zwingli – Zwingli was the most radical, so that Luther and Melancthon were anxious to disavow the Anabaptists. The epoch-making theology of Calvinism, Calvin's *Institutes of the Christian Religion*, was first written to prove to the King of France that the Protestants were good people and had nothing to do with such extremists as the Anabaptists. When the Baptist movement was in this cradle, nobody expected that baby to sit on the brakes of the chariot of progress.[7]

Lest there be any doubt about the radical perspective from which Rauschenbusch viewed church history, he further clarified his stand in the following words from the same address:

We were for a "reformation without tarrying," even if we had to leave the old church and break it in pieces. We were against clericalism and against all hierarchies. We were for the religious emancipation of the laity. We went as far as the most radical Calvinist in purging religion of superstition, and when he stopped we went on. The others reformed the Lord's Supper, and cleared it of the abuses which had grown up around it, but they feared to attempt the reformation of baptism, for they knew that would shake the foundation of church life. The abolition of infant baptism meant not simply the modification of one church rite, but a revolutionary reconstruction of the very conception of the church.

That is the kind of movement which our fathers initiated. They paid for their understanding with their blood, but the God of history has vindicated their daring. In the long, slow sweep of four centuries, the course of religious development for the Protestant world has been in the direction marked out by the swift rush of radical parties of the Reformation. That course has been fastest and most decided where Christianity has been allowed to follow its own genius with least hindrances from the conservatism of the past. Its triumph has been most complete in our own country.[8]

Surely there could not be a more consistent or thoroughgoing reading of modern ecclesiastical and cultural history than that embodied in this Anabaptist-centred conception. Rauschenbusch's conclusion that the Reformation radicals were determinative in shaping American life is in keeping with Ernst Troeltsch's conclusion that democratic institutions as a whole stem from this free-church background.

Baptists and Anabaptists

Up to this point I have emphasized the Continental radicals, and properly so, since Rauschenbusch's roots are there. Later he identified himself with the English left wing as well, lauding the Puritans and independents of England for their revolutionary ideas on a "free church." He was in tune with their proposal to create churches of believers who would unite freely on the basis of equality in little church democracies, repudiating both the help and interference of the state. While the Puritans did not at first hold this ideal, he says, it was in the "free life of the virgin continent [America that they] tended that way by a sort of spiritual gravitation," and thus congregationalism found its first large development in America.[9]

Rauschenbusch had an abiding faith in the creativity of radical Protestantism and free institutions – in this case through the Puritans. While he was less aware of the English stream of thought than of its continental equivalent, he had some awareness of it, as a report on his Boston lecture clearly indicates. The Anabaptists had been crushed in Germany, with tragic effects.[10] On the other hand, English Puritanism was vital and dynamic in its effect on society. He said it this way: "Religious life insofar as it affects political life in England is the humanitarian democracy begotten by Puritanism. German religion has been taught to confine itself to the inner life, the family and the personal calling. When religion affects political action in Germany it is by ecclesiastical considerations rather than by ethical spirit."[11]

As far as the Baptist church in America and England is concerned, its roots are clearly in English Puritanism. As Moehlman points out, the Philadelphia Confession of 1742 is closely related to the Westminster Confession of 1646. The London Confession of 1677 is largely a reproduction of Westminster, suggesting to Moehlman that the Baptists looked more to Calvin's Geneva than to Hubmaier's Zurich. Winthrop Hudson, emeritus professor of Colgate-Rochester Divinity School, holds strongly to this point. In an essay that completely denies any Anabaptist background to the Baptists, he blames Thomas Crosby's *History of English Baptists 1738–40* for launching the Anabaptist-Baptist connection – a connection that Rauschenbusch accepted and that most Baptists accept to this day.[12]

Hudson's view has met with formidable challenge. Ernst Troeltsch argued that the Cromwellian Independency generated the ideas of the separation of church and state, toleration of various churches alongside each other, the principle of voluntarism in the establishment of denominations, and freedom in both religion and culture. All of this, Troeltsch says, marks the end of the old medieval concept of culture and the beginning of modern, individual, nonecclesiastical culture. The fact that the Continental expressions of this transition were secular and rationalistic must not obscure the fact that in England, its religious roots lay in the Puritan revolution. He makes the crucial point that this is the result of revived Anabaptist and spiritualist movements in combination with Calvinism.[13]

Ernest A. Payne, a leading English Baptist historian, believed that the English Puritan left wing drew a great deal of its inspiration from the Swiss, German, and Dutch Anabaptists.[14] Likewise, Rufus Jones writes that the continental Anabaptists provided "the soil out of which all non-conformists have sprung, and it is the first plain announcement in modern history of a program for a new type of Christian society in the modern world, especially in America and England ... an absolutely free and independent religious society, and a state in which every man counts as a man, and has his share in shaping both church and state."[15]

Another version of Baptist history is that propounded by Robert G. Torbet, formerly of the American Baptist Board of Education and Publication. In his foreword, Kenneth Scott Latourette says that "nowhere else is there to be found in so nearly inclusive and up-to-date [a] fashion a summary of the people who bear the name Baptist."[16] Torbet concludes that "with respect to the relationship between Anabaptists and Baptists, it is safe to say that the latter are the descendants of *some* of the former."[17]

In summary, it appears that the position of Walter Rauschenbusch still has serious support in scholarly opinion. In any case, his kinship with both the continental and Anglo-Saxon left-wing Protestants is alive and his discovery of their relationship to social and political activity most important.

Meanwhile, the contemporary US Baptists and their counterparts in Canada are more interested in theological purity than origins, multiple or singular. The huge Southern Baptist church is awesome in membership, number of congregations, and budget: fifteen million members, thirty-five thousand congregations, and two billion dollars in the budget. The annual assemblies are always times for debates and crucial elections that determine direction and control by liberals or conservatives. James J. Thompson's *Tried by Fire* sets forth the necessity of combating the social gospel. The Rauschenbusch legacy is alive much more clearly in the northern or American Baptists, with 1.5 million members. William Henry Brackney's *The Baptists* represents this wing of the Baptist church.

KINGDOM OF GOD SOCIAL ETHICS

Walter Rauschenbusch represented two generations of authentic encounter with left-wing Protestant materials. This influence was bound to manifest itself when he began to construct his basic system of thought.

I have documented Walter Rauschenbusch's legacy of left-wing sectarian research and impact. His encounter with the sectarian viewpoint, especially that of continental Europe, became one of the bases of his social ethics. From boyhood he was aware of his father's interest in these prophetic and revolutionary Protestant movements. Though somewhat latent in the earlier years, this sectarian background assumed great importance as he sought to put together the outlines of his ethics.

I look now at how he employed the broad influence and perspective of the sectarian background in his systematic construction of the ethics of the Kingdom of God, an effort for which he was to become famous. While his ethics were unquestionably grounded in part in sectarianism, it is important to understand that he was not bound by any compact confessional limitation; nor was he confined by any lack of academic freedom, or by his father's more intense pietism. It is evident that he made the freest and most original use of his sectarian origins. Indeed, at times the sectarians would hardly recognize themselves in his formulations. Usually the forms of sectarianism are present, and sometimes its content; in all cases, the sectarian origins flow freely in and out of his basic perceptions. A pertinent example appears in his speech on "The Church and Money Power," in which he described Anabaptism as "the revolutionary kind of doctrine, brimful of social applications of Christianity."[18] In the same address he said that the Catholics and Lutherans represented the upper and middle classes, respectively, which were crushing the lower-class sectarian movements.

In addition, Richard Heath must be considered a probable influence in Rauschenbusch's development – upon the testimony of C.H. Moehlman, Rauschenbusch's successor to the chair of church history at Colgate-Rochester. Further, one must also take into account the contribution of Emile de Laveleye, a maverick crypto-sectarian Catholic who exerted a strong influence on Rauschenbusch's doctrine of the analogous role of the Church.

Part Two is basic to my discussion because the sectarian origins made possible Rauschenbusch's uniquely free selection and appropriation of materials for his Kingdom of God ethics. Without these sectarian origins, his approach to social ethics would be an insoluble puzzle.

While Rauschenbusch's method was eclectic, his conclusions were definite. He believed in the Kingdom of God as the reign of God coming through the progressive growth of love in society; the outcome would be a humanity organized according to the will of God. The role of the kingdom was dual: it was to be at once the master key to the mind of Christ and the basic principle of the new theology. Those who participated in it as disciples and apostles of Christ would experience cultural conflict as a result (since the ethics of the kingdom are incompatible with the selfish and materialistic organization of merely human society).

Rauschenbusch wrote that the function of the kingdom is to Christianize the social order by abolishing unjust privilege and changing semi-Christian social institutions. It exists as a universal sociohistorical reality struggling with three antagonistic or limiting forces – pietistic subjectivism, other-worldliness, and apocalypticism.

Perhaps Rauschenbusch's concept of the kingdom can best be understood in terms of its ethical and sociological impact. The sanctity of human life, the solidarity of the human family ("the fatherhood of God and the brotherhood of man"), the role of love as the law of life, leading the strong to stand with the weak – a love supplemental to justice and sometimes synonymous with it, these are the trends of Rauschenbush's social-ethics gospel that found acceptance in the laity. Since life operates in a solidaristic, socio-organic context, sin expresses itself in supersocial institutions, binding people together in the kingdom of evil – a common yoke of suffering. "Mammonism," or economic privilege, is the key to the social problem. Thus we have two opposing superforces, the kingdom of evil and the Kingdom of God; the latter comes to save us from the former.

Within this context it becomes necessary to redefine the role of the Church. The true Church is a disciplined and democratic voluntary association. It rejects sacramentalism and ceremonialism, hierarchial priesthood, Hellenized theologizing, and all alliances with the state. The Church has a direct effect on social institutions. As a democratic, voluntary association it stimulates democratic social institutions. Conversely, when it is autocratic and other-worldly it stimulates autocratic social institutions. Its sole reason for existence is to serve the Kingdom of God. When it fails to do this it is anti-Christian. At the same time, the Church can never fully contain the kingdom, whose natural habitat is all humanity.

This view of the Church and its relation to society demands a new evaluation of history. According to Rauschenbusch, the socioethical failure of the Church is not due to factors inherent in either the Church or history, but to temporary causes now inoperative. The kingdom comes in gradually rather than catastrophically. However, history shows distinct periods in which the approach of the kingdom is evident, of which the present moment is one of the greatest opportunities for hastening the arrival of the kingdom since the Renaissance and the Reformation.

Having listed the basic premises of Rauschenbusch's theory of the Kingdom, I shall now consider his theses one by one.

The Kingdom of God Defined

Rauschenbusch offers a number of related definitions of the Kingdom of God, the best of which defines it as the reign of God.[19] In the Taylor lectures at Yale he supported the view that "the Kingdom of God is humanity organized according to the will of God." In the same presentation he declared that, "since love is the supreme law of Christ, the Kingdom of God implies a progressive reign of love in human affairs."[20] Further, there is his frequently quoted statement that "this doctrine [the Kingdom of God] is the social gospel."[21] Finally, there is his equation of the kingdom with the ideal social order and the perfect ethic: "Jesus bade us 'seek first the Kingdom of God and his righteousness,' and he obeyed his own call. The main object in his life was the ideal social order and the perfect ethic."[22]

Rauschenbusch saw the Anabaptists as part of a larger movement beginning in the twelfth century and including the Franciscans, Waldensians, Lollards, and Taborites, among others. Anabaptist radicalism, he thought, constituted "the first stirrings of Christian democracy, express[ing] lay religion and working-class ethics" and "the religious awakening of the common people and their cry for the Reign of God on earth."[23]

He proceeds to show that all of these movements were rife with apocalyptic excitement, suggesting "a new era, a new judgment on the Church, and a golden age for all the world." The main parties of the Reformation did not build their foundations squarely on the Kingdom of God, although the radical parties did. Nevertheless, the Reformation as a whole helped social Christianity by destroying medievalism and arousing the masses.

Another discussion of the Anabaptists reveals how the Rochester social prophet interpreted their contribution to the reign of God on earth:

The Anabaptists believed in a religious transformation of social life. To understand them one must understand their times. There was a revolt of class against class, party against party everywhere. The Anabaptist movement was a religious movement with social aims. The Anabaptists entertained the social revolutionary hope under Biblical guise. Christ was to come and rescue his poor and oppressed people, and, in place of the present reign of the wicked, set up the reign of the saints. It was a passionate hope for speedy relief from intolerable oppression.[24]

The citations verify that the reign of God on earth was a concept that Rauschenbusch found not only among the Anabaptists but also among the forerunners of the Reformation. To this he added the progressive or evolutionary growth of love that would gradually moralize the whole social order, a concept derived more from the Enlightenment than from the left-wing groups.

Leading scholars of Anabaptism agree that the Kingdom of God is one of the major motifs of the left wing of the Reformation, although the form it took then was somewhat different from Rauschenbusch's adaptation of it. The left-wing groups rejected the kingdom as the sole theme but accepted it as one of the main themes. They also rejected the synthesis between the kingdom and evolutionary thought: the early Anabaptists affirmed the reign of God primarily in terms of the *koinonia* (fellowship of believers); this reign in the *koinonia* had radical implications for society as a whole but was not to be equated with the moral standards of that society.

On the other hand, since Rauschenbusch applied the term Anabaptist to all the groups in this general category, he could have found roots for his position in the chiliastic groups, since their periodization of history held many radical implications. Or he could have based his position on the work of Balthasar Hubmaier (1440–1528).[25]

Rauschenbusch's strong kingdom-mindedness was rooted in the Continental left wing, as was his definite sense of two kingdoms in conflict. In a later chapter I will examine the integration of this sectarian motif with the kingdom motif of the idealist theologians and philosophers.

This kingdom emphasis reflects in part the evangelical-biblical-community type of Anabaptists, with whose literature Rauschenbusch was familiar. And yet he avoids limiting the kingdom to the *koinonia*, visualizing it rather as breaking into the entire social order. Here he moved towards the aggressive sects, both continental and English, climaxing in the neo-Calvinist or Puritan types. Chapter 5 will show the extent to which this universalism and catholicity came from Calvinist and Anglican sources. The present chapter will throw more light on this same problem from the idealist philosophers of the Enlightenment. It will also show how Rauschenbusch used liberal biblical hermeneutics to reinterpret the millenial teaching of early Christianity as a call to an earthly, redeemed society.

Role of the Kingdom

A second concept developed by Rauschenbusch was that of the role of the Kingdom of God, which he visualized as the key to the mind of Christ and the primary material principle of the new theology. The Kingdom of God is the greatest truth of the mission and message of Jesus Christ, he maintained. On his trip to Europe in 1891, this belief came to Rauschenbusch as a new revelation, like the emerging summit of some great mountain of the Alps.[26]

Convinced that the Kingdom of God ought to be dominant in biblical studies and in Christology, Rauschenbusch was also ready to make it dominant in theological formulations:

> The old theology is essentially the theology of the Reformation. The formal principle of the Reformation was the Bible; its material principle: justification by faith. That is to say, it took its guidance from the Bible and had for its object personal salvation. But back of the Bible lies the Holy Spirit which inspired it; back of the individual to be saved lies humanity of which he is a part. The formal principle of the new gospel must be the Holy Spirit; the material principle must be the Kingdom of God. Thus we shall not go back to Paul alone, who inspired the Reformation, but to Jesus Christ, who founded Christianity by preaching the Kingdom of God in the power of the Spirit.[27]

Rauschenbusch's emphasis on the kingdom in this radical sense is in line with the individual quality of American Christianity, as H. Richard Niebuhr points out in *The Kingdom of God in America*.[28] In the light of Niebuhr's book, it is clear that Rauschenbusch made the kingdom the primary motif of his theology against the background of the American scene where the same theme, variously interpreted, was also central. Specific evidence for this American influence in Rauschenbusch's outlook will be discussed in chapter 5.

H. Richard Niebuhr's friendly placement of Rauschenbusch in the context of America's kingdom-mindedness is derailed somewhat in his *Christ and Culture* (1951), where the Rochester social prophet is interpreted as a Ritschlian who presented the Christ *of* culture. Rauschenbusch's Christology clearly reflected the new theology: the divine nature of Jesus is based on free acts of will rather than on a passive inheritance of the divine essence, on character rather than on nature.[29] Salvation "is the voluntary socializing of the soul,"[30] since Jesus represents the "democratizing of God."[31] In this process of salvation, one enters into the total life of humanity through Jesus, who was perfectly bound up with the life of humanity. The collective sins that killed Jesus brought him into conflict with the whole life of humanity in the kingdom of evil. When his God-consciousness and life is accepted, one begins to live righteously. At this point the Kingdom of God comes to stand in opposition to the kingdom of evil. Obviously, something other than left-wing elements entered into Rauschenbusch's interpretation.

Rauschenbusch's emphasis on the role of the kingdom must be seen as a rejection of various kingdom concepts stressed by other Christian leaders: the spiritualization of the kingdom taught by Origen and the pietists; Augustine's equation of the kingdom and the Church; the tendency of the Reformers to equate the kingdom with the invisible church; and the emphasis on eschatology found in the writings of Johannes Weiss and Albert Schweitzer.[32]

Under the stimuli of his sectarian background and of American theology generally, and under the impact of liberal Ritschlianism, Rauschenbusch made the role of the kingdom preeminent as the key both to Jesus and the new theology. He was consequently forced to reject some ancient and well-known patterns in seeking to delineate the role of the kingdom.

Rauschenbusch's initial religious experience was divided into two parts: conversion and discipleship. Of conversion he said: "I am out in a far country and I want to get home to my country and I do not want to tend hogs any longer; and so, I came to my Father, and I began to pray for help and got it; and I got my own religious experience."[33]

From the age of seventeen, as noted earlier, when he underwent this touching pietistic experience, he "wished to preach and save souls." He resolved to live literally by the spirit and teaching of Jesus and described the new discipleship experience as one of following Christ in life and in death and thereby helping to redeem humanity.[34] This experience of the meaning of discipleship occurred in his seminary course in Rochester and was evident to others. His biographer maintains that "this contact with Jesus and his decision to live Christ's way of life, had as much to do with his social enlightenment as anything else. Like the Apostle Paul, Walter Rauschenbusch met Jesus – and all life was different. Jesus changed Walter Rauschenbusch, and Walter Rauschenbusch changed the course of American Christianity."[35]

BROTHERHOOD OF THE KINGDOM

Every stage of Rauschenbusch's life was controlled by his concept of discipleship. His first organized attempt to express social concern was the founding of the Brotherhood of the Kingdom in 1892 under the leadership of Leighton Williams, Nathaniel Schmidt, Samuel Zane Batten, and himself. Its aim was to "permeate modern social movements with the social ideal and to attempt this by emphasizing Jesus' teaching of the Kingdom of God, the central ideal of the

Gospel." Its 1893 pamphlet on the "Spirit and Aims of the Brotherhood" contains the following guidelines for members: (1) emulate the ethics of Jesus; (2) propagate the thoughts of Jesus to the limits of your ability in private conversation, by correspondence, and through pulpit, platform, and press; (3) lay special stress on the social aims of Christianity, and endeavour to make Christ's teaching concerning wealth operative in the Church; (4) take pains to keep in contact with the common people and to infuse the religious spirit into efforts for social amelioration. This platform clearly indicated to members the necessity as well as the possibility of following Christ.

A lecture delivered at Brown University by the father of Leighton Williams apparently played a part in the development of the Brotherhood of the Kingdom. In this address, entitled "Jesuits as a Missionary Order," Williams portrayed an ideal society of missionaries that should combine self-sacrifice of a Protestant type with a true Society of Jesus.[36]

What we encounter here is a radical emphasis on the imitation of Christ, based on the Jesus of the synoptic Gospels and mediated through an Anabaptist stress on discipleship and modern concepts of social concern. A revealing experience in this connection was Rauschenbusch's attendance at the famous Oberammergau Passion Play in Bavaria. He was amazed at the "evangelical purity" of the play. He explained this by the "rationalism" of Weiss and Daisenberger and the tendency of the Gospels themselves to make believers less ecclesiastical and more Christian. He was pleased in many ways with the impersonation of the Christus, feeling that it was probably as satisfying as human nature could make it. Yet Rauschenbusch was not entirely satisfied. He missed the Christ of the Gospels, whose task it was to set up the reign of God on earth, and whose dominant characteristic was a passionate love for people and for righteousness.[37]

Rauschenbusch's eloquent review of the world's most famous passion play makes sense only against the background of his quest for the synoptic Jesus who can be followed, obeyed, and imitated. It is, by implication, an attempt to make the lordship of Christ real to the ethical realm, both personal and social. It is a protest against docetism in any form in order to make the humanity of Jesus both real and contagious. To be sure, it runs the risk of emptying Christ of all divine meaning in a desperate attempt to conserve his humanity.

Rauschenbusch adapted this concept of discipleship and applied it to a larger system of Christian social thought. He correlated discipleship with the kingdom concept, thereby socializing the meaning of the term. This emphasis is evident in *Christianizing the Social Order*, in which he speaks of the Kingdom of God as "the lost social ideal of Christendom" and says that "a social interpretation of ... personal discipleship will bring us into closer spiritual agreement with the original aim of Christianity."[38] The clear implication is that Jesus is to be followed not only in personal ethical issues but in the larger social challenges as well.

At times Rauschenbusch seems to have shifted the focus from the historical Jesus to union with God in the same way that Jesus had union with God. This point still stands despite contemporary disapproval, such as that of President Strong of Rochester Theological Seminary, who mildly criticized *A Theology for the Social Gospel* for leaving out the "union with Christ," or Christ mysticism, which was the foundation of Strong's *Systematic Theology*.[39] Rauschenbusch replied that his own theology was as Christocentric as Strong's. In his "Why I Am a Baptist" series, he declared that "to become a disciple of Jesus means to learn to think of God and life with Him as Jesus did, and to let all life be transformed by that new faith and knowledge."

In any case, both the Christocentric and theocentric concepts of discipleship assume that one can fully follow, obey, and initiate the divine object. This seems to be the case whether the stress is on Jesus Christ or on God the Father.[40] It is precisely this point that Visser t' Hooft underscores as the essence of the sectarianism of the earlier social gospel in general and of Rauschenbusch's concept in particular.[41]

But discipleship is more than an ethical relationship between Christ and the individual, or between Christ and the social order. The authority of Christ implied in discipleship extends to all of history, particularly when Christ is stripped of false accretions from theology and sacramentarianism. In his "Introduction to the Study of History" (1905), Rauschenbusch says: "The spirit of Jesus is the ultimate canon by which every historical personality, institution or movement must be judged, and our personal absorption of his mind and spirit is the ultimate qualification for a really useful study of the history of the church."[42]

The emphasis is on the essence and spirit of Jesus, purged of all accretions. This represents a union of the more primitive sectarian elements with modern thought. In a sermon published in 1909, Rauschenbusch affirmed that "a truth familiar to Jesus and to his disciples was the pure spirituality of the new religion. To strip religion of all forms and make it purely a matter of love to God and man was so immense an innovation that we have hardly come in sight of it yet."[43]

A NEW APOSTOLATE

The new social movement would demand a new discipleship or apostolate as well as a new evangelism. Here Rauschenbusch likens the situation to apostolic times, when there was a deep "fellow-feeling for social misery and from the consciousness of a great historical opportunity." In the midst of this, Jesus bade his disciples to "pray for laborers for the harvest and then made them answer their own prayers by sending them out two by two to proclaim the Kingdom of God." Were the situation repeated today, Jesus would create a new apostolate to meet new needs in a new harvest time of history.[44]

What is new about the new apostolate? First, ability and ambition are still to lead, but they must be yoked to the service of all. "The old way to leadership was to knock others down and climb up on them; the new way is to get underneath and boost."[45] Service is the key, and service is not incompatible with ability and ambition when tied to the larger social good.

Second, selfish acquisition of money is ruled out in the new apostolate. "Freely ye received; freely give. Get you no gold, nor silver, nor brass in your purses; no wallet for your journey, neither two coats, nor shoes, nor staff; for the laborer is worthy of his food."[46] Rauschenbusch cites Francis of Assisi, Pastor Waldo, Wycliffe, John Wesley, and William Booth as illustrations of the principle that support is only enough to live in health and no more. The Christian ministry is now under this law of leadership, where once the priests were upper class, domineering, rich with unearned incomes, and pervaded by graft. The general trend is "toward intelligent service on plain pay," as with educators, judges, scientists, and doctors. This is also true in politics (unless there is graft). The big problem, he says, is with business. Can it be brought under the law of service, or is commerce constitutionally incapable of this moral axiom? Actually, the only question is whether "business leaders will voluntarily turn their backs on such misuse of power or have a change forced on them."[47]

Third, "the apostolate of a new age must be the work of the sower." The sower sows new truths. Although he may never see the results, he can wait, because the powers of life are on his side. This is like leaven in the soul; like the mustard seed becoming a tree. A perfect example is that of Robert Owen, whose cooperative communities failed but whose ideas stimulated Chartism, the Rochdale co-ops, and other radical movements. The new apostolate will lead people slowly but surely into a new way of life.

Fourth, the new apostolate will not be discouraged by suffering and opposition, both of which are inevitable. Rauschenbusch cites

Charles Kingsley and F.D. Maurice, English Christian socialists who were bitterly assailed and misunderstood at the time of their ministries, but who were later acclaimed as the finest products of their time. The same is true, he says, of Rudolph Todt, the German pastor who showed that the New Testament and socialism have a close affinity. The new leaders will not be surprised by opposition, suffering, and rejection. Indeed, these will be expected as part of normal experience.

Fifth, and perhaps most startling, was the principle that the new apostolate is not limited to Christians or to churchmen. This is clearly delineated in Rauschenbusch's book on social work, *Unto Me*, published in 1912. With his usual eloquence he writes that social workers "are in the direct line of apostolic succession ... They are doing with the large resources of modern organization what He did in Galilee ... They are doing Christian work when they do social work, even if they themselves disclaim religious motives or even repudiate religious faith."[48] Anticipating objections to this inclusive concept of discipleship, he boldly answers that the experience of social workers "is more peculiarly Christian than any other kind of religious experience" and that they "bear their griefs [those of the poor and downtrodden] and carry their sorrows like the one who was a man of sorrows and acquainted with grief." Even as Jesus collided head on with the selfish interests of the ruling classes, so will those who attempt in modern days to assist the poor and the weak.[49] This radical oceanic Christianity (to use Vergilius Ferm's phrase) was not spelled out only in terms of social workers. The major stress was on the special mission of socialism in the larger sense of following Christ even when he is not consciously accepted.

Sixth, the new apostolate will go beyond the sins of the disposition and the sins of the flesh to the social sins. Rauschenbusch points out in his essay on "The New Evangelism" that, while in the past the Church boldly condemned "drunkenness, sexual impurity, profanity ... Sabbath-breaking, dancing and card-playing and theatregoing ... it has not been successful." The gap between the community and the Church has narrowed to the extent that today "the morality of the church is not much more than what prudence, respectability and good breeding also demand."[50] Regarding the relation of the Church to large social questions, he says the Church is silent ("dumb") on the most pressing questions arising in politics and business. When it does speak out, he laments, it often comes down on the wrong side.[51]

Thus, the new apostolate yokes ambition and ability to service, rules out selfish acquisition of money, does the work of a sower in planting radical new ideas, will not be discouraged by opposition and suffering, is not limited to Christians, and will follow Christ in rejecting social as well as personal sins.

Furthermore, the new social order will make it easier to follow Jesus. Rauschenbusch and subsequent advocates of the social gospel favoured the idea that in the present unregenerate social order one cannot follow Christ, but that when the new social order comes it will facilitate rather than hamper discipleship. In *Christianity and the Social Crisis*, Rauschenbusch lists six "ifs" that constitute the hopes of the social gospel for a new context in which the new apostolate can function: if production could be organized on the basis of cooperative fraternity; if distribution could at least approximately be determined by justice; if all men could be conscious that their labour was contributing to the welfare of all and that their personal well-being was dependent on the prosperity of the commonwealth; if predatory business and parasitic wealth ceased and all men lived only by their labour; if the luxury of unearned wealth no longer made people feverish with covetousness and simpler life became the fashion; and if time and strength were not used up either in getting a bare living or in amassing unstable wealth and there was more leisure for the higher pursuits of the mind and the soul.[52] If these probabilities were to become actualities, he postulated, the impact would be revolutionary. Rauschenbusch declares with sheer joy that the "Cooperative Commonwealth [might] give us the first chance in history to live a really Christian life without retiring from the world, and [might] make the Sermon on the Mount a philosophy of life feasible for all who care to try."[53]

Social reconstruction is crucial in Rauschenbusch's view. If the social order goes down, the Church goes down with it. If the Church can cooperate in changing the social order, then it will rise to the newer and higher life. If the "ifs" are taken care of, then following Jesus and expressing the Sermon on the Mount are genuine possibilities.

Part of the foregoing is logically inconsistent with the emphasis on following Jesus in the face of suffering and opposition. Nevertheless, the development of the new apostolate and discipleship in response to the kingdom is a characteristic aspect of Rauschenbusch's modified sectarianism. He insists that Jesus can be followed both in personal and social situations, in small-scale and in large-scale groups.

Rauschenbusch owed much of his emphasis on discipleship to the Continental left wing. In his Boston address on "The Prophetic Character of the Anabaptist Movement," he maintained that their "prophetic power and grandeur" stemmed from the fact that they took

Jesus Christ as their leader and the Holy Spirit as their inward light. He then challenged his audience to follow their lead.[54]

In addition to the influence of the Reformation radicals on his views on property, there is considerable evidence that Rauschenbusch was also influenced by Tolstoy, Russia's greatest sectarian radical. His four major books all contain quotations from Tolstoy, whom he regarded with glowing approval. Thus, in *Christianity and the Social Crisis*, he writes: "When the religious teachings of Tolstoy first became known ... they gave many of us a shock of surprise by asserting with the voice of faith that these [the teachings of the Sermon on the Mount] were the obligatory and feasible laws of Christian conduct."[55]

Finally, the emphasis on the necessity of a friendly social order to make discipleship possible is clearly indicated in Rauschenbusch's analysis of the fateful crushing of the Anabaptists. His essay on "The Influence of Historical Studies on Theology" makes this important point: "The Anabaptist movement was the most purely religious movement of all the movements and that was stamped out because the social classes within which it spread did not command enough political power to protest it. Any theory of religious and moral movements which separates them from the patriotic and social movements of the nations is wholly contradicted by history. The more we comprehend history, the more we see the organic and inseparable unity of all life."[56]

Elsewhere, this idea is spelled out more sharply along class lines. Rauschenbusch shows how both the Peasants' Rising in 1525 and the Anabaptist movement expressed the social and religious ideals of the common people, and yet were quenched in streams of blood. It is true that truth is immortal; nevertheless, to quote Balthasar Hubmaier, "for a definite historical victory a given truth must depend on the class which makes that truth its own and fights for it."[57] Pre-Reformation radicals lacked this support and thus were destroyed by the papacy. Lutherans and Calvinists made such alliances, however unsavoury, and triumphed: "The classes within which Anabaptism gained lodgement lacked that concrete power, and so the Anabaptist movement, which promised for a short time to be the real Reformation of Germany, just as it came to be the real reformation of England in the Commonwealth, died a useless and despised death."[58]

Further, Rauschenbusch discovered in the sectarians the roots of two more of his discipleship theories: (1) that the acquisitive spirit is ruled out in a life of simplicity and voluntary poverty; and (2) that the crushing of previous radical movements calls for the embodiment of great religious truths in a social movement whose triumph will eventually cooperate with discipleship instead of going against it.

Although Rauschenbusch's *Why I Am a Baptist* reaffirms the Baptist concept of a gathered, disciplined congregation, he seems to set aside this more sharply defined concept of the Christian life in favour of a broader moral definition that accepts as Christian those with implicit or explicit faith, whether inside or outside the Church. The roots of this idea may be found in the Christian socialism of Europe.[59] Leading contemporary scholars of Anabaptism agree with Rauschenbusch that discipleship is a basic theme of the Christian life. H.S. Bender long contended that discipleship was the major motif for Anabaptists. Bender stressed that the Continental left wing did not accept the discipleship of Thomas à Kempis's *Imitation of Christ*, which is "basically ... mysticism mixed with socialism." In Thomas, moreover, "the social dimension is almost completely lacking and criticism of the total social and cultural order with a view to the establishment of a full Christian order in the brotherhood and church of the living Christ in the midst of the present world is missing." Actually, "Thomas à Kempis and all those many who follow in his train evade the conflict with the world, avoid the constructive labor of establishing the true church, and thus escape the real cross-bearing experience of true discipleship. There is more kinship between Thomas and the later Pietists than between Thomas and the Anabaptists."[60]

Arising in the context of the threat of banishment and the death penalty, Anabaptism could not provide the soil for an ethic of responsibility. Rauschenbusch took part of this ethic from the liberal concept of responsibility and ascribed part of it to the Anabaptist influence amplified by the Puritan and free churches. With less tyranny and oppression in America and England, the concern for social action and social responsibility developed freely. However, the Continental radicals are the source and fountain-head of his stress on sectarianism; nothing is more characteristic of this emphasis than his concept of discipleship.

W.A. Visser t' Hooft was one of the first to detect the sectarian dimension in Rauschenbusch and, more generally, in the early social-gospel thinkers, but he never followed through on the insight because he believed that the idealistic scientific Enlightenment elements predominated. He described and then criticized the methodology of the discipleship approach that characterized the American social movement:

The general method followed is to deduce a number of principles from the teaching of Jesus and confront the social order with each of them in turn. There is no clearly systematized scheme in which all these principles are put in their logical place ... The strength of the method lies in its flexibility and readiness to take account of reality in all its diverse forms. Its weakness lies in its lack of coherence and unity ... The one principle from which they may all be said to derive is that of brotherhood ... The fact of the Divine Fatherhood and human brotherhood is the only natural law.[61]

Over and against this, Visser t' Hooft suggests that in the primary Catholic and Protestant conceptualization, natural law is valid in the state of sin; Rauschenbusch and his followers saw the absolute natural law of the New Testament as valid only in the state of perfection.

Another attack on the discipleship ethic of the early social gospel was made by James Dombrowski in *The Early Days of Christian Socialism*.[62] He accuses its exponents of assuming that the recovery of the pure ethical teachings of Jesus by scientific research would transform society. Dombrowski asserted that because the leaders of the new social ethic were middle-class liberals rather than working-class radicals, they overlooked objective social conditions that would not yield to ethical idealism.

It is unfair, however, to class Rauschenbusch with those who disregarded sociological problems. Most of his career was spent in developing a theology of institutions. To be sure, Rauschenbusch was optimistic. He was a scholar, not a proletarian leader of the leftist movement. He did underestimate the element of self-interest in every ethical pretension. He was a liberal rather than a radical, who believed that the pure essence of Jesus would have a tremendous effect on human culture.

For Rauschenbusch the response to the kingdom was discipleship and apostolate, leading to the cross and cultural conflict. This is a basic theme in his teaching. It is a theme shaped by considerable sectarian influence.

CHRISTIANIZING THE SOCIAL ORDER

The function of the kingdom is to Christianize the social order through the abolition of unjust privilege and the transforming of semi-Christian institutions. To Christianize the social order means "bringing it into harmony with the ethical convictions which we identify with Christ." The kingdom is adapted "to inspire and guide us in Christianizing the social order because: It is a religion for this earth and for this present life; it wastes no time on mere religious paraphernalia; it gives religious value to the plain man's job; it deals with both bodies and souls; and finally, it demands an ethic for public life. Therefore, we must survey those areas of life which have been Christianized."[63]

By "Christianize" Rauschenbusch does not imply perfection but a basic constitutional change that permits an institution to be squared with the demands of Christian morality. Four institutions must be essentially (although not entirely) changed: the family, from despotism to democracy; the Church, from despotism and superstition to morality; public education, from aristocracy and un-Christian methods to democracy; and the state, from special privilege to personal liberty and equal rights. This program leaves the economic order of mammonism as the final crucial domain for Christianization. The poisons of the current economy infect every part of the body politic, including the Church.

In each case, "the fundamental step toward Christianizing the social order ... is the establishment of social justice by the abolition of unjust privilege. Logically, this would be the first step; ethically, it is the most important step; practically, it is usually the last and the hardest."[64] Therefore, the function of the kingdom is to further Christianize a semi-Christian social order by abolishing unjust privilege, as part of the process of bringing it into harmony with the ethical convictions of Jesus Christ.

Once again, Rauschenbusch ascribes this conception to the sectarians. Observations like the following document this point: "The Anabaptists believed in a religious transformation of social life ... The Anabaptists entertained the social revolutionary hope ... The Anabaptist movement was a religious movement with social aims. Anabaptism expressed most thoroughly the demand for the abolition of abuses in the government of the church ... It was almost consistent and thorough in purifying the worship of the church of ceremonialism. So far from destroying the standards of the moral law, the Anabaptists as a body sought to raise it."[65]

Rauschenbusch's material on Puritanism is scantier than that on the Continental radicals, partly because he considered the second to be the product of the first. Nevertheless, certain materials show that he rooted his concept of Christianization in Puritanism as well as in Anabaptism. For example, on 30 November 1908, he shared a platform with Washington Gladden in Boston, giving an address that was subsequently reported in the *Springfield Daily Republican*. In this address he developed the concept of the English Puritans under Cromwell as "the prophets and creators of the modern world." He made the following affirmations: (1) In America these principles have triumphed more completely than elsewhere and are now accepted in large part by churches that formerly opposed them. (2) The industrial revolution demands that the principles that were victorious in the Reformation nonconformists and the French Revolution be extended to contemporary industrial and economic orders. (3) The Baptists and Congregationalists are pledged by their past history to affiliate themselves with the new extension of democracy. And (4) if we do this we will be spared an ugly social struggle and will "be the pioneer of the kingdom of God among the nations."[66]

It is obvious that Rauschenbusch used the term "extension" here as a synonym for Christianization. There is a kind of inherent drive that reaches its highest intensity in certain periods of history – an inherent drive towards ever wider areas of Christianization and socialization. The left-wing Christian movements were originally responsible for these secular movements, which now have a momentum of their own. Thus, the modern church, in a somewhat Marxian fashion, has only one option: to cooperate with its democratic offspring through Christianization and extension or go down in defeat at the hands of reactionary opposition.

In historical terms, Christianization moves from the Anabaptists to the Puritans to socialism. The fundamental function of the kingdom is to assist this dynamic historical movement through the removal of unjust privilege in the last remaining citadel of abuse – namely, the economic order. The malleability, plasticity, and pliability of the social order is assumed throughout. The reform of the Church is assumed to be no different from the reform of the social order. It awaits only the committed decision of the new apostolate.

Again, Rauschenbusch's utilization of the left wing received broad confirmation in historical scholarship, but there were definite reservations on some points. H.S. Bender assesses the meaning of the central emphasis of the Anabaptists:

In essence the discipleship which the Anabaptists proclaimed was simply the bringing of the whole life under the Lordship of Christ, and the transformation of this life, both personal and social, after His image. From this point of view they subjected the whole social and cultural order to criticism, rejected what they found to be contrary to Christ, and attempted to put into actual practice His teachings as they understood them, both ethically and sociologically ... This absolute discipleship applied to all areas of life ... It meant a Christianizing of all social relationships, a substituting of the simplicity and sincerity of Christ for the pride and vanity of the world ... Implicit in the basic Anabaptist theology of discipleship was a new order which was bound to come as the discipleship was practised.[67]

At the same time, the Continental Anabaptists tended to have a strong eschatological expectation, since their hopes for society as a whole were pessimistic within history. At this point Rauschenbusch borrowed from the Puritan stream of Christian thought, with its emphasis on "the renewal of the soul in God, a conscience void of offense, the will of God for the church and society."[68] His Boston address of 1908 emphasized the creative character of the Puritans' idea of Christianizing the social order. ("Christianize" may be inaccurate if it is taken to mean the full Sermon on the Mount ethic; perhaps "democratize" or "moralize" would be better terms.)

Of course contemporary literature on Puritanism was not available to assist Rauschenbusch in delineating the relationship of Puritanism to Wycliffian dissent, to Calvin, Zwingli, and Bucer, to the sectarian left in Switzerland and Holland, or to the whole economic order. The writings of Max Weber, R.H. Tawney, Perry Miller, M.M. Knappen, William Haller, B.R. White, and others proved increasingly rich and illuminating. They suggest an extremely complex relationship between Puritanism and Anabaptism. This particular problem is not fully settled, although Irvin Horst's studies at Amsterdam made an important contribution.[69]

AN HISTORICAL KINGDOM

The location of the kingdom in time is historical. It is rooted in the theocratic ideal of Israel, which meant "the complete penetration of the national life by society."[70] This ideal provided a contemporary focus for the work of the kingdom. When the outlook of the Jewish leadership became one of individualism and withdrawal, Jewish prophecy declined into "apocalyptic dreams and bookish calculations." The prophets' consciousness of the kingdom is sombre; hence their rejection of lullabies for the sounding of the reveille.

While Jesus was profoundly religious and not basically a social reformer, he did present a modified version of the historical message of the prophets: "The Kingdom of Heaven is now close at hand" (Mark 1:15). He offered his kingdom message to all humanity, not only to the Jews, thus universalizing the historical concern. He also insisted that the fundamental realities of the kingdom were present now. The kingdom must be fully consummated in the future, but this is only an amplification of what already exists.

Two other factors helped make the kingdom a historical reality. First, the ethics of the kingdom are based on love, and love, to use Rauschenbusch's phrase, is a "society-making" force. Love creates fellowship, organism, togetherness, and immanence. Second, the radical social hopes of the primitive church found brilliant expression in a unique society where conventional barriers broke down. History was invaded by a dynamic new movement that included

Christian democracy with its genuine expression of community; an intensive program of welfare services and mutual aid; and a general stirring of divine discontent, opening up new possibilities for social change.

Thus the spirit of primitive Christianity did not spread only sweet peace and tender charity, but the leaven of social unrest. It caused some to throw down their tools and quit work. It stirred women to break down the restraints of custom and modesty. It invaded the intimacies of domestic relations and threatened families with disruption. It awakened the slaves to a sense of worth and a longing for freedom which made slavery doubly irksome and strained their relations to their masters. It disturbed the patriotism and loyalty of citizens for their country, and intervened between the sovereign State and its subjects.

Our argument here is simply this, that Christianity must have had a strong social impetus to evoke such stirrings of social unrest and discontent. It was not purely religious but also a democrative and social movement. Or to state it far more truly: it was so strongly and truly religious that it was of necessity democratic and social also.[71]

Here we find a theocratic prophetism concerned with current issues that is derived from the Old Testament, which locates the kingdom historically. Out of this grows the viewpoint of Jesus, who universalizes the present reality of the kingdom for all people. Jesus based his work on the ingredient of love, made provision for human need in mutual aid, and launched a powerful new movement resulting in a series of reverberations within history. This, says Rauschenbusch, is the new wine fermenting and bursting the old wineskins.

This is not to say that the kingdom is located only in society and not in the human heart. In his exegetical note on the *entos humon* of Luke 17:20–1, Rauschenbusch states: "The Greek phrase may mean either 'within you' or 'among you.' In either case it is an assertion of the presence of the kingdom and a contradiction of the catastrophic expectations."[72]

Thus Rauschenbusch lays the foundation for his argument, which recognizes the origin of the kingdom in the individual, but offers serious qualifications and warnings against the mystical and pietistic illusions that it lies solely within the individual. Though he concedes a certain inner dimension to the kingdom, he locates it primarily within history: it is a concrete, societal, historical experience. In fact, Rauschenbusch saw two major perils confronting a true understanding of the location of the kingdom: the pietistic truncation of the kingdom as solely within, and the other-worldly, apocalyptic focus of the kingdom in heaven rather than on earth.[73]

The focus of the kingdom within history and the rejection of pietism and other-worldliness have their roots in Anabaptist thought. This is made clear in Rauschenbusch's remarkable address to the German department of Rochester Theological Seminary on 12 September 1902 entitled "Die Geschichte der Idee des Reiches Gottes." After locating the roots of the kingdom, he traced its subsequent historical development. Augustine, he said, made the error of identifying the Church with the kingdom. The mystics, such as Tauler and Boehme, joined with the pietists in locating the kingdom within the hearts of men; however, the pietists also defined the kingdom as the invisible communion of the reborn. While Rauschenbusch preferred the concept of the invisible congregation to the Roman identificationist formula, he actually rejected both, crediting St Francis with the correct formulation of the kingdom as having an historical focus.[74] He credited the pre-Reformation monastics and sectarians – and their successors – with the rejection of subjective pietism and observed with considerable satisfaction the rejection of a purely personalistic ethic by the Calvinist-Puritan movement.

Rauschenbusch's address contains a synthesis of Anabaptist content (following Christ, accepting the Sermon on the Mount, and apostolic foundation) with a neo-Calvinist focus in relation to the whole community: a focus that he said was universal not tribal, historical not apocalyptic or heavenly; it started inwardly, but stressed the concrete outwardness of corporate life.

In his rejection of subjectivism, millennialism, and other-worldliness, Rauschenbusch was in line with what Robert Friedmann has shown to be one of the definitive struggles of the Anabaptists and other left-wing groups. In fact, Friedmann argues that pietism sapped the ethical vitality of Anabaptism in less than a hundred years through an emotional, individualistic subjectivism that made its peace with the *status quo* of social institutions.[75]

In one of his typical outlines, Friedmann puts it this way:

Pietism	Anabaptism
1 Experiential Christianity	1 Concrete or existential Christianity
2 Experience of one's own sinfulness, conversion, enjoyment of grace and edification	2 Imitation of Christ, discipleship, obedience and martyrdom

	Pietism		Anabaptism
3	The "sweet" Christ	3	The "bitter" Christ
4	Godliness (*Gottseligkeit*)	4	God-fearing (*Gottesfurcht*)
5	Group of redeemed individuals turning more to denominational-type church	5	Closely knit community with individuals
6	Emotionalism	6	Stern, austere frame of mind
7	Peace with the world	7	Nonconformity

The contrasts brought out by this listing uphold the point made in chapter 3, that while pietism operates in conflict with sectarianism, there is an affinity between the two. It might appear from this analysis that there were no pietist influences – which is not the case, despite Rauschenbusch's vigorous rejection of certain basic errors of pietism. His critics have charged that in refuting these errors, Rauschenbusch made the opposite mistake of negating the transcendence of God. This is implied in certain passages, but others suggest that Rauschenbusch was trying to protect himself against this very charge. It is clear to me that both aspects are present. But Rauschenbusch's defences of God's transcendence are inadequate in view of the sharp concessions he made to immanentism.

The main point, however, remains: Rauschenbusch holds that the Kingdom of God is located within history as a sociohistorical reality struggling with pietism, other-worldliness, and apocalypticism.

A RADICAL ROLE FOR LOVE

In his Taylor lectures, Rauschenbusch joined in the traditional evangelical emphasis on the death of Christ as the supreme revelation of God's love.[76] Elsewhere, however, he insists that this centre of love in the cross must find expression in ethical activity. To him, love of God was inseparable from love of people. We love our neighbour out of gratitude for the love God shows us. Our love takes shape in concrete patterns of social action. "The love of man is our concrete object lesson in the kindergarten of love, and if we learn that well, and as fast as we learn that well, the love of God grows in us and we become religious."[77]

Carrying this thinking over into the social realm, Rauschenbusch says it is to be expected that "those who are engaged in social work with a really loving spirit will find religion growing in them."[78] This is consistent with his thesis that discipleship is not limited to Christians or church members in the formal sense. A single line from his

Taylor lectures sums it up: "We love and serve God when we love and serve our fellows, whom he loves and in whom he lives."[79]

Rauschenbusch assigns a radical role to love in the kingdom. Indeed, love's task is all-encompassing: it is the force that creates society – cooperative organizations are "a remarkable demonstration" of this force. Thus, love is the key to sociology; it is the elemental force, the basic ingredient that brings and then binds humans together. Social institutions and culture in general are the necessary or potential expression of love. Where such expression is only potential, love steps in to complete its work. Love relates us to society. The kingdom is the realm of love because it moves the strong to stand with the weak in an affirmation of the sanctity of life.

Rauschenbusch had the strong prophetic feeling that Christians must emulate Jesus and the prophets and openly identify with the oppressed and rejected elements of society. "Love alone," he writes, "creates enduring loyalty and persuades the individual to give up something of his own for the common good of society." Through love one is moved to sacrifice by identifying with the downtrodden classes of the earth. This identification is evidenced in Jesus, as Rauschenbusch argues in his little book for college students, *The Social Principles of Jesus*.[80]

It is love that gives structure to the feeling of solidarity and forges positive, explicit identification with the unfortunate people at the bottom of society – a relationship that implies a certain delight in the sanctity of life.[81] Solidarity, identification, sanctity of life – all are love's work as it relates to society. It is love that makes society a creative force and binds individuals into communal groups. Love relates to society through close identification of the strong with the weak. It is guided in this identification through its own experience of illumination. The immediate task of love is to become socialized through the Christianization of the economic order.

In his commentary on 1 Corinthians 13, Rauschenbusch asks a number of crucial questions. Must we live permanently in a loveless industrial world, or do we dare to be Christians? Have we faith enough to believe that the Christian doctrine of love is the solution to the big modern questions? Dare we assert the futility of everything in our great world of commerce and industry that leaves love out? Do we dare to undertake the readjustment of all social life to ensure its obedience to the law of love? It is at this point that Rauschenbusch outlines the work of love:

The severest task and the most urgent task of love today is in the field of business life. Unless love can dominate the making of wealth the wealth of our nation will be the ferment of its decay. There will be no genuine advance for human society until business experiences the impulse, the joy, the mental fertility of free teamwork. As long as industry is built on fundamental antagonisms and the axle of every wheel is hot with smothered resentment, there can be no reign of love and no new era of civilization. Our age is asking leaders of the business world to take a great constructive forward step and to found business on organized love.[82]

Standing against any charge that he might have lost all contact with reality is Rauschenbusch's strikingly realistic analysis of just what this hope is struggling against. The following passage is an outstanding example of the union of stark realism and radical idealism that characterized his outlook:

With Christian instinct men have turned to the Christian law of love as the key to the situation. If we all loved our neighbor, we should "treat him right," pay him a living wage, give sixteen ounces to the pound, and not charge so much for beef. But this appeal assumes that we are still living in the simple personal relations of the good old times, and that every man can do the right thing when he wants to do it. But suppose a business man should be glad indeed to pay his young women the $12 a week which they need for a decent living, but all his competitors are paying from $7 down to $5. Shall he love himself into bankruptcy? In a time of industrial depression shall he employ men whom he does not need? And if he does, will his five loaves feed the five thousand unemployed that break his heart with their hungry eyes? If a man owns a hundred shares of stock in a great corporation, how can his love influence its wage scale with that puny stick? The old advice of love breaks down before the hugeness of modern relations. We might as well try to start a stranded ocean liner with the oar which pulled our old dory from the mud banks many a time. It is indeed love that we want but it is socialized love. Blessed be the love that holds the cup of water to thirsty lips. We can never do without plain affection of man to man. But what we most need today is not the love that will break its back drawing water for a growing factory town from a well that was meant to supply a village, but a love so large and intelligent that it will persuade an ignorant people to build a system of waterworks up in the hills, and that will get after the thoughtless farmers who contaminate the brooks with typhoid bacilli, and after the lumber concern that is denuding the watershed of its forests. We want a new avatar of love.[83]

It is a socialized love that emerges. It is essentially a love that places the responsibility for human misery upon social institutions. The older love is outmoded not because it is love but because it is merely personal and individual. In other words, it is the sociology not the ethics of love that needs alteration.

For Rauschenbusch love relates itself to other ethical principles as well; justice is a minimal precondition of love. Both love and justice are needed to restore right relations when injustice occurs. This aspect of his thought is difficult to describe because part of his analysis is ambiguous. In his pre-Niebuhr, pre-Gutierrez era, the leading social thinkers did not distinguish sharply between love and justice. At times Rauschenbusch's references to justice seem unrelated to previous discussions about love; at times he does relate them. Perhaps it would be illuminating to say that for Rauschenbusch there was no inherent conflict between love and justice. It would be more accurate, however, to say that he saw grave tension between love and injustice. While Niebuhr stresses that justice in the function of doing justly is in tension with love functioning as love, Rauschenbusch says that injustice "sterilizes" love, that injustice destroys the solidarity among humans – with a consequent breakdown of love.

By the same token, love seems to play a primary role in motivating people to destroy injustice. In a sense love is the precondition of justice. Where injustice occurs, justice demands both personal and social restoration.[84] He appears to say, first, that justice must be done, either by restoration of property or by a change of attitude through forgiveness, and second, that love must bridge the gap; the result may never be less than just.

The courts are necessary, says Rauschenbusch, for the conduct of social groups and for effecting large-scale changes such as adequate taxation of land values. His view on the role of love in effecting such changes is difficult to discern. Nevertheless, love and justice maintain a dialectical relationship, with love as the precondition of justice and justice as the minimal basis of love. Love has the function of abolishing injustice and of expressing itself institutionally.

This is where inconsistencies appear. In *Dare We Be Christians?* Rauschenbusch stresses love as the all-important ethical reality.[85] In *Christianizing the Social Order*, first love and then justice are the key ethical concepts. However, the dominant pattern in his thinking remains: that love is the all-important reality, both in its negative role of abolishing injustice (because injustice destroys solidarity), and in its positive role of finding expression in major social institutions. While the other two patterns are also present – love and justice as synonymous and dialectically related – they are not referred to as frequently as the first.

Conversely, Rauschenbusch sees coercion as the symbol of love's failure. This point is clearly established in *Dare We Be Christians?*, where he maintains that "love can usually dispense with force." He believed that democracy had softened "the horrors of criminal law and it will yet bring us a great lessening of militarism," and he predicted that if ever America "draws toward its ruin" it will come at a time when it "bristles with efficient arsenals and hired fighters." The constant use of military violence, he says, "is still in the despotic state. It needs democratizing and Christianizing."[86]

While recognizing the frequency with which love collapses into coercion, this statement fully assumes that love is both desirable and possible. Physical coercion is not inherent in the social fabric. It is a temporary, pathological development that *must* be driven out by love because it *can* be driven out by love.

WAR AND PEACE

The development of Rauschenbusch's thought with regard to war and social coercion went through three periods. In the first phase he saw value in various American wars in terms of advancing social change, releasing new and creative tendencies in American life, and promoting freedom in general. The second phase came during the First World War, when he met ruthless anti-German hysteria with a proposal roughly equivalent to the pre-World War II Neutrality Act, which banned the sale of munitions.[87] The third period arrived when he officially joined the Fellowship of Reconciliation (FOR), a Christian pacifist organization. An address he delivered at a meeting of FOR on 10 March 1917 was declared by Vida Scudder to be the best analysis she had ever heard on the ethical problem of war.

It is true that his letter to Cornelius Woelfkin of 1 May 1918, written shortly before his death, seemed to imply support for the war. His Boston address to the Fellowship, however, appears to be his final public word on the subject. It emphasized that war should be set among the social evils, all of which are closely connected at base; that love, as the supreme principle, makes reconciliation a present duty; and that Jesus and war are in utter conflict.

As for coercion in the social struggle, Rauschenbusch maintained a pragmatic pacifism during the period before he joined FOR. While not ruling out force in every instance, he believed that "force is not as effective as it looks ... The slow conflict of opposing forces is God's method of educating a nation."[88] The fact that the ruling classes could play the game of violence better than the working classes was cited as an additional argument against the use of force. Rauschenbusch always emphasized the necessity of basic structural changes: "The idea that violence can suddenly establish righteousness is just

as utopian as the idea that moral suasion can suddenly establish it."[89]
He offered a unique combination of a love ethic and social realism.[90]

THE ORIGINS OF LOVE

In looking for the origins of Rauschenbusch's concept of love, the
pro-New Testament left wing again comes into the picture. Unfortunately, his two books dealing most directly with love are small and
wholly without footnotes, something highly unusual in his otherwise
profusely documented writings. *Unto Me*, his book on social work,
contains a long section on the meaning of love but makes no reference
to any other books or writers. *Dare We Be Christians?* is based on
1 Corinthians 13 and naturally contains many references to biblical
material; the only nonbiblical writer it quotes is Tolstoy. That Rauschenbusch was deeply indebted to Tolstoy has already been established.

Rauschenbusch was immersed in the Scriptures, particularly the
synoptic Gospels as interpreted by the late nineteenth century critical
apparatus; he bypassed the Weiss-Schweitzer upheaval. His desire to
remain in the spirit and essence of the synoptic Gospels must, of
course, have contributed to his emphasis on love. And his studies
on the Continental Anabaptists must surely have reaffirmed his
emphasis on love and the rejection of violence.[91]

In connection with Conrad Grebel's letter to Thomas Müntzer,
which he translated and interpreted, Rauschenbusch wrote as follows:

Grebel and his friends regard nonresistance as the unquestionable Christian
duty against oppression and persecution. They feel trouble impending. They
face the thought of suffering and death with a spiritual exaltation that thrills.
They are the little flock among wolves and must suffer in meekness. Here
they clash with Muenzer. He was the angry voice of the on-coming social
democracy, and his religion only served to make him angrier and bolder.
They, on the other hand, utter the thought of the gospel and of the medieval
sects.[92]

All of Rauschenbusch's major books refer to St Francis of Assisi.
In *Christianizing the Social Order*, he remarks in a footnote that "Sabatier's *Life of St Francis of Assisi* is still the classical interpretation of
that wonderful soul." The following affirmations from Sabatier's book
enter into Rauschenbusch's concept of love: the apostolate, originally
quite primitive and without hierarchy (see chapter 5, "The First Year
of the Apostolate"); the radical emphasis on love, both from God
and for one's neighbour; the emphasis on enduring suffering; the

renunciation of property and the embrace of Lady Poverty; and the tragic struggle with institutional Christianity.

However, to find the sources for his sociological concept of love, one must study his relationship to liberalism, which made love the basic element in the whole of human society. His writings contain several references that suggest that he understood the sacrificial character of *agape*, even though the motif was usually subsumed in his emphasis on "solidarity." Thus:

Christianity means love. Love means community of interests and solidarity of life. The family has always been used as a symbol of Christian relations because it is the social organization most completely based on love and exhibiting the completest community life and possessions. Hence, we speak of God as our father and men as our brothers. Now it should be the aim of Christianity to base all other human relations on the same fundamental principles on which the family is based. The family contains the utmost diversity of sex, age, ability, and education, yet it exhibits complete social equality among its members. It recognizes authority but the authority is unselfish and sacrificial authority. The family is organized on the basis of service and not exploitation.[93]

Following this general statement on the sacrificial character of familial love, Rauschenbusch goes on to illustrate *agape* in the family, comparing it to the ethics of economics: "I hold that a nation will be Christian in the measure in which it regards itself as a great family and thus treats its members on the basis of social equality, solidarity of interests and possessions, and mutual service."[94] It is clear from this that he perceived the character of love as sacrificial and that he demanded its fullest expression in the whole social situation.

Visser t' Hooft sees Rauschenbusch's interpretation as the universalization of the ethics of family life, in which "extension rather than intensity or depth of love becomes the criterion; the quantitative aspect becomes of greater importance than the qualitative," and love "has to be toned down for its expansion to the ends of the earth."[95] Indeed, in *Christianizing the Social Order*, Rauschenbusch advocates that "instead of the policeman theory, a family theory of the state should be adopted."[96] Visser t' Hooft and others notwithstanding, surely Rauschenbusch made one of the boldest attempts in Christian social thought to construct a political and social ethic in terms of love.

THE JUST SOCIETY

Walter Rauschenbusch develops a realistic sociology embodying a solidarity-based doctrine of institutions; his sociology of the kingdom portrays life as operating in a solidaristic, socio-organic context in which sin expresses itself in superpersonal social institutions bound together in the kingdom of evil. This kingdom is to be countered with the Kingdom of God, which must deal with social groups in its pattern of salvation.

It is at this point that Rauschenbusch reworks the doctrine of Original Sin. His cogent arguments are that evil is transmitted both socially and biologically; that the evil of one generation is caused by the evil of the generation that preceded it; that sin and evil are wrought into social institutions, which then become superpersonal forces imposing their sinfulness on the individuals related to them; that these institutions are a form of collective selfishness perpetuated by the profitable quality of evil; that although past generations are represented in the collectivity of evil, the sources of evil are now present and active; that the all-pervasive character of the kingdom of evil makes it impossible to deal with by any purely individualistic means; and that the evil that has beset the network of social institutions is not inherent in these institutions; hence radical change is both desirable and possible.[97]

On the contrary, the doctrine of salvation must incorporate the sociology of the Kingdom of God even as the doctrine of sin incorporates the kingdom of evil. Therefore, while personal salvation is still important, the social gospel starts where personal experience leaves off; for the individual is to be fully redeemed, there must be salvation of the superpersonal forces of society. For these composite social personalities or institutions, "the love of money is the root of all evil."[98] He finally draws the conclusion that is basic to his whole system: "If unearned gain is the chief corrupter of professions, institutions, and combinations of men, these super-personal beings will be put on the road to salvation when their graft is in some way cut off and they are compelled to subsist on the reward of honest service."[99]

The Church is the social factor in salvation because it is a superpersonal institution; as such it must be expressive of the living Christ. In describing the corporateness of the Church, Rauschenbusch expresses his characteristic contempt for a purely noninstitutional and nonsocial approach. "What chance," he asks, "would a disembodied spirit of Christianity have, whispering occasionally at the keyhole of the human heart?" He states firmly that "nothing lasts unless it is organized, and if it is organized of human life, we must put up with the qualities of human life in it."

This in a nutshell is Rauschenbusch's sociology. On the positive side it is a sociology of love, since love makes and creates solidarity. Functionally it is a sociology of institutions, stressing the decisive role of the superpersonal forces expressed in social organization.[100]

Rauschenbusch himself traces the heart of his sociology to the sects, both before and during the Reformation, as well as to some larger currents in the mainstream of the upheavals of the sixteenth century. He particularly roots the ideal of "the poverty of the church" in the sects. Most of the reformers, he says, were trying to cleanse the Church of graft and the resulting idleness and vice rather than change its doctrine. "The ideal of the 'poverty of the church' which was common to men so unlike as Saint Bernard, Arnold of Brescia, Saint Francis and all the democratic sects, must be understood over against the vested wealth, the graft, and semi-governmental power of the church."[101] As far as the mainstream of the Reformation is concerned, property was again seen as a key issue. Because the Church refused to divest itself of its possessions and vested interests, these were forcibly secularized in all countries that officially adopted the Reformation. "The sinecures mostly disappeared. The bishops lost their governmental functions. Everywhere the reform movement converged on this impoverishment of the Church with a kind of collective instinct."[102]

At the 1893 meeting of the Baptist Congress in Augusta, Georgia, Rauschenbusch read a paper on "The Church and Money Power," in which he suggested that someday a church historian should throw aside the tradition inherited from papal and monarchical days and write a history on the simple but profound principle *Ubi Spiritus Christi, ibi ecclesia* (Where the spirit of Christ is, there is the Church). He commented that such research would probably find the bulk of Christian history in the account of the heretical movements and would show how much social leaven was contained in all the reforming movements of the Church. He made special mention in this regard of the Waldensians, Savonarola, Wycliffe, the Bohemian Brethren, the mendicant orders, Quakers, Anabaptists, and Mennonites.[103]

He continued in the speech to analyze the Reformation from a class perspective, pointing to the fact that the population of Germany took sides largely according to social standing. The nobility stood by the Catholic church and supported the *status quo*. The lower nobility and city dwellers followed Wittenburg and the Swiss reformers. It was a middle-class movement; in most cities where the new doctrine carried the day the political situation was simultaneously revolutionized. The monopoly of civil power held by the Catholic priests and nobility was overthrown and power given to the Lutheran or Reformed burghers. It was only in Anabaptism that reform ideas finally took hold of the proletarian masses. There the ideas proved to be revolutionary, brimful of Christian social applications. "That Catholics and Lutherans united in crushing out the Anabaptists is by no means solely due to theological convictions, but to class interests aroused to fury," says Rauschenbusch. "The middle class began to come into its inheritance at the Reformation, in religion, politics and social enfranchisement. The lower classes have had to wait till our own generation; they have now achieved their political rights; slowly they are also achieving their social rights; and in so far as Christianity is really sharing in the people's movement, it is recalling the church to its ancient hostility to money power."[104] While the proletarian movement was crushed in the sixteenth century, Rauschenbusch regarded the rise of the labour, socialist, and cooperative movements of his day as the final rising of the working classes, a phenomenon that would be consolidated through the agency of the new religious movement of the social gospel.

Current Anabaptist research deals more precisely with the class composition of the left wing than did the scholarship of seventy-five years ago. In 1850, Friedrich Engels made Anabaptists part of the struggle in his study of the Peasants' War. The 1955 doctoral research in Zurich by Paul Peachey on the economic and social backgrounds of the Anabaptists concludes that while the Reformation, the Peasants' Revolt, and Anabaptism all shared in the social, political, and religious stirrings of the early sixteenth century, Anabaptism did not spread among the Swiss peasantry until months, and in some cases years, after the peasant uprising.[105] This study stresses that the radical factor in Anabaptist sociology was the rejection of the medieval *corpus Christianum*, which had been retained by the reformers. But the overall impact of Peachey's study is to sharpen rather than destroy Rauschenbusch's perception of the Anabaptists as being related to weighty social issues, with deep roots in the lower classes.

In the United States, Rauschenbusch's sociology came as a needed corrective to the subjectivism and individualism of American pietism. This was, in fact, one of his outstanding contributions. His identification with the sectarians provided part of the material for his sociology. This is clearly seen in his burning conviction that the sectarians, preceded by the Franciscan type of monastics, purged the Church of the curse of money in their ideal of Church poverty. The fact that Rauschenbusch was a church historian constructing an ethical system is significant because he had a more sensitive outlook towards the economic corruption of the Church in the past.

THE CHURCH
AND THE KINGDOM

For Walter Rauschenbusch the true church is a disciplined, democratic, voluntary association that has a direct effect on social institutions. In fulfilling this role, the Church realizes its sole reason for existence, namely, to serve the Kingdom of God. In his Yale lectures, Rauschenbusch explained that those who stand for the new social ethics have been among the most active critics of the churches because they have realized most clearly both the great needs of American social life and the Church's potential ability to meet them. In fact, he says, "their criticism has been a form of compliment to the Church. I think they may yet turn out to be the apologists whom the Church most needs at present. They are best fitted to see that while the Church influences society, society has always influenced the Church."[106] This picture of the mutual interpenetration of church and society is basic to Rauschenbusch's thought.

Rauschenbusch discovers a new emphasis on the Church – due not to a renascent Anglican Catholicism but to "a combination of purified Protestantism and modern social insight." He ascribes much of this purification of Protestantism to the liberal theologians of Germany and America. In any case, the net effect is that the individualism of Protestant theology, with its long-standing evil effects, is overcome.

Nowhere does Rauschenbusch set forth more clearly a sectarian concept of the Church than in his 1905–06 series of essays on "Why I Am a Baptist." He is humble about his Baptist connections, declaring that he does not want to foster Baptist self-conceit because that would grieve the spirit of Christ. Nor does he want Baptists to shut themselves up in their little shells and be indifferent to the ocean outside. He admits that Baptist church organization is faulty in many ways, that it creaks and groans as it works along, but that it is built on noble Christian lines; hence it is very dear to him. He is a Baptist, but he is more than a Baptist: "All things are mine, whether Francis of Assisi, or Luther, or Knox, or Wesley; all are mine because I am Christ's. The old Adam is a strict denominationalist; the new Adam is just a Christian."[107]

He goes on to outline the pattern of the Church through his Baptist orientation: (1) It is a voluntary association of Christ followers guided by discipline and definite standards of moral and spiritual achievement.[108] (2) It is a Christian democracy. The people are sovereign. The power of the Church is carried out by ministers and officers strictly in the name of the people. All aptitude for leadership is encouraged but it must serve the people and be reviewed by the people in the Church from time to time. (3) It recognizes no priestly class. The minister is not essentially different from the laity. (4) It has no hierarchy within the ministry, no hierarchy of vicar, rector, bishop, archbishop, and pope. (5) Its churches have home rule. Each church is sovereign in its own affairs. (6) It rejects all alliances with the state. However, this does not mean that spiritual life has nothing to do with secular life. Separation means the state will not dictate to the Church on spiritual affairs, that it will not hamper the work of the Church, and that the Church will not introduce ecclesiastically based considerations into politics.[109]

The second part of his doctrine of the Church is already implied in the foregoing: the Church has a very real effect on social institutions. The kind of church he advocates will mould, shape, and influence the surrounding culture in the direction of democracy. Even as the Church was and is continually influenced by society, so it will exert its own influence on that society. Rauschenbusch holds that church organization is of the utmost importance for the social institutions of the culture. While he concedes that the Church inevitably borrows from the state, he laments the fact that "the Catholic Church by its organization tends to keep alive and active the despotic spirit of decadent Roman civilization" and that "the aristocratic republicanism of the Calvinistic churches ... has perpetuated itself wherever Calvinism went." The democracy of the Congregational churches, originating in the democratic passions of the English revolution, has also perpetuated itself, in a more positive way. Because the action of religion on people's minds is profound, he believes that people accustomed to democratic church organization will find self-government in the civil community that much easier and any government from above unpalatable.[110]

Rauschenbusch locates the heart of his ecclesiology in primitive Christianity and left-wing Protestant history, particularly in Continental Anabaptism and the Puritan synthesis of Calvinism and sectarianism. He suggests that the farther down one goes in the class structure, the closer one comes to the left-wing forces of the Anabaptists, and that the interpenetration of these forces and the lower classes gives us the nearest thing we have to a truly Christian church and culture. The lower classes need the sectarian church and the sectarian church needs the lower classes. He always correlates polity and politics against the background of class: "In the English Revolution the political attitude of each section was quite accurately graded according to its ecclesiastical radicalism. The Episcopalians were for the king; the Presbyterians were for a strong Parliament; the Independents were republicans, and vice versa."[111]

Quite characteristically, Rauschenbusch bases much of his ecclesiology on the early church community. "Wherever Christianity came," he says, "we see a new society nucleating."[112] He calls this "the society-making force of primitive Christianity."[113] He loved to emphasize the revolutionary impact of the early church.[114] It had a communitarian dimension that he admired: "They were social communities with a religious basis ... They prayed together but they also ate together. They had no church buildings but met in the homes of their members ... they had no official clergy distinct from the laity. They were democratic organizations of plain people."[115]

Rauschenbusch was also influenced by Richard Heath and Emile de Laveleye. Written in a polemical style, Heath's *Captive City of God* is a radical attack on the alienation of the Church from the working classes through materialism, middle-class apathy, and capitalistic injustice. The Church is portrayed as apostate. Heath uses figures to show that on the Continent, in Great Britain, and in the United States, the working classes were basically lost to the Church. This is due, he claims, "not so much to doubts about the truth of the Christian religion as to a settled conviction that the churches do not truly represent it."[116] Contemporary Christians, says Heath, "are so infected with the business spirit that they know of none but its ideals and cannot imagine any order of things not governed by its rulers."[117]

This apostasy, says Heath, is true of both the Anglican church, which is inherently incapable of reaching the people, and nonconformist churches, which are temporarily incapable of doing so. The Church of England does not, never has, and never can preach the gospel to the poor, because it is united with the state, and the English state is an oligarchy constituted for the protection of property and the maintenance of the power of the wealthy few over the impoverished many. In addition, the English church condones war, penal sadism, and other evil policies.[118]

The nonconformist churches are also ineffective because they are plagued with mammonistic middle-class prejudices. Heath cites with approval a conference between Nonconformity and labour in 1867 where labour accused the dissenting churches of engaging in religious commercialism, promoting class distinctions in places of worship, and hindering free speech. Ministers were accused of being members of the dominant class and acting in its interests.[119]

What is the answer to such captivity? First, says Heath, the free churches must demonstrate democracy within themselves and let it flow out into the social order, thereby producing an example of a truly divine society.[120]

Both Rauschenbusch and Heath combine pessimism about the empirical churches with unbounded optimism about the creative role of a radical, prophetic, proletarian, democratic church. Both are sectarian with specific roots in Anabaptist and Puritan life and thought, and both lay great stress on the original, normative pattern of the early church. *The Captive City of God* has a chapter on "Early Christianity and the Democratic Ideal," which makes much of the antiproperty communism of the early church and the generally dynamic and creative role of the primitive *koinonia*. Though Heath at times portrays the Church as only the more inspired dimension of a democratic society, he returns to the theme of the great role of the Church, emphasizing that it "exists to be a City in which a Divine Society may develop. It has to witness for God and the Kingdom of Heaven."[121]

Heath's Kingdom of Heaven is a perfect equivalent to Rauschenbusch's Kingdom of God. It is the reign of God coming to earth, preferably to the Church first of all and then to society, but in any case to the whole culture. Heath is perhaps more reluctant than Rauschenbusch to see the separation of human concerns from the Church. Both agree that culture has corrupted the Church but that a radical sectarian church could lead the masses in redeeming the culture. Heath strongly believed that any such option was forever closed to the Church of England and similar state churches. There can be do doubt that Rauschenbusch's ecclesiology was influenced by this left-wing English Baptist and student of Anabaptism.[122]

Emile de Laveleye (1822–92) was a Belgian economist with a background in the Roman Catholic church. He was chiefly associated with bimetallism and primitive property, but Rauschenbusch was particularly influenced by his book *Protestantism and Catholicism in Their Bearing Upon the Liberty and Prosperity of Nations* – a book so insignificant by some accounts that it is usually missed in the list of his literary contributions. A cursory reading suggests the radically Protestant character of this book and reveals why de Laveleye is referred to four different times in *Christianity and the Social Crisis*. It also suggests why de Laveleye is reported to have left the Roman church later in his career.

Like Heath and Rauschenbusch, de Laveleye believed that religion is highly creative in the political realm, leading to the organization of state forms borrowed from religion.[123] His book provides a critique of economic and political life and praises the creative and healthy interaction between Protestantism (particularly left-wing) and economic and political life. While Catholic countries must rely on Renaissance paganism, he says, Protestant countries find no such dichotomy between morals and religion.

The Christianity of Penn and Washington, writes de Laveleye, is a better cement for the foundation of a state than the philosophy of Verginaud, Robespierre, and Mirabeau. He also praises Roger Williams, whose name, while little known outside the United States, "deserves to be inscribed amongst those of the benefactors of mankind ... he was first to sanction religious liberty as a political right."[124] He contrasts this with the experience of France, which persecuted, strangled, and banished "those of her children who had become Protestants."[125]

De Laveleye repeats his analysis over and over: (1) Free and representative government is the logical consequence of Protestantism; absolute government is the consequence of Rome. (2) Protestantism unites a nation; Catholicism divides it in dangerous, angry conflict. (3) Protestantism diffuses knowledge; Rome tends to suppress it. (4) Protestant countries initiate education and science, which lead to prosperity; Catholic nations do not and thus have more poverty. (5) The highest Protestant ethic is moral duty; for Rome, it is honour. (6) Protestantism tends to keep its intellectuals; Rome alienates them. And (7) the Puritan and left-wing Protestants are the most creative in society.

Once again, here was support for Rauschenbusch's vigorous ecclesiology: state forms and economic forms are borrowed from religious forms. Religious institutions are dominant, whether for good or for evil. Free Protestantism is the most desirable form for attaining a democratic end.

In the original reference to Richard Heath in *Christianizing the Social Order*, Rauschenbusch also recommends H.C. Vedder's *Socialism and the Ethics of Jesus*, especially the chapter on "The Social Failures of the Church."[126] Henry Vedder was a fellow Baptist who held the chair of Church History at Crozer Theological Seminary. Vedder dedicated his *Reformation in Germany* to Rauschenbusch with these words: "To the prophet of the New Reformation to whom this story of an older struggle for liberty is inscribed with all esteem and affection."[127]

Vedder finds the roots of modern socialism among the Anabaptists, although he is careful to point out that not all Anabaptists were collectivists and that they were more inclined towards communism in the primitive sense than to socialism. He feels that the tragic outcome of the Moravian Anabaptist communists (later known as Hutterites) is suggestive both negatively and positively. Vedder believed that Luther was uninterested in ethics and that Calvin's theology tended towards aristocracy and monarchy. This suggests that it was the Anabaptists who had a dynamic view of life that demanded cultural and ethical changes. "The Anabaptists were despised and rejected for the same reason that Jesus was rejected and despised – they announced a gospel that, if accepted, would have required and produced a reorganization of society on the principle of human brotherhood." Sixteenth-century Europe, he said, "was no more ready for such a gospel than twentieth-century Europe is."[128]

Here is one more influence in Rauschenbusch's sectarian ecclesiology: the left wing is the most creative because in seeking to recreate itself in the society it develops democracy and community. The left wing and conventional capitalist culture exist in radical conflict.[129]

This, then, is Rauschenbusch's ecclesiology: the true church is a disciplined, democratic, voluntary association that has a direct effect on social institutions; it is rooted in the sectarian churches and is influenced by Richard Heath, Anabaptist scholar and nonconformist from England, Emile de Laveleye, a Roman-nurtured anti-Catholic who saw churches as master blueprints for the culture, and Henry C. Vedder, Baptist scholar of the left wing and proponent of Christian socialism. Few concepts are more important to Rauschenbusch than his concept of the Church. One final but crucial idea remains.

THE KINGDOM IN HISTORY

Walter Rauschenbusch believed that the Kingdom of God comes by evolutionary gradualism and by distinct periodizations, of which his own time was one of the richest in all of history.[130] When he published his first major work in 1907, he was living in the climactic fourth period of history – one of a series of epochs that started with the Renaissance:

The modern emancipation of the intellectual life began in the Renaissance of the fifteenth century and is not finished yet. The modern emancipation of the religious life began in the Reformation of the sixteenth century and is not finished yet. The modern emancipation of the political life began in the Puritan revolution of the seventeenth century and is not finished yet. The modern emancipation of the industrial life began in the nineteenth century and is not finished yet. Let us have patience. Let us have hope. And above all let us have faith.[131]

What was it about his own time that made it so great and momentous a period in history? For one thing, past reasons for the Church's failure to respond to Christianization in the social order had either disappeared or been weakened. They were inherent neither in the Church nor in history. Rauschenbusch lists nine such reasons: the impossibility of any social propagandizing in the first centuries after Christ; postponement of Christianization until the Lord's coming; the Church's hostility to the Roman Empire and its civilization; its ascetic tendencies; monasticism; sacramentalism; dogmatic interests; the disappearance of church democracy; and lack of scientific comprehension.[132]

Of particular importance to Rauschenbusch was the setting aside of the idea that the Kingdom of God must slough off apocalypticism if it is to become the religious property of the modern world.[133] While there are apocalyptic dimensions in the New Testament, he maintained that these were not in the mind of Jesus.[134]

Progress is evolutionary but not inevitable. "History laughs," he said, "at the optimistic illusion that nothing can stand in the way of progress." The important point is that it is the substitution of the evolutionary for the apocalyptic that makes this a key period, a brilliant climax to the series starting with the Renaissance. In saying this, Rauschenbusch attempts to define the original historical context of eschatology, which he says has always been influenced by social causes; it was nurtured among the Jews by political oppression and among the early Christians by persecution. Rauschenbusch memorably says that the Jews and early Christians "wept and prayed our eschatology into existence. Our Apocalypse is wet with human tears and must be read that way. Ever since, some sections of eschatology have been vivified, others modified, and some consigned to oblivion through the pressure of social causes. Has not the social consciousness of our age, speaking through the social gospel, also a right to be heard in the shaping of eschatology?"[135] Thus, a historically conditioned apocalypse meets the new historical conditions of the social gospel's eschatology.

The foregoing gives the roots of Rauschenbusch's concept of periodization. The Renaissance will be discussed in the next chapter; socialism will be treated more fully in the chapter on Calvinist and Catholic transformationism. This leaves three characteristic foundations for the origins of periodization: the primitive apostolic church, the Anabaptists, and the Puritans (especially as interpreted through the Baptists and the Congregationalists).

Rauschenbusch viewed the early church as a revolutionary movement that jolted Judaism out of its ethnocentricity and legalism – a movement that challenged a hedonistic culture. It tore down the existing barriers "with irresistible force" and "brought men together by a new principle of stratification." Fraternalism, democracy, communism, even the political implications of millennialism combined to make the primitive church one of the most seminal movements in history.

I have shown how Rauschenbusch accepted the Anabaptist movement as a unique force in history. In his essay on "The Freedom of Spiritual Religion," he notes that "in the long, slow sweep of four centuries, often by devious and pathetic ways, the course of religious development for the Protestant world has been in the direction marked out by the swift rush of the radical parties of the Reformation."[136] "Swift rush" is a vivid phrase for the special power of the Reformation period.

Speaking in Boston in 1908, Rauschenbusch included the Baptist and Congregational Puritans among those who moulded a distinct period of history and then defined his idea of a revolutionary era. The local press reported him as follows: "The speaker made it plain that he meant by 'revolution' not a transitory violent outbreak, but a large historical change in the fundamental convictions and institutions of a nation or an age. It might last a century or two."[137]

Revolution, then, is a synonym for period and period means a large historical change in the fundamental convictions and institutions that may last several centuries. If we couple this with Rauschenbusch's theory of ascending periodization from the Renaissance through the twentieth century, we discover his concept of history. It is interesting to note that he does not limit historical pediodization to the distinctly religious periods, despite the great importance he assigns to them. He includes the Renaissance as well as the Reformation, the socialistic-industrial revolution as well as Puritanism.

Rauschenbusch owed two immense debts to sectarianism: his early start in sectarian research, and the architectonic structure of his Kingdom of God ethic, in which he freely used sectarian motifs. To be sure, he adapted, modified, and selected from the materials at hand, rejecting the tragic concept of history and the tendency towards withdrawal that he found in the nonaggressive sects; he also regarded the unfolding of the kingdom as more urgently important than redemption, contrary to the view of the sectarians. But the sectarian impact on the formation of his ethics was very great indeed.

It must be borne in mind, however, that some of the synthesized concepts (based in large measure on sectarian teaching) remained in tension for him: the discipleship emphasis versus the institutional outlook; love as fulfillment versus tragic love; pessimism about the empirical churches versus hopefulness about the role of the creative radical church; the periodic view of history versus his tendency to think in terms of progress; the emphasis on discipleship versus a nonliteral view of the Bible; and Baptist sectarianism versus a genuine catholicity of outlook on church questions. Despite the problem posed by these residual conflicts, the sectarian factor was too basic to his Kingdom of God ethic to be ignored.

The next chapter examines the role of liberalism in the intellectual development of Walter Rauschenbusch.

CHAPTER FIVE

The Influence of Social and Religious Liberalism

Walter Rauschenbusch is widely known as a Christian social thinker whose origins were primarily in liberalism. H. Richard Niebuhr regards this as his weakness, since it was the Christ-of-culture type of idealism that lost its power of transcendence over culture. By contrast, Ralph Henry Gabriel considers this "social thinker" label a high compliment, since the Rochester prophet overcame the romanticism of Charles Sheldon and the dogmatism of George Herron to articulate the religious side of the American democratic faith.[1]

Niebuhr and Gabriel are representative interpreters of two conflicting schools of thought, both using liberalism as their key insight. Despite the popularity of this emphasis, the interaction of the liberal motif with other factors bears further investigation, particularly since additional research reveals the originality of the normative formulation of Christian social concern at the beginning of this century. In the fuller context now available, Rauschenbusch emerges not as a carbon copy of contemporary liberalism but as a creative thinker who freely appropriated materials from many streams of influence.

I shall devote special attention to Albrecht Ritschl in order to illustrate one of the main examples of Rauschenbusch's free and independent encounter with a major liberal mind. Rauschenbusch and Ritschl may be compared and contrasted on at least nine different issues. Above all, my analysis is centred around the theme that linked them together – the Kingdom of God motif. That Ritschl was a strong influence does not imply that Rauschenbusch uncritically and completely accepted his ideas; on the contrary, Ritschl has no bearing on Rauschenbusch's sociology, political ethics, or doctrine of the Church, and Rauschenbusch opposes Ritschl on various sectarian themes (discipleship and the doctrine of the Church, for example).

I shall attempt to show how Rauschenbusch freely criticized liberalism from the standpoint of other motifs as well, and shed light on the various affirmations of freedom that shaped his ethics. Here it is necessary to stress a basic division between the theological, biblical, and historical liberals and the socioeconomic progressives. This division corresponds to the twofold definition in my introduction of Rauschenbusch as a social thinker whose origins were in liberalism. From the theological side came the attack on the Hellenization of theology, rejection of confessional dogmatism, an anti-metaphysical outlook, stress on the historical Jesus, a view of redemption as secondary to the teleology of the kingdom, solidarity in sin and salvation, rejection of the forensic atonement, gradualism, and optimism. The liberal theologians influenced Rauschenbusch before the socioeconomic thinkers, since he encountered them during his graduate studies before embarking on more vigorous ethical and social encounters.

From the socioeconomic thinkers and movements come six formidable contributions to Rauschenbusch's ethics: a theology of social institutions, an economic interpretation of ethics, the value of socialism, the doctrine of progress, a historical perspective stressing the uniqueness of the new social concern, and an eclectic spirit.

The number and diversity of his liberal influences also pose questions concerning the other theologically liberal leaders who preceded him. For example, the idea of discipleship had been emphasized in America by various liberals since the days of Horace Bushnell, yet there is a difference between thinkers who stemmed directly from Puritanism and those who, like Rauschenbusch, reflected a sectarian background. The children of Puritanism start with a transformationist vision rooted in the sovereignty of God in His kingdom. This essentially Calvinist approach, which put strong emphasis on the historical Jesus, was modified by the neo-Ritschlianism that swept across America. To this modified theology was added an institutional analysis of liberalism and the overall climate of critical methods and optimistic social hopes.

Rauschenbusch, on the other hand, began with a pietist and sectarian emphasis on discipleship, love, and the Kingdom of God, and on the Church as a democratic, voluntary fellowship. Consequently, he rejects quietism, borrows transformationism from the Puritans and evangelicalism, and exchanges part of his sectarian theology for that of the neo-Ritschlians. Like the children of Puritanism, he adds the institutional analysis of liberalism, its democratic philosophy of history, and much of its methodology. But these liberal emphases provide the least common denominator between W.D.F. Bliss, Washington Gladden, Richard T. Ely, and other American social prophets, though once again, there is marked interaction, fostered by the free atmosphere of American church and cultural life.

Rauschenbusch equates the beginning of our own age with that of the eighteenth-century Enlightenment, suggesting that the impact of science on religion is very great and that this demands basic changes in religion. These changes will, of necessity, bring us closer to Jesus.[2] While his utterances are not all as uncritical as this one, it is evident that he often drank deeply from the cup of liberalism. It is unfortunate that the pattern of his biblical outlook was formulated without the benefit of the cogent criticisms of contemporary New Testament interpretation made by Johannes Weiss and Albert Schweitzer.[3] Had these been part of Rauschenbusch's thought he might have been less vulnerable to attack. However, I refer to Rauschenbusch as an "Enlightenment liberal" in order to associate him with the most accurate and meaningful category of liberalism.

Against the background of many orthodoxies, Europe had seen cruel and ravaging religious warfare. There was a deep longing for some kind of common ground that would subsume a humane concern for the welfare of people and the richness of human life. The answer appeared in the Enlightenment, which stressed a unifying rationalism and produced a universal religion and ethics. Starting in the Reformed countries in the mid-seventeenth century, the movement reached France in the eighteenth century and later spread to Germany and the United States. Far from encouraging an atheistic scepticism, it was a moralistic secularization of the Christian tradition with a sharp focus on an earthly utopia.

Sidney Mead and James Nichols identify three different Enlightenment groups in terms of their attitude to revealed religion: (1) rational supernaturalists, the largest group in Britain and America, represented by the philosopher John Locke, Archbishop Tillotson, American Unitarians, and, in the first half of the eighteenth century, many articulate English Anglicans and Presbyterians, whose basic belief was that revelation was a corroboration of natural religion; (2) Christian deists, who were a shade more radical since they wanted to purge Christianity of all irrational and peculiar elements (Kant and the neo-Kantians, hence Rauschenbusch, would be located in this second category); and (3) anti-Christian deists, who had no hope for a rationalistic Christian church because they believed that Christianity was inherently linked with bigotry, persecution, and superstition (Voltaire hoped to see the last king strangled with the entrails of the last priest).[4]

It is against this background that we see Rauschenbusch being influenced by the Christian deists, who were more liberal than the rational supernaturalists and less sceptical than the anti-Christian deists. Indeed, there was never a time when he was not speaking as a convinced Christian and an active churchman.

With regard to the origins of his liberal thinking, Rauschenbusch's family background is perhaps less important than it is in relation to the influence of pietism and sectarianism. Yet one must not underestimate the very early origins of political liberalism in the Rauschenbusch family, which supported the German revolution of 1848. The *Zeitgeist* of Germany and America (primarily of New York and Rochester) was basic to his development.

His self-image is that of a participant in a groundswell of liberal affirmation; this is essentially compatible with his allegiance to other previously accepted strata of truth. His Kingdom of God image becomes the catalyst that integrates these widely scattered elements into a coherent whole. It was around the Kingdom of God motif that he selected and rejected original materials. Albrecht Ritschl was his main theological mentor, although, as already mentioned, this was a free and creative encounter. Immanuel Kant and Friedrich Schleiermacher were also important for his theological development, while H.C. King, Washington Gladden, and W.A. Brown were less so. Julius Wellhausen was a crucial interpreter of the Bible, in contrast to Ernest Renan and Emil Schürer. In history, Adolph Harnack stands out above all others. And in the socioeconomic sphere, Henry George and Edward Bellamy are highly important while Giuseppe Mazzini, John Ruskin, Sidney and Beatrice Webb, and Theodore Roosevelt are less important.

My main purpose here is to show more clearly how liberalism constituted an original influence on Rauschenbusch's ethics. The picture will be that of liberal content poured into the moulds of sectarianism and pietism. Even here, however, there must be some qualification, since some of the content of sectarianism is retained in terms of discipleship and of the doctrine of the Church.

SETTING A LIBERAL DIRECTION

Before taking up the theological, biblical, historical, and socioeconomic thinkers in a more systematic fashion, it is important to outline the origins of Walter Rauschenbusch's social ethics in the experiences that started him in the direction of liberalism and kept him growing in that direction.

In an excellent characterization, Blake McKelvey has observed that "the religious stirrings in Rochester around the turn of the century both influenced and reflected the career of Walter Rauschenbusch."[5] Apparently it is difficult to know when he was shaping Rochester's outlook and when he was reflecting that city's environment.

Among the experiences that particularly influenced Rauschenbusch in the direction of liberalism were those of his family during the German revolution of 1848. His father was deeply moved by the democratic student movement, which eventually culminated in an ill-fated revolution and was followed by the Bismarckian reign of blood and iron. August Rauschenbusch arrived in the United States in 1846, several years before a stream of liberal Germans who were destined to enrich American liberalism in many ways. Rauschenbusch's uncle, Wilhelm, risked his professional reputation as a lawyer to defend students who took part in the 1848 revolt. Hence the Rauschenbusch family had a liberal strain running through it, along with pietism.

A.S. Zucker vividly depicts the distress of refugees from the German revolution.[6] August Rauschenbusch, Carl Schurz, and H.L. Mencken are typical of some who emigrated to the United States. August and, more clearly, Walter Rauschenbusch represent the attempt to express a passion for democracy within the context of the Christian faith. Carl Schurz displays the democratic faith through political action in a secular-idealist context. H.L. Mencken, who graduated from Knapp's Institute in Baltimore (a school founded by one of the Forty-Eighters), symbolizes the German free thinker endowed with literary and intellectual gifts.

The Forty-Eighters were anti-ecclesiastical because of their bitter experiences with the reactionary state church of Germany. Moreover, they had been deeply affected by the Enlightenment. Their common creed was an impassioned faith in liberty, democracy, and national unity in terms of an optimistic and rationalistic progressivism. In America it found expression in a touching faith in humanity and in democratic institutions.

While some of these refugees found in the more democratic churches of America an alternative to the hidebound ecclesiasticism of Europe, the true expression of German Protestant progressivism in America came, as described in chapter 3, in waves of immigration after the 1848 upheaval. It led, for example, to the union of pietism and ecumenical liberalism in the *Evangelischer Kirchenverein des Westens*. This became the evangelical denomination in which the Niebuhr family of Missouri found an increasingly liberal American Protestantism.

Thus, August's nurture and the favourable timing of his departure from Germany assured Walter Rauschenbusch of a legacy of political progressivism and philosophical rationalism, for August was part of the most liberal contingent in the long history of German immigration. In addition, there is the tendency towards political liberty in Württemberg pietism, as suggested by Ritschl. While this will not be pursued in detail here, it may be the clue to the receptivity of a genuinely pietistic family to political liberalism.

Another factor in the Rauschenbusch family background is its pattern of cultural development under a regimen of travel, encounter with beauty through the fine arts, classical education in the Continental manner (a brilliant intellectual life rooted in three or four generations of family eminence), and the stimulus of knowing America and Europe almost equally well from childhood through maturity.

This social and cultural potential found room for development in Rochester, which was and remains a vital middle-sized city with a long history of vigorous theological and social liberalism. The following summary documents the sweep of this movement from the early period of Rauschenbusch's career to the mature years, when he was one of the acknowledged leaders of the local progressive movement.

The Rochester Years

Walter Rauschenbusch was born in Rochester in 1861, a decade before the open defence of evolution by Newton Mann, the minister of a local church. Rauschenbusch grew up in a city where the most controversial liberal ideas were being proclaimed. There were few places in America where the son of a Baptist minister would be exposed to such a critical milieu. Indeed, McKelvey reveals that in the early part of his career Rauschenbusch was overshadowed by "several more dramatic prophets of the new day who were already on the scene ... beginning with Newton Mann, defender of evolution in the 1870s and culminating with the Reverend Paul Moore Strayer, close associate of Rauschenbusch at the end of this period."[7]

In 1880 the Rochester presbytery ejected the Plymouth church led by Byron Adams. The building was later converted into a people's clubhouse. Billiard and pool tables were installed in the former Sunday-school rooms and dancing was permitted. Lectures on social problems alternated with musicals to replace Sunday worship. A weekly paper called *Here and Now* was published. Rauschenbusch was keenly interested in this experiment in social Christianity and appeared on the platform together with Richard Ely, Henry Lloyd, Golden Rule Jones, and others. In 1902 the pastor resigned to become a socialist organizer in New England.

Algernon Crapsey, another local minister and organizer of St Andrew's Episcopal Church as a haven for the poor and oppressed, began a series of lecture-sermons in 1904 on the historical relationship between religion and the state. In the tenth address he denounced the contemporary commercialism of both church and state – a theme Rauschenbusch had previously lectured on from the same pulpit. In his presentation, Crapsey questioned the virgin birth. The bishop removed him from St Andrew's two years later, and the defrocked pastor promptly organized a successful forum on social issues in a local theatre. Crapsey and Rauschenbusch were close friends, although Rauschenbusch was to be bitterly attacked by this bold Episcopalian liberal for being a noninterventionist during the First World War.

Rauschenbusch was a popular lecturer (as well as committee member and organizer) at all the liberal forums, held most often at the Labor Lyceum, which was started in 1896 as a Sunday-afternoon discussion group devoted to questions of interest to working people. The scheduled topics covered the spectrum from God and the Bible (with views ranging from agnosticism to devout belief) through temperance, peace, socialism, the class struggle, and anarchism. Rauschenbusch frequently discussed the socialist question, meeting all comers. He candidly criticized the dogmatic, brittle thinking of certain socialist parties as contributing to the corrosion of the genius of socialism.

In his biography of Rauschenbusch, McKelvey makes a suggestion hitherto unrecognized as a possible genesis for the writing of *Christianity and the Social Crisis*. He believes that the Rochester Labor Lyceum was the anvil on which Rauschenbusch hammered out his social ethics, which ultimately received wider expression in the book that made him famous.

In 1901 Rauschenbusch became a member of a committee charged with drawing up a charter for the local federation of churches. His committee recommended that the word "evangelical" be omitted so as not to exclude the Jews and Unitarians. While the committee finally failed to agree on the suggestion, the incident suggests Rauschenbusch's liberal temperament. In 1904 a local branch of the Brotherhood of the Kingdom was organized, drawing together the socially minded ministers of the town. Annual meetings of the local chapter brought in such nationally known speakers as Josiah Strong of New York, whose theological platform was identical to that outlined in Rauschenbusch's books.

A strong institutional church movement in Rochester was led by Brick Presbyterian, organized in 1898, and by the Unitarian church under the leadership of William C. Gennett. There were also some creative offshoots of the Church, such as the Salvation Army (organized in 1896), the Baden Street Settlement of 1901, the YMCA and YWCA, and various social agencies that numbered thirty-nine under a United Charities organization in 1910. The city's numerous reform movements included Clinton Howard's Prohibition Union, the suffragist Political Equality Club, and a special committee set up by the YMCA and chaired by Rauschenbusch to investigate social conditions in the city. The committee's report revealed that the average wage in manufacturing was $498 per year for men and $267 for women. Twelve recommendations were made, all of them relevant and progressive. In addition to its liberal movements, Rochester held a great revival in 1907, led by Wilbur Chapman, with two hundred thousand people attending two hundred meetings.

What emerges here is an unusual community well suited to providing a liberal social prophet with a superb local base for leadership, the expression of his convictions, exchanges with other socially concerned people, and, above all, an opportunity for continuous lecturing well to the left of the conventional church meeting. These public forums played an important part in Rauschenbusch's intellectual development, giving him a chance to test his ideas before receptive audiences. Moreover, most of his addresses were fully covered by a sympathetic local press, thus enlarging his platform immensely.

The New York Years

In New York City Rauschenbusch's individualistic pietism broke down under the pathological collectivism of the city. "Clean, kindly, religious men," he wrote, "stoop to methods so tricky, hard and rapacious, that we stand aghast whenever the curtain is drawn aside and we are shown the inside facts ... Men do not want to do these things, but in a given situation they have to, if they want to survive or prosper, and the sum of these crooked actions give an evil turn to their life."[8]

At the same time he discovered, through the works of Henry George, political action and the beginnings of a basically socialist institutional criticism. His first published reflection on these topics was in a paper dated 12 December 1887, which implied that no amount of personal integrity or enforced reform could deliver New York (or the United States, for that matter) from the death-knell of capitalism and industrialism. In New York he also discovered new Christian co-workers in Leighton Williams and Nathaniel Schmidt, with whom he founded the Brotherhood of the Kingdom. With these new colleagues he could discuss social questions in a new theological context; the fact that all of them started from a Baptist base gave them a common frame of reference. The Brotherhood of the Kingdom developed his great gifts for social analysis and criticism and gave him a new literary medium.

Seven years after arriving at Hell's Kitchen (the name by which the area surrounding his New York City church was known) Rauschenbusch married Pauline Rothe of Milwaukee, who shared his new theological and social views. Together they created a home that undergirded Walter's prophetic life. Pauline's support perhaps compensated for his loss of hearing one year before he left New York – a tragedy, but one that increased his sympathy for the physically handicapped and may have furthered his scholarly career, since reading became easier for him than conversation.

It was in New York that he discovered a completely new range of authors: Henry George, Richard Heath, Emile de Laveleye, Tolstoy, Mazzini, Ruskin, Sabatier, Ragaz, Kingsley, Maurice, Bellamy, Gladden, and many others. This broadening of literary experience became evident in his Rochester books some years later.

It was also during this period that he took one of his most fruitful European trips to study sociology and the teachings of Jesus in Germany, and to inspect cooperatives, the Salvation Army, and other social institutions in England. He investigated Fabian socialism in the home of Sidney and Beatrice Webb.

The New York parish experience involved Rauschenbusch in a strike, in which he opposed the antilabour leadership of the Reverend A.J. Behrends, who used the sanctions of the Church against the workers.

Family roots in the German liberal revolution, his American relocation to Rochester (where liberalism flourished early), and the sharp intellectual, religious, and social impact of New York City were basic to Walter Rauschenbusch's development as a leader of the social gospel. Indeed, it was his historical destiny to be in places where vigorous historical forces were being unleashed. In Germany he experienced the early, confident phase of Ritschlianism; in America he entered the same powerful phase of liberal theology and social concern. He met liberalism in America and abroad as a militant, aggressive, fighting faith. To give a leader a firm grasp of the dynamic *Zeitgeist*, nothing can equal direct involvement in key centres of influence during the earliest phases of Rauschenbusch's development. Rauschenbusch fortunately had such involvement, and when his experience interacted with his previously acquired convictions, he was able to give the American social gospel its definitive expression.

LITERARY ORIGINS

No evaluation of the impact of liberalism on Walter Rauschenbusch's thinking can be considered complete without an investigation of the theologians, biblical scholars, and historians who influenced him. Much of the theological side of his Kingdom of God ethics came from Kant, Schleiermacher, and Ritschl (on an ascending scale of influence). As usual, he was critically selective. Yet there is a sense in which certain aspects of Rauschenbusch's thought are a commentary upon these three towering German figures.

Rauschenbusch's pietism no doubt helped prepare the way for those who emphasized experience, rejected Protestant scholastic theology, and used the scientific methods of historical and literary criticism. Walter's father entered the University of Berlin in 1834 at the age of eighteen, thus bringing to the father-son team an early encounter with Kant and Schleiermacher. Schleiermacher's work was well known even before his death in Berlin in 1834. Ritschl's career as a thinker had not yet begun, since he was only twelve in the year of Schleiermacher's death. Walter himself entered the gymnasium in Gütersloh in 1879; when he went to Berlin in 1883, the works of Kant, Schleiermacher, and Ritschl were available through Mommsen, Curtius, and others.

Immanuel Kant, like Walter Rauschenbusch, was a child of pietism who turned to liberalism — at least theologically. From pietism Kant acquired an emphasis on the practical and moral priorities of religion. From the Enlightenment he received his rationalism, which was for him not so much a historical and empirical quest as a metaphysical and universal outlook. Indeed, he distrusted history as a vehicle of truth and grounded religious faith on the inmost moral consciousness. He essentially expounded a "religion of good works, in which religion is loved for its own sake — a religion of pure humanity which is the true religion of Christ."[9]

It was with enthusiasm that Rauschenbusch received the Kantian idea that "the eighteenth century marked the adolescence of the modern spirit." He also agreed with Kant's concept of the Kingdom of God. The system expounded by Kant strikes many other familiar chords in the readers of Rauschenbusch's works. It is a deistic conception of natural law with a collective societal culmination in a Kingdom of God or ethical commonwealth. The details of Kant's concept of the kingdom in the third part of his book on religion (the part recommended by Rauschenbusch) are as follows.

(1) A juridico-civil state (condition) of nature is the relation of people to each other in which they all stand alike under coercive

public juridical laws. (2) An ethical-civil state of nature is that in which persons are united under noncoercive laws, i.e., under the laws of virtue alone. (3) Mankind must leave the ethical state of nature to become a member of the ethical commonwealth or kingdom because the juridical state of nature amounts to a war of all against all, while the ethical state of nature is one in which the good principle, residing in every individual, is continually attacked by the evil that is also there to be found. (4) The people cannot be the source of good law because the general will sets up external legal control, whereas morality is inward. Hence an ethical commonwealth can be thought of only as a people under divine commands, i.e., as a people of God living under the laws of virtue. (5) The idea of a people of God can only be realized (through human organization) in the form of a church. By "church" Kant meant primarily the complete organization of humanity under the moral law in a universal society. He contrasted the historical-ecclesiastical church with the pure religious faith of reason in a universal church and rejected most of the historical forms of the church, including the sectarian.

Here, then, is a familial organization of humanity in a voluntary, universal community of moral law, which is to say, the Kingdom of God. In the transition from historical to universal faith, worship recedes into the background, since it contains no moral worth; indeed, an evil person can worship. Moral faith assumes the predominant role. The atonement (which one cannot accomplish for oneself) is also rejected. The humiliating distinction between laity and clergy disappears because true freedom will result in equality. In addition, Kant believed that, whereas morality had formerly been expounded in biblical terms, it is better that the Bible be expounded according to morality. Lest there be any mistake that this is radically moralistic, Kant's last line in *Religion Within the Limits of Reason Alone* declares that "the right course is not to go from grace to virtue but rather from virtue to pardoning grace."

These, then, are the elements of Kant's teaching that Rauschenbusch found particularly significant. Other similarities in their thinking included the concept of the kingdom as a gradual triumph of moral values among humanity as a whole; a common desire to purge Christianity of all irrational elements, pushing back to the rational essence of religion; redemption as secondary to the coming of the kingdom; the family as the ultimate symbol of human community; a sense of the tension between their contemporary state of religion and culture along with a sense that the highest inner drives of the culture were consummated through religion.

There are several points of difference between Kant and Rauschen-busch. Kant's ultimate category is law while Rauschenbusch's is love. Kant offers no equivalent of Rauschenbusch's response to Jesus in terms of discipleship and apostolate. Moreover, he broke quite radi-cally with the Church whereas Rauschenbusch remained active in the Church all his life, drawing upon its vocabulary and symbols despite a prophetic anti-ecclesiasticism spelled out in sectarian terms. Rauschenbusch had a deeper interest in history and a richer concept of historical forces, and where Kant was a systematic, philosophical thinker, Rauschenbusch was topical and homiletical. Kant had no sociology of institutions commensurate with Rauschenbusch's and, in particular, no sense of the creative role of a gathered, democratic Christian fellowship. Despite these differences, however, I conclude that the Enlightenment liberalism of Kant was fundamental to Rau-schenbusch's thinking.

Friedrich Schleiermacher may be regarded as the bridge between Kant and Ritschl in terms of their influence on Rauschenbusch.[10] Rauschenbusch quoted approvingly Otto Pfleiderer's assertion that "the Protestant theology of our age rests on the foundation laid by Schleiermacher; all theologians – some directly, some more indirectly – are seeking to establish connections between the religious person-ality of the individual and the common consciousness of the church."[11] He also pointed out that "Schleiermacher was one of the really creative minds in the history of Protestant theology, a man who set new problems and made old problems profounder, thus fertilizing the thoughts even of those who know nothing of him."[12] Rauschenbusch reaffirmed Ritschl's statement that Schleiermacher should not be known primarily for his "subjective view of religion," the feeling of dependence on God as against the dry intellectualism of Enlightenment rationalism. Rather, Schleiermacher ought to be known for his concept of solidarity. This emphasis on corporateness, as well as his Christology, appears to have influenced Rauschenbusch greatly.

In his Yale lectures, Rauschenbusch quoted at length from Schleier-macher's *Der Christliche Glaube* to show the racial and societal dimen-sion of sin. Sin is something wholly common, not pertaining to individuals separately but "in each the work of all, in all the work of each." Schleiermacher maintained further that "the congenital sinfulness of one generation is conditioned by the sinfulness of those who preceded, and in turn conditions the sin of those who follow."[13]

Rauschenbusch is eager to find support for his thinking on sin because the solidaristic view of sin and salvation is at the very heart of his kingdom theology and ethics. Schleiermacher developed and expanded the Kantian collectivism through a social dimension of the Christian faith modernized by solidaristic insights. He rejected the Augustinian sense of guilt and inherent corruption in favour of an incapacity for good, which is linked with the guilt of the race. Redemption becomes the restoration of God-consciousness through Jesus Christ. Rauschenbusch acknowledged his debt to Schleiermacher on this insight as well. According to the German theologian, humanity in the Kingdom of God comes from a spiritual unity and fellowship with God. Christ was the first to live fully within the consciousness of God and to share his holy and loving will; by so doing he set in motion a new beginning of spiritual power that pervades the common life within the organized totality of the race.

Here was the small start of the Kingdom of God within the human race. Now the relation between God and humanity changes from antagonism to cooperation. This is not a forensic proposition but a new factor in the bloodstream of the race. Thus, "when men would learn to understand and love God, and when God could by anticipation see his own life appropriated by men, God and men would enter into spiritual solidarity, and this would be the only effective reconciliation."[14] In this description of Schleiermacher's view, one notes the weakening of forgiveness as a factor in redemption. Rather, there is the emphasis, as in Rauschenbusch, on the communal or societal factor. The social dimension and God-consciousness are available in the Church. Through them the individual passes from the evil state of God-forgetfulness to God-consciousness.

Rauschenbusch agreed with Schleiermacher's concept of sin as rooted in the social and racial oneness of people everywhere. This is the characteristic solidarity motif. There is also a common emphasis on religious experience rather than on miracles, revelation, or dogma. Both rejected forensic Christologies in favour of the divine-human solidarity renewed through the new God-consciousness of Christ.

But there are differences between Rauschenbusch and Schleiermacher as well. Rauschenbusch believed that Scheiermacher was inconsistent in his analysis of redemption and the kingdom. At one time the redemptive theme had priority, at another the kingdom theme was dominant. Rauschenbusch thought the kingdom must be central at all times. A second difference is that while Schleiermacher lacked a full-orbed sociology, Rauschenbusch believed that a sociological analysis was fully compatible with the Schleiermacher system; in fact, he thought of himself as making the logical inference in social ethics from the basic direction of Kant, Schleiermacher, and Ritschl.

Finally, Schleiermacher held to German nationalism, which in fact destroyed a vital social ethic based on his theology. Koppel Pinson concludes that Schleiermacher rejected a world state, accepted the monarchy, and identified the state with people and soil in the concept of *Volksstaat*.[15] Rauschenbusch's life as the American son of a German immigrant in the late nineteenth and early twentieth centuries made it easier for him to transcend these nationalistic beliefs. During the First World War he suffered over the prevalent anti-German hysteria. While he loved German culture, he never succumbed in any degree to a view of the state as an organism.

The theologian who most deeply influenced Walter Rauschenbusch was Albrecht Ritschl (1822–89), who taught at Bonn and Göttingen. A comparison of the two reveals striking similarities. Indeed, H. Richard Niebuhr places Rauschenbusch squarely with Ritschl, though Rauschenbusch, he believes, had greater moral force and less theological depth. In other words, Rauschenbusch thought more clearly than Ritschl on ethical questions without, however, possessing the theological insight of Ritschl, who was nonetheless influential in the former's thought process. Niebuhr considered Ritschl the quintessential exponent of the Christ-of-culture philosophy. It is important to test this concept, since it sheds much light on Rauschenbusch's handling of the same question.

Rauschenbusch pays high tribute to Ritschl. As early as 1892 he said that the sage of Göttingen had done the most effective work in making the Kingdom of God central in theology. In his last book, published in 1917, Rauschenbusch still placed Ritschl at the top of an ascending scale of kingdom theologians, above Kant and Schleiermacher. He lauds Kant for being the first to recognize the importance for ethics of the Kingdom of God. Schleiermacher was the first to apply the teleological quality of Christianity to definitions of its nature; yet Schleiermacher wavered ambiguously between personal redemption and the Kingdom of God. Rauschenbusch concluded, therefore, that it was Ritschl who did more than anyone else to bring the Kingdom of God to the forefront of theology.

To study the relation between Ritschl and Rauschenbusch is to observe the tremendous impact of Ritschl on Rauschenbusch's ethics, particularly in terms of the Kingdom of God. Yet Rauschenbusch did not find his discipleship and apostolate in Ritschl. He rejected Ritschl's union of church and state and his patriarchal monarchism. He could not find a sociology in Ritschl and sought it instead in the post-Ritschlian liberals. A comparison of their Kingdom of God concepts will, however, bring to a specific focus the interaction of these two figures in the master theme of the kingdom.

The definition of the Kingdom of God   We have seen that Rauschenbusch defined the kingdom as the reign of God coming through the progressive growth of love in society, leading to a humanity organized according to the will of God. In other words, it is a universal moral fellowship of humanity that comes gradually through the power of love. Many statements in Ritschl's works suggest the precise definition of the kingdom found in Rauschenbusch.

The role of the kingdom   To Rauschenbusch as well as Ritschl, the kingdom is the master key and the most important material principle of the new theology. However, Ritschl did not nail down his view of the kingdom as the master key to the mind of Christ without some development in his thinking. In his major work, *The Doctrine of Justification and Reconciliation*, he first subordinates redemption to the kingdom as the key to the work of Christ. Then he coordinates the two in his famous statement that "Christianity is not to be compared to a circle which should run about one centre, but to an ellipse, ruled by two foci."[16] In later statements, the foci are identical. However, in *Instruction in the Christian Religion*, the characteristic Ritschlian position is finally assumed; now the Kingdom of God is both the key to the mind of Christ and the regulative principle in his theology. The vacillation found in *Justification and Reconciliation* (originally published in German in 1870–74) disappeared several years later with the publication of his *Instruction*, in which he makes it quite clear that the kingdom is both the key to Christ[17] and the greatest fact about Christ for Christian community: "The kingdom of God is the divinely vouched for highest good of the community founded through His revelation in Christ; but it is the highest good only in the sense that it forms at the same time the ethical idea, for whose attainment members of the community bind themselves together through their definite reciprocal action."[18]

One also notes in Ritschl's kingdom concept a tension between the kingdom and nature. What he accepts as given is "man's self-distinction from nature and his endeavour to maintain himself against it or over it." In another key sentence, he says that "the kingdom of God, even as it now exists in the world is the present product of love-inspired action, is supra-mundane, in so far as we understand mundane to mean natural, naturally conditioned and divided existence." This, of course, had a direct bearing on the Christ-of-culture dimension of Ritschl's theology. In any case, the role of the kingdom is primary for Rauschenbusch and Ritschl alike.

The response to the kingdom   In Rauschenbusch the response to the kingdom is discipleship and apostolate. He socializes discipleship in order to save it from an individualistic interpretation. He focusses usually on the need to follow Jesus but sometimes, in a more mystical fashion, on union with the Holy Spirit. He stresses the pure essence of the teaching of Jesus as the norm for the Christian life and calls for a broader definition of discipleship in relation to the new social movements outside the Church. Furthermore, he believes that a new social order would make it possible to follow Jesus.

There are points of contact with Ritschl in this, but again, there are also substantive differences. In Ritschl we find the same emphasis on the historical Jesus and on the pure essence of his teachings, a rejection of christological speculation regarding the two natures of Christ, and an emphasis on Christ's teleological mission rather than his nature or origin. Ritschl also sought to underscore the social dimensions of sin and redemption: Christ did not come to save individuals but to establish the kingdom through community. Later I will show that Ritschl had not logically inferred an adequate sociology from this socialized theory. Yet the intensely social nature of his view of the work of Christ derives from a moral faith interpreted within the experience of the Christian community.

Ritschl's rather rigid historicism made him dissent from a direct spiritual contact with Christ in the present. Chapter 6 in *Justification and Reconciliation* outlines his objections to the Christology of the reformers. He believed that an exclusive emphasis on redemption often led to a pathological response, falsely rigorous, and he is the avowed enemy of all monastic and pietistic practices of the devotional life. Rauschenbusch corrected the subjectivity of pietism with a more objective and sociological concept of discipleship. Moreover, he was exposed to a radical criticism of the institutional church. Hence, he could not agree that Christ could not be known apart from his historical existence in the Christian community. Indeed, Rauschenbusch accepted the *kairos* of his time through socialism and social movements where Christ was more truly present than in the Church, although he continued to hope that the Church would respond to the divine call to structure society with an analogous Christian democracy.

Perhaps this is the real issue between Rauschenbusch and Ritschl: for the former the response to Christ was both individual and social; the latter demanded a church leading in socioinstitutional action; for Ritschl the response to Christ demanded Christian community but excluded radical social, political, and economic changes.

The function of the kingdom   To Walter Rauschenbusch the function of the kingdom was to Christianize the social order by abolishing unjust privilege while at the same transforming semi-Christian social institutions. It was in the context of this idea that he made his ill-fated attempt to measure the Christianization of major American institutions, concluding that four out of five such institutions (family, church, school, and home) were already essentially sound and that only the economic order remained to be Christianized. While there are indications of this position in Ritschl, Rauschenbusch displayed both his independence and his greater sociological and ethical depth in reconstructing the Ritschlian background.

In Ritschl, humanity comes into human culture with a drive towards the good but becomes corrupt through evil associations, which are mediated by society through social inheritance. Obviously, the creation of sound social relationships will change human life. To preach forgiveness of sins to individuals is to go back to the Old Testament or Catholic perspectives. Forgiveness is always offered in terms of community. Against this background, Rauschenbusch could easily develop his idea of Christianization, singling out the structural parts of the culture for clues to their moral health. This would be an extension of Ritschl. But Ritschl also emphasized the idea that men and women realize their highest good in the kingdom. His theory of self-realization is predicated on the reality of freedom in the kingdom. Eternal life is given a present, historical definition.

Moreover, Ritschl believed that the basic issue is between human beings and nature rather than between human beings and God. He used this doctrine to rationalize nationality, arguing that Christianity must win over nations as a whole and that it cannot be antinational. He also attacked what he called the pietistic critique of state churches.[19] Certain nations are destined for Christianity. What is more, Ritschl attributes the diversity of nations to different spiritual endowments as well as to acquired moral dispositions. The unhistorical (Australian aboriginals) and the particular-historical (China and India) lack an inner disposition towards Christianity. He does not deny a priori the possibility of extending the Christian community over nations that are not world-historical outside of Western civilization, since scientific proof is not available, but he does imply a scepticism about this possibility.

The point is that Ritschl could not conceive of any individual apart from nationality, or of any individual apart from the Christian community. Individualism is dead; collectivism is a fact. Christ brings to fruition the cultural destiny of certain peoples (but not necessarily of all peoples) and the rich historic-communalism of the Christian faith; out of their meeting comes what God has intended.

Missing here, of course, is the awareness of tension and conflict between Christ and culture. H. Richard Niebuhr once observed that

Ritschl's view was more like the gospel according to St Immanuel than the gospel according to St Matthew or St Paul. While Rauschenbusch was steeped in German culture and had a genuine feeling for America's democratic destiny, he did not place his faith in an ethnocentric nationalism. While he maintained a much sharper sense of tension with the culture, he also tended to see Christ bringing to fruition the master cultural trends of his time – such as an awakened working class seeking a socialist culmination of its hopes.

The scope and location of the kingdom   Rauschenbusch made one of the outstanding attempts of modern Christian history to construct an ethic of love. He defined love as a society-making ingredient, a dynamic power that relates people to the community by causing the strong to stand with the weak, a power whose task it is to be socialized in the process of taming the economic order. For him love involved justice; coercion led to its failure. Ritschl defined the kingdom as "a fellowship of moral action prompted by love." More than a chance remark, this is a central affirmation. As for God, Ritschl says that he is "either conceived as love or not at all" and that he "has revealed Himself to the Christian community as love."[20] The law of love in correlation with the kingdom is the very foundation of the Ritschlian system. While he does not elaborate on its use as extensively as Rauschenbusch does, there is no essential difference between the two.

The sociology of the kingdom   Rauschenbusch sees life as operating in a solidaristic, socio-organic context in which sin expresses itself in social institutions bound together in the kingdom of evil. This kingdom is to be countered with the Kingdom of God, which must deal with social groups in its pattern of salvation. Ritschl placed a strong emphasis on teleology; it is basic to his outlook. He ascribed his pioneer teleologic conception to Schleiermacher. Sin is social; it is not purely an individual matter.[21] It was on this theological idea that Rauschenbusch built his sociological concept of sin. He once indicated that Ritschl was "born too early to get sociological ideas."

The ecclesiology of the kingdom   Rauschenbusch believed that the true church was a disciplined, democratic, voluntary association with a direct effect on social institutions; in making this impact the Church realizes its sole reason for existence, namely, to serve the kingdom. It is at this point that the distance between Rauschenbusch and Ritschl is the greatest. Rauschenbusch clearly borrowed his idea of the Church from the left wing rather than from Ritschl.

Two cornerstones are apparent in the Ritschlian view of the Church. First, he distinguishes between moral and devotional life, a distinction based on the larger difference between the Church and the kingdom. The community of believers constitutes the Church when it is engaged in public worship or devotional action; the community of believers constitutes the Kingdom of God when its members are acting morally towards each other in everyday life. Thus, the kingdom is given a purely moral definition separate from sacraments and piety. Second, the kingdom is identified with the invisible church. The Church temporal is visible to the naked eye; it belongs to the world. The kingdom, although moral, is supramundane. While the two spheres are related, they are not identical. They are, however, mutually dependent and reciprocally serviceable.[22]

Ritschl is primarily interested in the relationship of the Church to the kingdom. He solves the problem by stripping the Church of any dynamic function and giving the crucial moral responsibility to the kingdom. Although few theologians have made corporateness more crucial to Christianity, neither Catholics, reformers, nor sectarians will accept this formulation. Ritschl has constructed a status for ethics that is independent of the Church. The latter exists in terms of piety but not in terms of ethics.

While Rauschenbusch shared Ritschl's sense of tension between church and kingdom in making the former serve the latter, he did not want the Church operative solely in terms of piety.

The philosophy of the history of the kingdom   As already noted, Rauschenbusch believed that the kingdom came by evolutionary gradualism and distinct periodizations, his own day being one of the most auspicious periods in all of history. In general, Ritschl shared the gradualist concept.

After Ritschl, several other theologians played secondary roles in the development of Rauschenbusch's thinking. They had a later impact and their contributions were less structural. The evidence suggests that Josiah Royce was the most important. His great teaching career at Harvard (1881–1916) coincided with Rauschenbusch's most creative years. In the Taylor lectures at Yale in 1917, Rauschenbusch rated Royce as the most outstanding American thinker on the Church in relation to salvation.[23]

Royce writes that humanity is divided into two different grades or levels: individuals and communities. He puts great importance on the religious and moral truth "that a community, when unified by an active indwelling purpose, is an entity more concrete and less mysterious than any individual man, and can love and be loved as a husband and wife love."[24] He restricts the term "love" to individual relationships, applying the term "loyalty" to the love of an individual for a community.

Second, Royce affirms the burden of sin: "The individual human being is by nature subject to some overwhelming moral burdens, from which, if unaided, he cannot escape. Both because of what has been technically called original sin and because of the sins that he himself has committed, the individual is doomed to a spiritual ruin from which only a divine intervention can save him."[25] He "cannot unaided win the true goal of life. Help must come to him from some source above his own level."[26]

Third, salvation comes not through the person of Christ but by membership in a community that has salvation. The individual members give this community loyalty, identifying themselves with its life, appropriating its memories, experiences, hopes, spirit, and faith. This is the atoning and saving power of the true community, and it is available in Christianity.

In the preface to *The Problem of Christianity*, Royce makes it quite clear that he is an explicit modernist. He bases his stand on the fact that the Church rather than its founder is viewed as the central idea of Christianity. Moreover, he affirms a religion of experience – not the religious response of individuals as described in *The Varieties of Religious Experience* by William James (to whom Royce says he owes a great deal of inspiration), but rather social religious experience. Loyalty depends upon this corporate encounter. He severely criticizes James's belief that the religious experience of a church must be "conventional," calling this "a profound and a momentous error."[27]

Rauschenbusch was pleased with Royce's basic argument, but vigorously rejected "the slighting of Jesus" as one of the most unsatisfactory elements in his thought. Indeed, Rauschenbusch declared that "a proper evaluation of Jesus as the initiator would have been the natural and necessary consummation of this entire doctrine of salvation by loyalty."[28] Yet his deep sympathy for much of Royce's thinking as an absolute idealist is significant and basically in line with the Kant-Schleiermacher-Ritschl Enlightenment continuum. Royce is closer to Hegel than to Kant, even though he objected to a glib use of Hegelianism as characteristic of his position and emphasized the contribution of Charles Pierce, William James, and even Schopenhauer.

The American theologians known to and read by Rauschenbusch were all essentially Ritschlians who contributed nothing new to his thought, although they confirmed the general trend of his theology and perhaps tightened the connection between theology and the emerging social gospel. In *Christianizing the Social Order*, Rauschenbusch pays tribute to three pioneers of Christian social thought in America: Washington Gladden, Josiah Strong, and Richard T. Ely. He says that "these men had matured their thought when the rest of us were young men, and they had a spirit in them which kindled and compelled us."[29] Of the three, only Gladden would qualify as a systematic theological thinker, although he was essentially a preacher with literary gifts. His theology, as Charles Hopkins points out, stemmed directly from that of Horace Bushnell, which, in turn, strongly resembled the teaching of Ritschl. Frank Foster also says in his *History of New England Theology* that both had the same point of departure, the same detailed results, and a common reaction against a repulsive orthodoxy.[30]

Rauschenbusch both quoted from and recommended the writings of other American Ritschlians: William Newton Clark's *Outline of Christian Theology*, William Adam Brown's *Christian Theology in Outline*, Gerald B. Smith's *Social Idealism and the Changing Theology*, Henry Churchill King's *Reconstruction in Theology*. As previously noted, these books contained nothing that Rauschenbusch had not already found in Ritschl and amplified in his own thinking. However, they could be recommended to his American readers, since they were written in English and generally more attuned to the American mind.

All the familiar themes are here: the kingdom as the master theme, the community as the religious unit, religious experience as more valuable than doctrine, the growing social consciousness, value judgments as the source of knowledge, a playing down of the miraculous, little interest in the Trinity or the incarnation, a sympathy for science, an emerging sociology, and an optimistic view of humanity and history. It must be concluded that Rauschenbusch's legacy from the Enlightenment, mediated by Christian Ritschlian theologians, is basic, genuine, and far reaching.

In addition, one must take into account the impact that liberal scholars had on Rauschenbusch's intellectual development. He was a bilingual first-generation German American. He was educated in America at the University of Rochester and its seminary. In Germany he attended the gymnasium and spent two years at a university. Hence he was always keenly informed on scholarly trends in Europe, particularly in Germany. He followed the major trends in biblical criticism as a child of the times. His was not a dutiful following of the current "line" in biblical criticism, but a joyous sense of having discovered a new truth capable of contributing greatly to the social message of the Christian faith. In his outburst of delight over the rich new period of history that was to realize the promise of the Renaissance, the Reformation, and the prophetic expectations, he noted that the Bible shared in the new social interpretation. The following words indicate the zest with which he welcomed the new approach to the Bible:

The first self-styled scientific life of Christ was written in 1829 by Karl Hase who observed, "Christians had always bowed in worship before their Master, but they had never undertaken to understand his life in its own historical environment and his teachings in the sense in which Jesus meant them to be understood by his hearers. He had stood like one of his pictures in Byzantine art, splendid against its background of gold but unreal and inhuman. Slowly, and still with many uncertainties in detail, the figure is coming out of the past to meet us. He has begun to talk to us as he did to his Galilean friends, and the better we know Jesus, the more social do his thoughts and aims become."[31]

Even more specifically, Rauschenbusch found the main themes of his theology in biblical criticism: the centrality of the kingdom of Jesus; the central ethical concern of the prophets, of whom Jesus was the chief; evolutionary development from lower to higher forms; and Pauline and Johannine elements as Hellenistic accretions on the simple teachings of Jesus. Among the scholars who affected his biblical outlook, Julius Wellhausen (1844–1918) exerted crucial influence. In one passage, after showing how Jesus appropriated the essential spirit of the prophets, and that "in the poise and calm of his mind and manner, and in the love of his heart, he was infinitely above them all," Rauschenbusch appends a footnote saying that "this superiority is beautifully expressed in Wellhausen's *Israelitische und Judische Geschichte*, Chapter XXIV."[32] While one is accustomed to thinking of Wellhausen in terms of Old Testament criticism, he in fact did most of his writing on New Testament themes. The volume referred to here was written about the time Rauschenbusch first entered university in Germany.

Wellhausen's approach is characteristic of Rauschenbusch: the kingdom is a present spiritual entity outside the context of the apocalyptic, leading to a fellowship of spiritual men seeking a higher righteousness.[33]

Two major scholars whose writings would have altered the basic orientation of Rauschenbusch's biblical outlook and whose position might have protected him from severe attacks later on were Johannes Weiss and Albert Schweitzer. Johannes Weiss (1863–1914) was an almost exact contemporary of Rauschenbusch. His *Die Predigt Jesu vom Reiche Gottes* was first published in 1892, at the very outset of Rauschenbusch's first period of study at a German university.

Albert Schweitzer's *Von Reimarus zu Wrede* (*The Quest for the Historical Jesus*) was published in 1906, one year before Rauschenbusch's second stint in Germany but probably after he had already written *Christianity and the Social Crisis*, which appeared in print in 1907.

Since Weiss's eschatology was written in 1892, it must surely have been known to one as thorough in his reading as the bilingual Rochester historian.[34] Fourteen years later, when Schweitzer appeared on the scene, Rauschenbusch still had twelve of his best years ahead. On the other hand, by the time Schweitzer's bomb exploded, Rauschenbusch had set his mind on a view of history which he either could not or would not change. Conrad Moehlman suggests that Rauschenbusch was aware of the attack on his position, but would not yield. The new eschatological concept would have meant a radical reworking of his entire theological, historical, and ethical outlook, since his was a developmental, gradualist, evolutionary view of life. In any case, the American *Zeitgeist* was hardly in keeping with an outlook more akin to Melville, Kierkegaard, and Dostoievski than to Emerson, Ritschl, and Tolstoy.[35]

American Influence

Walter Rauschenbusch singled out the works of two American scholars as recommended reading on the social aims of Jesus. For those who read only English he recommended *Jesus Christ and the Social Question* by Francis G. Peabody of Harvard, and *The Social Teachings of Jesus* by Shailer Mathews of Chicago. He rated Peabody as more sympathetic and Mathews as more incisive.

Shailer Mathews represents a shift that might have taken place in Rauschenbusch's thinking had he lived after the First World War instead of succumbing to cancer in 1918.[36] Mathews's book, published in 1897, was a compilation of a series of articles he had written for the *American Journal of Sociology*. He had called his series "Christian Sociology," uniting his interest in sociology and biblical theology. So far as he was aware this was the first volume in English in its field – although this is accurate only as regards the first presentation of the new liberal concept of the kingdom "as a social order to be progressively reached."[37] It is significant that thirty-one years later, in 1928, he rewrote the book under the title *The Social Teachings of Jesus*, in order to incorporate an eschatological view of the kingdom. Could this have happened to Rauschenbusch if he had lived for seventy-eight years like Mathews did (1863–1941) instead of only fifty-seven years?

Rauschenbusch recommended Mathews's book even more highly than Peabody's widely used work. Mathews wrote discriminatingly on the meaning of the kingdom; he was aware of the Scylla of literalism and the Charybdis of modernization of the simple gospel records. He stated clearly that Jesus did not believe in a kingdom that was political or theocratic, as the Christian socialists believe. Nor did he accept the view that Jesus taught the kingdom as a figure of speech merely to indicate a perfect method of life for the individual – a subjective interpretation that he found in Tolstoy's *The Kingdom of God is Within You*. He likewise rejected the eschatological view of the kingdom as untenable, eventually revising his book accordingly. However, by 1897 he believed that the eschatological position was historically conditioned. For Mathews two facts remained: Jesus thought of the kingdom as a concrete reality rather than as an idea; and this reality is not to be left as an unattainable ideal but must be progressively realized.[38]

This reveals once again the congenial soil in which the new social ethics took root. One is impressed by Mathews's attempt to protect his kind of idealism from glib optimism and oversimplification; at every point he tried to secure the maximum protection from possible attacks on his position. Yet his is still the voice of a Christianized Enlightenment idealism rediscovering the Christian ethic. His intellectual honesty, however, forced a serious modification of this outlook by 1928.

Francis G. Peabody, the other American scholar cited by Rauschenbusch, published a social interpretation of Jesus in 1900. There was nothing particularly new in this erudite work, which contained a definitive bibliography. However, the book is a valuable commentary on the alertness and catholicity of the American Protestantism of a century ago as it responded to the social implications of Jesus. According to Peabody, Jesus is more than an economic reformer, even though his sayings on wealth are very hard to follow. Jesus issues a summons to the kingdom and demands the whole life of the follower.[39] The mechanism of the social order is adapted for the conveyance of social energy. The teachings of Jesus will give ample power to transmit energy. The kingdom is gradually realized and is the finally perfected community of disciples. The socialist movement is of great significance. Jesus can contain the socialist progress within his kingdom, yet the kingdom is more than socialism.

The erudition of Peabody's book and its reference to the best in German scholarship no doubt appealed to Rauschenbusch. It confirmed his gradualist, moralized view of the kingdom and placed considerable emphasis on the economic factor in the growth of the reign of God. Peabody was an idealist of the Ritschlian type.

This brief survey of Wellhausen, Mathews, and Peabody and of Rauschenbusch's many European mentors shows that he was oriented towards liberalism, rationalism, historicism, scepticism, and prophetic moralism. He existed in a most difficult transition period in biblical studies, arriving on the scene of creative scholarship and leadership just before the occurrence of major shifts brought about by archaeology, historical agony, disillusionment with scientism, and the collapse of naive optimism together with the recovery of the uniqueness of biblical categories.

Rauschenbusch's critical views of the Bible were basically those of the Enlightenment, yet he helped reveal ethical resources in Holy Scripture that had been obscured by an orthodoxy devoid of an adequate ethic or sociology. This result was arrived at in part through his contact with the works of the liberal historians. Earlier I mentioned that Richard Heath and Emile de Laveleye gave Rauschenbusch a sense of the crucial, creative role of Christianity in history. Perhaps this was the most important aspect of his approach to history – a factor rooted in his sectarian background. However, he was also greatly influenced by Adolph Harnack, one of Ritschl's most devoted followers.

Harnack and Troeltsch

Adolph Harnack (1851–1930) was born only ten years before Rauschenbusch and thus was a contemporary during his mature years. An avowed follower of Ritschl, he is the most quoted author in Rauschenbusch's books and unquestionably gave the Rochester seminarian his basic method for research into church history. The frequent references to Harnack are usually more than footnotes; they are acknowledgments of a vast debt, with citations of whole sections from his writings.[40]

To some extent Harnack employs analogy to find the reflected image of a given institution projected into the culture in which it exists. However, instead of seeing the democratic sect projecting itself into a democratic culture, Harnack invariably sees a pagan culture projecting its image onto the Church. For example, Rauschenbusch quotes Harnack as saying that when the early church lost its vigour, the culture wrought itself into the Church; hence, the Roman Catholic church is still the religious replica of the Roman imperial organization.

Most decisive of all Rauschenbusch's comments on Harnack is a declaration he made in his last book: "We shall not get away again from the central proposition of Harnack's *History of Dogma*, that the development of Catholic dogma was the process of the Hellenization of Christianity; in other words, that alien influences streamed into the religion of Jesus Christ and created a theology which he never taught or intended. What would Jesus have said to the symbol of Chalcedon or the Athanasian Creed if they had been read to him?"[41]

Harnack's perspective obviously opened the gates for a radical attack on previous theological formulations, both Catholic and Protestant (all of the former and most of the latter). Looking at the historical method Rauschenbusch took from his fellow Ritschlian will help to explain one of his most restricting blunders, namely, the placing of social concern in Christian history as something basically contemporaneous except for the early church and the Reformation radicals. It will also explain his vulnerability to the theology of the Enlightenment; in Harnack's methodology most Christian doctrine is regarded as null and void.

Harnack described and rejected the classical Catholic dogmatic methodology: the assumption of the divine origin of a succession of Christian and pre-Christian writings, and of an oral tradition; the abstraction from these documents of logically formulated propositions of faith, mutually connected and expressed for scientific and apostolic purposes, the contents of which are the knowledge of God, the world, and the divine provisions for salvation; the proclamation of this structure (dogma) as the content of Christianity, the believing acknowledgment of which *must* be required of every mature member of the Church and *should* be the condition of blessedness held in prospect by religion.[42] This outlines the source, method, and religious value of dogma.

He then compared Protestants and Catholics on those three points. Protestants have rejected the notion that oral tradition is equal with Scripture. Protestants seek a direct return to a pure understanding of the Word of God, although they largely fail to do so. This teleological method made Catholic Christianity vulnerable to corruption through a decadent Greek intelligence. The Catholic conception of the value of theology made heaven and earth dependent on assent to a creed rather than on faith in Christ. The net effect was to provide a movement for the maintenance of the Catholic church. Distinguishing between origin and development, Harnack makes the former the logical formulation of a proposition of faith that is then enforced by the Church. In the Catholic church the Logos (Greek)

Christology originated at the end of the third and beginning of the fourth century.

The history of dogma teaches four lessons that Rauschenbusch quite clearly absorbed. First, the assertion of the churches that dogmas are exclusively the exposition of Christian revelation is not confirmed by historical research. On the contrary, dogmatic Christianity (the dogma) in its conception and execution is a work of the Greek spirit on the soil of the gospel. Second, historical research reveals that the Church was compelled always grudgingly to conceal the work of the theologians, thereby putting them in a bad position. Third, dogmatic Christianity has experienced far-reaching transformations, first at the hands of Augustine and then Luther. Fourth, the history of dogma, while exhibiting the process of the origin and development of dogma, yields the most appropriate means of freeing the Church from dogmatic Christianity and hastening the unceasing process of emancipation that began with Augustine.[43]

The foregoing suggests the method that Harnack bequeathed to Rauschenbusch. Orthodoxy is attacked not because it has a given ingredient of divine revelation but because it is culturally conditioned and yet will not admit its origins. Its method of abstracting propositions from its mixed ancestry must be replaced by a context that subsumes all the causal factors, both human and divine. Harnack calls for a new theology that does not return to Catholicism, but combines the Jesus of the synoptic Gospels with certain motifs from the Enlightenment.

Rauschenbusch found the German historian's positive theology attractive. For example, the basic emphasis of Harnack's *What is Christianity?* is almost identical with that of Rauschenbusch's *The Social Principles of Jesus.*[44] Both books were bestsellers; both were attempts by the authors to place in popular form the essential emphases of their more scholarly works. Harnack declared that "theologians of every country only half discharge their duties if they think it enough to treat the Gospel in the recondite language of learning and bury it in scholarly folios."[45]

What is Christianity? What are the leading features of Jesus' message? The answer, according to Harnack, is as follows: the parables are the kernels of Jesus' Kingdom of God message. Harnack's kingdom is less prophetic than Rauschenbusch's, but the definition rests essentially on the same gradualist ground. The kingdom is also more internal and less radically external than in the Rochester interpretation; the emphasis is on God the Father and the infinite value of the human soul. The fatherly providence of God is affirmed, in a somewhat pietistic sense. Harnack calls this the restful aspect of the message of Jesus, disavowing a sense of tension and antithesis; love and mercy are ends in themselves and not secondary to worship. The all-important root and motive of ethics is one and one alone, namely, love. Religion is the soul of morality, and morality is the soul of religion. The definitive expression of Jesus' religion and ethics is the Sermon on the Mount.

Rauschenbusch's answer to the same question – What are the leading features of the message of Jesus? – is, first, the Kingdom of God and its coming; second, the value of life and the sacredness of personality; third, the spiritual solidarity of all men, creating the sacredness of fellowship; fourth, the leading of love, which impels the strong to identify with the weak and suffer for the kingdom's sake when conflict arises. These are similar to Harnack's basic affirmations.

Rauschenbusch used Harnack's works intensively and praised them lavishly. He used the same basic method of historical research and reached strikingly similar conclusions, although Rauschenbusch's more sectarian feeling for the analogous impact of democratic churches in a democratic culture is one crucial theme that was not developed by Harnack. Nevertheless, the latter had a significant impact on the liberalism of Rauschenbusch, since he destroyed all the classical theological formulations of Christianity as Hellenistic accretions. Harnack must therefore be considered as one of the major influences on the origins of Rauschenbusch's social ethics – particularly in a negative way by what he demolished, namely, orthodox theology, and in a positive way through the crucial role of theological method.

The role of Ernst Troeltsch, on the other hand, is somewhat ambiguous. Rauschenbusch referred to Troeltsch's *The Social Teaching of the Christian Churches* as "monumental" and as "the first and chief attempt to apply the methods of the history of doctrine to the social via convictions and hopes of the churches."[46] Despite these superlatives, it is difficult to find any explicit references to Troeltsch in Rauschenbusch's writings, possibly because Troeltsch's great work arrived too late (1911 in German and 1931 in English) to be available during the most formative and functional years of Rauschenbusch's development. However, his remarks do suggest that Rauschenbusch recognized at once that Troeltsch's attempt to find the interaction of theology, ethics, and sociology was precisely what he was seeking to accomplish. Moreover, Troeltsch's typology of church-sect-mystic conveyed a great deal of what Rauschenbusch was trying to say but without as sharp or compact a typological formulation.

Troeltsch the historian, who saw the primary role of the sects in creating the modern world, and Troeltsch the theologian are not always coterminous. Actually, Troeltsch and Harnack are the last two great liberals of German theology and historiography. H. Richard Niebuhr considers Troeltsch "the leading theologian of the religio-historical school and a chief representative of non-sceptical relativism in philosophy of history."[47] H.R. Mackintosh views Troeltsch as reacting against Ritschl despite his neo-Kantian background. Troeltsch objected to Ritschl's neglect of apologetic questions arising out of natural science, his emphasis upon a final revelation mediated through history, and his tendency to ignore the new facts brought to light by the scientific history of religions.[48]

It seems doubtful that Rauschenbusch was prepared to follow Troeltsch into a nonsceptical relativism, since the former always had an unadulterated Jesus who could be reached by stripping off Hellenized theology. On the other hand, Troeltsch's systematic study of ethics, weighted towards the left wing, was a useful confirmation of Rauschenbusch's lifetime attempt to develop a context for ethical and theological struggles. Actually, Rauschenbusch's real inner drive was more in the direction of what Troeltsch did in the *Social Teaching* than what Harnack aimed for in *The History of Dogma*. His theology of institutions and their development was to receive great help from Troeltsch's work as historian.

With a major influence on origins from Harnack and a minor impact from Troeltsch, it is important to see what a dynamically liberating force church history proved to be in the ministry of Walter Rauschenbusch. In his essay "The Influence of Historical Studies on Theology," he notes that "history is a renovating and reformatory influence in theology."[49] He declares that "theology dislikes to discover that some golden candlestick which it has long lighted in honor of the Lord is only plated and the brass is wearing through." He urges the reader to follow Carlyle's wise exhortation: "When you find a lie, kill it tenderly, as though you loved it." Historical study, he observes, "is a truly catholic influence. It shows that every religious body has much to blush for in its own history and much to admire in others. Each church is but a partial reflection of the truth. But the church of Jesus Christ in its totality has sublime authority."[50]

Thus Rauschenbusch saw history as a basic part of his equipment in the development of a liberal social message in the Church. History was needed to renovate, reform, and recover the truth and to make Christians humble concerning their theological and ethical errors. From the left wing of the Reformation he received a radical sense of historical periodization and the principle of analogy between church patterns and cultural patterns. From the Enlightenment historians he received an attack on merely verbal orthodoxy and a concept of the cultural conditioning of theology – what Shailer Mathews characterized as transcendentalized politics and what Rauschenbusch would have viewed as transcendentalized economics.

There is probably no more fitting quotation with which to close this study of history than the following remark by Roger Lincoln Shinn:

There is little excuse for our generation, though it may have learned some things that the Social Gospel did not know, to sneer or condescend to Rauschenbusch. His purposes were so unquestionably generous and his enthusiasm so genuine that we would be foolish and ungrateful to forget his message. But since we have experienced a fury and intensity of history which he did not expect, and have found a persistent and demonic power in evil which he barely guessed at, we can recover powerful aspects of the Christian tradition which he ignored.[51]

LIBERAL SOCIOECONOMIC INFLUENCES

We are ready now to embark upon the second main section of this chapter, which deals with the influence of liberal socioeconomic thinkers on Rauschenbusch. The chronological setting for this section is roughly coterminous with the years of the New York pastorate. During this era many socioeconomic thinkers made major contributions to the formation of Rauschenbusch's ethics. Theologians, biblical scholars, and historians all prepared the way. The climax came from men labouring more directly in the area of ethics.

With regard to the proof of origins, the impact of Henry George is clear; Rauschenbusch himself testified that George was a solid, significant influence early in his awakening. The fact that Henry George was a successful writer as well as an effective politician made for a double impact during the Hell's Kitchen pastorate. Just as no other theologian equalled the influence of Ritschl on Rauschenbusch's origins, so no other socioeconomic thinker equalled that of Henry George, although others made minor contributions. "I owe my first awakening to the world of social problems to the agitation of Henry George in 1886 and wish here to record my lifelong debt to this single-minded apostle of a great truth." No testimony on origins could be clearer than this.[52]

Henry George's immediate effect was to stimulate Rauschenbusch as a writer. In 1887 he wrote a paper on George's ideas, inserting in the margin of the manuscript, "My first paper on the social question."[53] Even more striking is the fact that he committed to memory whole chapters of George's writings "so that much of his

[Rauschenbusch's] writings are tinged with George's ideals and philosophy."[54]

Rauschenbusch insisted that Henry George was more than a tax reformer; he was the prophet of a new social order. Charles Barker's book on George refers correctly to the "Triple Legacy of Georgism": the fiscal-reform Georgism of the single tax; the political commitment that entered into many varieties of reform activity; and the moral and intellectual perspectives that reconstructed religion, philosophy, and ethics.[55] Walter Rauschenbusch was influenced by all three of these legacies. He utilized the single-tax insight and supplemented it with socialism; he entered into George's mayoralty campaign in New York in 1886; he partook of the radical reconstruction of religion in Henry George, a former Episcopalian.

Daniel Bell saw George as "paramount in the authentic tradition of the great agrarian reformers of the United States."[56] George Geiger put him in the great liberal tradition of America.[57] His work is best seen in this context. In an address to the 1889 Baptist Congress in Toronto, Rauschenbusch made this point regarding George as an economist: "He is often called a socialist, but it is incorrect to call him so; he is not a socialist, but the strongest advocate of laissez-faire in the highest sense of the term. Therefore, he insists that artificial monopolies such as the tariff should be swept away, and that freedom should be given to the natural forces of society, and that natural monopolies should be owned and managed by the community."[58]

This is an expression consistent with the older liberalism, which sought justice through a natural harmony of forces, something that was now blocked by artificial monopolies. From George, Rauschenbusch accepted the principle that socializing the means of production is a necessary monopoly. What other convictions held by Henry George exerted an influence on Rauschenbusch?

The rational religion of the Enlightenment   Henry George was reared in a pious low-church Episcopalian home in Philadelphia where the King James Bible, the Book of Common Prayer, and regular church attendance were basic disciplines. A large family suffering from straitened circumstances in an era of depression, the Georges were seriously committed to the Church. Yet Henry George was never confirmed. While orthodoxy never became vital to him, he was always religious in spirit. Although he quit school at fifteen, George partook of the rich Franklinian legacy of adult education in Philadelphia and developed a brilliant literary style. He became philosophically devoted to Schopenhauer's concept of the will and spent

much time refuting Herbert Spencer. His *Progress and Poverty* ends
with a quotation from Plutarch that is purely Platonic.[59] He was also
influenced by Thomas Spence, Thomas Paine, Thomas Jefferson,
Baruch Spinoza, and John Locke.

The profound problem that led to the reconstruction of his religious
outlook was this: given a benevolent creator active in human affairs,
how can one account for the presence of want, suffering, and star-
vation? Stated in economic terms the question was, how can one
account for poverty in the midst of plenty? George's writings provide
a systematic answer to these questions.

Geiger writes that George's concept of God "was entirely divorced
from Christian revelation and Scripture, and was disclosed to man
only by the light of reason."[60] According to Geiger's survey, George
derived three basic convictions from the Enlightenment: natural law,
natural rights, and deism. He was indeed a Christian deist, standing
to the right of the anti-Christian deists and to the left of the rational
supernaturalists. He writes of his effort to purge Christianity of alien
elements and still retain the essence of the faith: "Though Christianity became distorted and alloyed in percolating through a rotting
civilization; though pagan gods were taken into our pantheon, and
pagan forms into her ritual, and pagan ideas into her creed; yet her
essential idea of equality was never wholly destroyed."[61]

While clinging to the belief that Christianity, almost in spite of
itself, has always retained some of its simple moralistic essence,
George was characteristically opposed to institutional Christianity.

While many basic themes of Enlightenment religion may be found
in the outlook of one who reacted against Episcopal piety, George
was not an irreverent Voltaire or a profane Mencken prodding the
believers with a sharp rapier. He was a prophet recalling people to
the grand simplicities of the faith as structured in an elaborate social
ethic. It is characteristic of Rauschenbusch that no one ever spoke to
his condition who did not combine a reverent religious spirit with a
prophetic, unorthodox outlook.

The Kingdom of God motif   Henry George was a lay preacher. In a
sermon in Glasgow in 1889, he spoke about the role of the kingdom.
He believed that the kingdom would come if people would only seek
justice, acknowledge the essential principle of Christianity (practise
the golden rule), live as though all are equally the children of one
Father and entitled to live their lives and develop their faculties, and
apply their labour to the raw material at hand.[62] He insisted that
early Christianity did not pray for the kingdom in heaven, but for
the kingdom on earth. The early Christians were not persecuted for

religious reasons, he says, but because they spearheaded a great movement for social reform, preaching the gospel of justice. Here, then, is a view of the kingdom defined in terms of reform and social justice, with the theological presupposition of the golden rule as equality.

Optimistic-utopian view of history   Coupled with George's view of the kingdom is a picture of what life will be like if liberty and justice are embraced. It will be "the Golden Age of which poets have sung and high-raised seers have told in metaphor! It is the glorious vision which has always haunted man with gleams of fitful splendor. It is what he saw whose eyes at Patmos were closed in a trance. It is the reign of the Prince of Peace."[63] This is indeed an eloquent picture of the perfect society, a great social hope that moved untold thousands to feverish activity because deliverance was a real historical possibility. Admittedly, Rauschenbusch was less utopian than this, but only in degree.

Fellowship and solidarity as key social realities   The basic law of social progress, says George, is the phenomenon of association and gregariousness, with ever-increasing communalism. As cooperation increases, less time is required for maintenance and more is available for real progress. Yet there is internal resistance to people's innate communalistic cooperation. This counterforce is inequality – not the product of biology but the creature of civilization itself. Specialized social growth tends to create inequality; with this integration comes unequal distribution of wealth and power. Now one side expends all its powers in maintaining existence based on a crude inequality. The other side keeps up inequality because it brings luxury, ostentation, and warfare. What is the key that will permit true association to be recovered? Association through equality is the law of progress, George declared, and the key to associational equality is land value. Since this is true, rent becomes cosmically significant: it is the tangible manifestation of the intangible power of association, the concrete material measure of the subtle and imponderable elements of gregariousness. Rent is the exchange rate for human development.

George made economics a branch of ethics, an emphasis that was destined to enter the deepest consciousness of the social gospel. The union of economics and ethics was brought about by a union of psychology with the social sciences so that human nature becomes a social variable, subject to the direction and conditioning of external forces. George based politics on economics; he interpreted the rise and fall of civilizations in relation to the economic process; he insisted on the attachment of religious significance to the land and the process of rental of the land; he pointed to the evil of poverty as the by-product of inequality; he offered a searing judgment on avarice and materialism; he maintained a sense of shame for mental energy wasted through debilitating poverty and inequality. Henry George fixed indelibly the mighty role of the economic factor in the human struggle for the good life. This viewpoint was equally characteristic of Walter Rauschenbusch.

A specific solution for the social problem Henry George was not given to glittering generalities; he left a legacy of specifics. He continually asked, Given certain religious presuppositions, given a view of history, given a concept of association as the basic fact of human life, then what is the precise inference for institutions in society? His specific proposal comes from *Progress and Poverty*: "I do not propose either to purchase or to confiscate private property in land. The first would be unjust; the second, needless. Let the individuals who now hold it still retain, if they want to, possession of what they are pleased to call their land. Let them continue to call it their land. Let them buy and sell, and bequeath and devise it. We may safely leave them the shell, if we take the kernel. It is not necessary to confiscate land; it is only necessary to confiscate rent."[64]

This proposal constitutes a definite solution for a basic problem of human life: the use of the land. It challenges classical economics. It led to an outstanding circulation of two million copies of his book, in fifteen languages. It stimulated municipal reform movements. Its moral presuppositions stirred Tolstoy in distant Russia. Above all, the vibrant personality behind these ideas awakened a pietistic Baptist person to seek a richer, more profound social ethic. Twenty-seven years later, in his first major book, Rauschenbusch wrote, "The brilliant books of Henry George, *Progress and Poverty* and *Social Problems*, are still worth reading. In his main contentions he has never been answered."[65]

George's concept of natural law was never fully utilized by Rauschenbusch since the latter emphasized love more than law, but its philosophical context was bound to influence his thinking. Rauschenbusch himself indicated that socialism seemed a fuller doctrine for his social ethic than did the single tax alone. Nevertheless, Henry George was typical of many who nurtured his thinking: emancipated Christians of the Enlightenment who sought a radical reorganization of society.

Rauschenbusch's biographers agree that he was also influenced by Edward Bellamy's *Looking Backward*,[66] a book that W.D.P. Bliss calls "one of the ablest socialist utopias ever written."[67] This is an all-time bestseller that rivals *Uncle Tom's Cabin* in influence.

Rauschenbusch's relation to Bellamy was not as close as to Henry George, yet it was significant. The difference is probably due the fact that George reached Rauschenbusch during those highly impressionable days in the New York pastorate, and that Rauschenbusch believed that no utopia could equal the richness of *de facto* living. Yet it is clear that Rauschenbusch refuted his attack by declaring that socialism was worthy of attention, pointing out that it was no longer mere theory but the actual guide for legislation in various countries of the world, especially England and Germany. The English reforms were mainly municipal while Germany's were largely national. He insisted that Bellamy's vision was not a bizarre creation of the author but the glorious dream of a whole generation of earnest seekers. Moreover, Bellamy's principles give hope and "to some of us who live among the people, life would scarcely be tolerable if we had no hope to buoy us up and give us patience in waiting for better days."[68]

Before proceeding to Bellamy's influence on Rauschenbusch, it is necessary first to review the clash between Henry George and Edward Bellamy. George's thinking originated in the long current of radicalism that has flowed from the American stream; Edward Bellamy's was rooted in the free-church background of the Baptists. Yet in a sense their ethical roles are reversed, with the Anglican affirming decentralization and the Baptist embracing socialism. Henry George represented an agrarian type of radicalism that was suspicious of state power. In 1889 he reviewed Bellamy's *Looking Backward* in his weekly paper, the *Standard*, charging that socialism promoted state power to an excessive degree. George wanted a revolution in property rights through the nationalization of land – but not the state management of economic enterprise.

Bellamy meanwhile represented an urban-industrial brand of socialism with two tenets: equality of income and nationalized production of all economic goods and services. His organizing principle was that of an industrial army, explicitly patterned after military organization as an outgrowth of his life-long fascination with military matters. In the light of George's criticism, it would be accurate to call George a liberal and Bellamy a socialist radical. Indeed, the view of the Nationalists (as Bellamy's party was known) was that George alerted the country to the need for socialization and Bellamy took it to its logical conclusion. George regarded rent from land as a public trust; Bellamy considered both rent and interest on capital as public trusts. George hoped to retain private management; Bellamy planned an industrial army.

Henry George also clashed with Thomas Huxley on the right, fighting Huxley's evolutionary-minded élitism and conservatism in the name of a natural rights philosophy in the Jeffersonian tradition. On the left he criticized the Bellamy socialism in terms of these same presuppositions. Yet Bellamy's socialism was far removed from the Marxian variety, since there was no suggestion of class war. Capitalist trusts were to be replaced by the logical next step – the Great Trust of the United States government.

It is significant that in spite of George and Bellamy's differences, Rauschenbusch's social concern grew up under the impact of these two effective mass propagandists in American social history. George always persisted in Rauschenbusch's affections and social outlook while Bellamy's more comprehensive and less narrow social doctrine remained part of his thought process as well.

Perhaps the disparity between George and Bellamy represented a kind of permanent dilemma to Rauschenbusch and, for that matter, to much of the social-gospel movement, if not to American democracy as a whole. It is the struggle between a liberalism that wants far-reaching social changes without the intervention of the state (because of its fear of the exercise of excessive power), and a socialism that wants to destroy competition utterly through the use of government power and then constructively to organize a socialist society with this same power. The symbol of Rauschenbusch's dilemma may well have been his refusal to join any socialist party, despite his synthesis of George and Bellamy.[69]

With this background one can now move to specific characteristics of Bellamy's thought as they are reflected in Rauschenbusch's outlook.

The rational religion of the Enlightenment expressed in the key concept of solidarity   According to H. Richard Niebuhr, Bellamy's religion represents both the affinity and the conflict between romantic liberalism and evangelicalism. The dream of progress is rooted in Christian faith but clothed in romantic ideas. Precisely this appears to be the case with Bellamy. His pious upbringing in the Baptist church persisted in terms of a deeply religious sensitivity, yet the content of his religion derived from the Enlightenment. He never ceased to read the Bible and to reconstruct his orthodox background. Walter A. Smith says the following represents the core of his religion: "Universal love is at once the seed and fruit, cause and effect of the highest completest knowledge. Through boundless love man becomes a god, for thereby he is made conscious of his oneness with God, and all things are put under his feet. It has been only since the Great Revolution brought in the era of human brotherhood that mankind has been able to eat abundantly of the fruit of the tree of knowledge and thereby grow more and more into the consciousness of the divine soul as the essential self and the true holding of our lives."[70]

This is a doctrine based on the loving self-realization of the individual in the universal consciousness of the divine. It is essentially pantheistic in its doctrine of God, Tolstoyan in its ethics, socialist in its economics and politics, and optimistic in its view of humanity.

In Dr Barton's long sermon in *Looking Backward*, Bellamy affirmed his belief that human nature is essentially good not bad, and that the natural inclination of people is to be generous rather than selfish, pitiful rather than cruel, and sympathetic rather than arrogant. He says also that humans are godlike in their aspirations and instincts.[71] His major statement on theological matters was his essay on "The Religion of Solidarity," written when he was twenty-three. He believed that in solidarity is found the only rational philosophy of moral instincts. He expresses a Whiteheadian sense of the oneness of the process of which the individual is a part:

It is the instinct of solidarity, however construed or unconfessed, which lends man a consciousness of greatness other-wise unaccountable ... It is this which renders it all essential for his comfort to feel that he is acting as a part of some universal plan or frame of things, thus making some sort of religion or philosophy indispensable to him, and rendering the notion of unconnected, isolated action abhorrent to his soul.

What an apotheosis of humanity will it be when men so realize the relation of their transitory lives as persons and as individuals to their eternal and unbroken life of solidarity as to count death but an incident of life, and no longer the dreary abyss of existence.

Time is not a vestibule of eternity but a part of it. We are now living our immortal lives. The present life is its own perfect consummation, its own reason and excuse.[72]

Thus Edward Bellamy spelled out the religious and philosophical foundations of the liberal religion of solidarity. It is a pantheistic faith, a rational approach that Arthur E. Morgan interprets as similar to the religions of the East. Morgan has no explanation for the origin of this emphasis but is quite sure that there runs through Bellamy's writing a strain that represents the thinking of India.[73]

Apart from the Bible, Bellamy was influenced, according to Morgan, by Plutarch's *Life of Lycurgus* in which the semimilitary organization of the state sounds like his industrial army. Other lesser influences were Joseph Bellamy (his grandfather), Robert Owen, John Stuart Mill, Charles Fourier, and François Fenelon.

The Kingdom of God motif One of Bellamy's favourite terms was Great Revolution; another was Great Revival. These terms suggested the Kingdom of God on earth, which he believed Christ bade men to hope and work for. His antiecclesiastical outlook is summarized in these words: "For many ages – almost, indeed, from the beginning of the Christian era – the churches had turned their backs on Christ's ideal of a Kingdom of God to be realized on earth by the adoption of the law of mutual helpfulness and fraternal love."[74] Thus he equates the Kingdom of God with the Great Revolution breaking out against money power. This is not far from Rauschenbusch's view, although it lacks his religious depth.

An optimistic-utopian view of history I have already dealt with Bellamy's doctrine of original nobility, temporarily perverted but guaranteed to snap back once a fully socialistic society is set up. At the end of chapter 26 in *Looking Backward*, Bellamy rapturously sings forth: "With a tear for the dark past, turn we then to the dazzling future, and, veiling our eyes, press forward. The long and weary winter of the race is ended. Its summer has begun. Humanity has burst the chrysalis. The heavens are before it."[75] This is typical of many passages in his writing that suggest the immanent, concrete possibility of a radical thrust upward, made possible once the nub of the problem – ruthless competition in an evil socioeconomic order – has been located.

The economic interpretation of ethics Most of the writings that influenced the earliest social-gospel thinkers emphasized economic forces as the crucial element in ethics. Deal with economics, they insisted, and you deal with the key issue. In *Equality*, Bellamy says, "Nothing can be in the long run or on a large scale sound economics which is not sound ethics."[76]

Socialism as the specific solution Bellamy stressed the idea that a religious solution must be comprehensive, offering analyses of everything from immorality to a specific economic program. His utopian socialism incorporated that specific program. This was the master answer that captured Christian liberalism to varying degrees and in various patterns.

A third thinker and writer with a similar impact on Rauschenbusch is John Ruskin (1819–1900). Sharpe notes that "Ruskin was constantly read not only for his superb literary style and his high descriptions but also for the social message of his revolutionary spirit – for this cultured, artistic, literary stylist could not only write about cathedrals and paintings, he was the prophet for a new social era."[77] Rauschenbusch read and enthusiastically quoted Ruskin's *Unto This Last*.

John Ruskin was a romantic anti-industrialist who, according to Troeltsch, represented the end of Puritanism and the beginning of a spiritual, aesthetic temper in English life.[78] He offered the English counterpart of immanentist mysticism. Ruskin stood for an emphasis on craftsmanship and the arts as an entrance into the good society, a mood reflected in the United States more recently by Lewis Mumford, Van Wyck Brooks, Waldo Frank, and the Catholic Worker organization. His criticism is rooted in the arts and crafts of the Middle Ages and is aimed at a cold, crass, banal, dull, and stultifying industrialism.

Ruskin changed the focus from specific issues like wages, hours, monopolies, corporations, single tax, and socialization to the total impact of capitalism as a way of life. The following emphases, explicit in *Christianizing the Social Order*, carry supporting quotations from Ruskin: capitalist industrialism is an ugly, antihuman system that demands systematic disobedience to the first principles of Christianity. It is inherently in conflict with everything Christian. Wealth is not necessarily a sign of virtue, nor poverty a sign of vice. The only wealth is life; all else is not wealth but "ill-th". Art has its roots in the moral life. Permanent ugliness is a product of sin and a producer of brutality. It is significant that this Ruskinian epigram adorns the opening paragraph of Rauschenbusch's chapter on "Commercialism and Beauty" in *Christianizing the Social Order*. He felt very strongly that capitalist industry and commerce were pathological in relation to beauty. Every word in this unique chapter breathes the spirit and influence of Ruskin; an economic system must be judged by what it does to human values as a whole rather than by strictly economic issues in the arena of the market.

Rauschenbusch was less influenced by Ruskin's constructive position than by his critical outlook, which was evident, for example, in Ruskin's belief that the principle of exchange abolished all distinctions of ability and fidelity, his tendency to oppose social movements that did not fight industrialism as much as unjust capitalism, and his hostility to America with its excessive trust in liberty and equality, bringing what Carlyle called "our clutterbuck Republic." Yet this affirmation of the virtues of the Middle Ages against nineteenth-century industrialism surely influenced Rauschenbusch without evoking a romantic reaction. Rauschenbusch, following Ruskin, interpreted ugliness as another manifestation of an unjust economic system.

Liberal influences in Rauschenbusch's ideas on economics were rounded out by the famous Russian novelist and pacifist Leo Tolstoy. Sharpe's biography makes seven references to the influence of this amazing figure. I am not aware of a single important book by Rauschenbusch that does not have a laudatory quotation from Tolstoy. The book most often cited is *My Religion*. There is a long quotation from this work in *The Social Principles of Jesus*, showing how Tolstoy's life was changed when he perceived that Jesus taught a way of life rather than the doctrinal vagaries of orthodoxy. It is here that Tolstoy spells out his unitarian, moralistic, pacifist, prophetic, agrarian, antiecclesiastical view of Jesus and formulates the problem of ethics. Troeltsch sees in Tolstoy a revival of the old radical-sect idea, shorn of the apocalyptic element, informed by Western pantheism, and in utter conflict with the whole Western technical-state tradition. The Russian boldly proclaims the realization of the Sermon on the Mount.[79]

Rauschenbusch explicitly drew the following points from Tolstoy: Tolstoy's life was radically changed when he discovered the simple teachings of Jesus; having been changed by his liberal acceptance of the Sermon on the Mount, he shocked Christendom by insisting that the Sermon was not millennial, other-worldly, or futuristic, but was rather for the here and now; he belongs in the prophetic "Jesus-strain" of those who announce God's will even when it impinges on commerce; and he preached and practised voluntary poverty as the heroic corollary of the moral condemnation of unearned riches.

The emphasis on the Sermon on the Mount is eminently clear in Rauschenbusch, especially in the most widely read of his books, *The Social Principles of Jesus*. But Tolstoy's teaching shines through most clearly in Rauschenbusch's radical attack on unearned wealth and the futile accumulation of money. Alongside his large-scale interest in social institutions one finds his personal equation with regard to riches. "The Tragedy of Dives," chapter 6 in *Christianizing the Social Order*, is the sort of critique that has tended to drop out of current social thought. Here he shows that rich people (he calls them "my rich brothers") are actually in a tragic position, struggling with superior forces that drag them down. It is a predestined struggle in which the guilty rich person wages a losing battle with the moral powers of the universe as they close in for retribution. A blind and hostile fate awaits the participants in this struggle, since they must obey two incompatible duties. In all sobriety, Rauschenbusch notes that "every rich man is the sad hero of a tragedy, and the more noble and wise and righteous he is by nature, the more tragic his fate."[80]

The writings of Tolstoy and Rauschenbusch contain some of the most devastating social criticisms of riches ever penned. Here is Rauschenbusch spelling out the terrible dilemma of the rich person, a passage difficult to equal in Christian social concern without going back to St Francis:

The social order as it is now places its beneficiaries in a position where they cannot escape wrong and unhappiness. If they obey its laws, they enrich their own life, but at the expense of others, and in the end their apparent advantage turns out to be their own curse. They escape from the necessity of work, but in time idleness undoes either them or their descendants. Their wealth seems to promise large means of doing good, but they find their philanthropy a heavy burden on themselves and a questionable blessing for others. Their money gives them power, but that power is an intoxicant that undermines their sense of human values. It piles up their pleasures, but the more they surfeit, the less pleasure do they feel. It offers them free scope for their intellectual life, but it rusts the mainspring of their intellect. It holds out happiness for their families, and does its best to ruin them. It assures them of security and makes them camp among enemies. It increases their sense of strength by surrounding them with inferiors, and thereby relaxes their virility. It forces leadership on them, and yet chills the love of people which is the condition of leadership. It seems to win all the powers of this world to their side, but it puts them on the wrong side in the final verdict of God, of humanity and of their own souls. This is the tragedy of Dives.[81]

George, Bellamy, Ruskin, and Tolstoy were all children of the Enlightenment and antiorthodox in their theological and philosophical presuppositions. Each, however, contributed a different aspect to Rauschenbusch's socioeconomic thinking. Henry George awakened him to the need for economic change and political action, with a focus on the land problem through a more liberal limitation on the use of state action. Edward Bellamy supplied a thoroughgoing socialist solution. From John Ruskin he derived his emphasis on the total impact of capitalism on human personality and his quest for what Thorsten Veblen calls the instincts of craftsmanship. Leo Tolstoy offered voluntary poverty as an inference of the Sermon on the Mount and prophetic warnings on the ill effects of riches.

Rauschenbusch learned further from Giuseppe Mazzini (1805–72). One may wonder at first glance what a German-American Christian socialist could learn from an Italian nationalist. Rauschenbusch himself supplies the answer. He calls Mazzini a prophet "to whom God has given an eye for the lessons of the past and an ear which he has laid on the beating heart of his own generation, and who, therefore, is able to tell what shall be." He regarded Mazzini's *Essays* as a religious book, to some "a book of devotion."[82] Sharpe contains five references to Mazzini as one who influenced Rauschenbusch. This is not surprising when it is recalled that Mazzini reached the hearts of a number of American liberals. Jane Addams recalled her father's sadness in 1872 when he heard of Mazzini's death. Rauschenbusch quotes with approval Mazzini's statement that "every great revolution demands a great idea to be its center of action; to furnish it with both lever and fulcrum for the work it has to do."[83]

A brief survey of Mazzini's contribution to Rauschenbusch's thinking retraces some familiar themes but also unearths some new motifs. Like many of Rauschenbusch's mentors, Mazzini had experienced a transition from an inherited orthodoxy to theological liberalism. Born into an austere and devout Jansenist Catholic family, he moved to a moralistic conception of God as morality, justice, love, guide to history, and teacher of humanity. He had a pantheistic concept of God interchangeable with law – natural and human. He also had a great reverence for Jesus within a unitarian framework.[84] Like Bellamy, Mazzini believed in the idea of a utopian theocracy emanating directly from the people, levelling all hierarchial arrangements, both secular and ecclesiastical. The following suggests something of the intoxicating religion of humanity that informed Mazzini's vision: "The Holy Church of the Future, the Church of the Free and Equal will give its blessing to every forward step that is taken by the Spirit of Truth. It will be one with the life of Humanity. It will have no popes and no laity, but just believers. All men will be priests with differing functions. And there will be a new heaven and a new earth."[85] This upward surge of humanity towards a new heaven and earth is a typical Enlightenment equivalent of the Kingdom of God. Its base is the assurance that emancipation from superstition, hierarchy, and other alien influences will permit the innate goodness of humanity to express itself in a Holy Commonwealth as deep and broad as the sweep of life itself.

Mazzini was a contemporary of Karl Marx (1818–83). He examined and rejected the revolutionary class struggle and an internationalist brand of socialism in favour of an approach to socialism that subordinated it to nationality. The denationalized socialism of Marx was impossible to Mazzini. He wrote to the Italian workers:

Without a country you have no name, no identity, no voice, no rights, no membership in the brotherhood of nations – you remain just the bastards of humanity. Soldiers without a flag, Jews in a world of Gentiles, you will win neither trust nor protection. You will have no sponsors. Do not be misled into trying to achieve your emancipation from an unfair social condition until you have freed your country. You will not succeed in such an effort. Only your country, the blessed land that stretches spacious and rich between the Alps and the Southern rim of Sicily, can realize your hopes for a better lot.[86]

Although a socialist, Mazzini based his concept of nationality on the idea that God grants a specific task to a given people in the larger progress of humanity. Basically, he advocated republican government on the ground of national unification, opposing the subordination of national interest to considerations of class. He saw this process of unification as an essentially revolutionary struggle against the monarchial class oligarchy that fought to suppress the upsurge of the people's nationalism. He regarded nationality as a necessary prerequisite to any higher state of being.

It is difficult to determine which parts of Mazzini's vision influenced Rauschenbusch. Both men rejected conventional religion, although this was more far-reaching in Mazzini, who, formally speaking, ceased to be a Christian. There was a common celebration of the upsurge of righteousness among the people insofar as it freed them from their acquired bondage. They shared a common rejection of Marxism while embracing kindred aspects of socialism. And it may well be that Rauschenbusch's feeling of kinship for Mazzini included something of his appreciation for a nationalism wholly emancipated from the reactionary egocentricity of warring monarchs and Machiavellian diplomats. It is possible that one who has learned to think within the German context – as Rauschenbusch had – can never embrace a rootless internationalism or minimize the part played by particular nations in this phase of human history. While never succumbing to any of the Hegelian pre-Fascist nationalistic *Geiste*, Rauschenbusch may have been aware of the role that each nation must play in the realization of the Kingdom of God. If so, he surely saw it not in terms of an autonomous tribalism but rather as part of the whole kingdom.

Rauschenbusch believed that the character of the United States was largely formed by the Christian influence of the free churches and the Puritans. This gave Americans a feeling for political democracy that is part of their heritage. Now it was their destiny to move on to industrial democracy. God speaks through the negative crises of labour exploitation, unequal distribution of wealth, low worker morale, bad health, inequality, growing class distinctions, the collapse of the family, a tainted moral atmosphere, and the lessening of democracy. On the positive side, the new social movements call for fulfillment of a national destiny.

In Mazzini's writings are found some cardinal convictions that may have betrayed Rauschenbusch into his Christ-of-culture concept. To Mazzini religion was strictly instrumental in national self-realization. Anyone who believes this is a cultural religionist or a cultural Christian. Clothed in Mazzini's flaming Latin passion, these convictions sounded like the fury of an Amos; as a matter of fact, they were more likely a synthesis of a romantic nationalism with the pantheistic myths created by Mazzini himself. On the other hand, there was a sober, monastic kind of integrity in Mazzini that emphasized the vast chasm between good and evil and the ominous retribution for wrong-doing. Rauschenbusch's empathy with any sincere prophet was immediate.

Outstanding among the minor influences on Rauschenbusch was the Fabian movement, as exemplified by Sidney and Beatrice Webb. Rauschenbusch lived with the Webbs during a trip to England in order to study cooperatives and Fabian socialism. Fabianism arose between 1865 and 1885 as an alternative to Marxism and Owenism. Marx believed that class struggle and revolution would come after an apocalyptic twist of history delivered the economic apparatus to the messianic working class through the state. But the working classes in England were rising to power, the national conscience for social change was growing, a democratic state was open to the possibility of reform, and freedom of assembly and the press permitted searching social criticism and overt organization. Therefore, why wait for the lid to blow off? Socialism begins *now* – whenever the capitalist class admits collective bargaining on the one hand and state intervention on the other.

The socialism of the Webbs was based on the Ricardian theory of rent, a neo-Georgian doctrine, and the growing social conscience of the nation. Sidney Webb's research genius led him to investigate particular evils and seek a socialist solution implemented by legislation. Harry Laidler summarizes the Fabian attack as follows: "The mission of the socialist was, therefore, to acquire knowledge by means of specialized research into the various manifestations of economic and social life, to acquaint themselves with the machinery of legislation and administration, and to put their knowledge and experiences at the disposal of all political agencies."[87]

This was basically Rauschenbusch's approach to the socialist challenge. He remarked in his 1901 speech on "Dogmatic and Practical Socialism" that "the attitude of the dogmatic socialists reminds me of certain Christians, whom we call Millennarians." Practical socialism is liberal, intelligent, and immediate, as the Fabians insist. Yet Rauschenbusch placed this in a much more dramatic context – a theory of periodization and the Kingdom of God.

Another lesser influence was purely American – the Bull Moose progressivism that formed the political climate of Rauschenbusch's mature years. *Christianity and the Social Crisis*, published in 1907, makes four references to then President Theodore Roosevelt, one of which reads: "The present movement for federal and state interference and control over corporations, of which President Roosevelt is the most eminent exponent and leader, is an effort to assert the ownership and mastership of the people and to force these stewards of public powers back into the position of public servants."[88]

Roosevelt's administration was preceded by Bryan's great campaign of 1896 and followed by the administration of Woodrow Wilson. During Rauschenbusch's key years in Rochester, liberal politics had able, colourful leadership. At that time it seemed that popular democracy was finally putting political pressure on the money interests. Rauschenbusch quotes the *Boston Common* as saying that the Progressive Platform of 1912 was "an adaptation of the more imminent teachings of socialism for middle class neophytes," adding that "out from among the lowly and despised once more has come a message of guidance for humanity."[89]

Another writer who must be considered is E.A. Ross, pioneer sociologist of the University of Wisconsin and the most quoted social scientist in the works of Walter Rauschenbusch. In *Christianizing the Social Order*, he quotes from Ross's *Sin and Society* four times and *The Changing Chinese* once. These books combine the wrath of a crusading reformer with the social scientist's awareness of corporate guilt for evil-doing. One of the chapters Rauschenbusch quotes is "Sinning by Syndicate," which suggests the organized, societal fashion in which sin takes place. Other passages show how private money interests are behind public corruption, how big business gags investigation and criticism, and how professors teach an amoral, triumphant lawlessness to college students. The quotation from the book on China argues that China's familial culture has never created a public mind that transcends the circumscribed domestic circle.

Franklin H. Giddings of Columbia is the only other American sociologist quoted by Rauschenbusch, who used a reformist reference by Giddings to the power of the concentrated wealth of the time.

In *The Social Principles of Jesus*, Rauschenbusch affirmed his belief that "the development of what is called 'Social Christianity' or 'the social gospel' is a fusion between the new understanding created by the social sciences, and the teachings and moral ideals of Christianity."[90] Against the background of the reformist zeal of Ross and Giddings and cast in a social framework, Rauschenbusch could discern a real affinity between Christianity and the social sciences. Today, however, most social scientists would not recognize themselves in the role of reformers. No longer do they issue judgments on social questions or clothe their findings in moralistic semitheological vocabulary. More typical of what was to come in social science was William Graham Sumner (1840–1910) of Yale, an ex-minister who became, in 1876, the first American teacher to introduce a clearly defined course in sociology. Sumner was a social Darwinist who believed that social change was automatic, depending strictly on the ratio of people to land. His famous essay "The Absurd Effort to Make the World Over" breathed a completely different spirit than that pervading the departments at Columbia and Wisconsin.

Against this determinism there have always been American social scientists who saw more interaction between human freedom and socially conditioning factors. Rauschenbusch, quite understandably, was an interactionist, particularly before the cult of objectivity cut the nerve of reformist impulses. Perhaps it was significant that the first seminary courses in ethics tended to be titled "Christian Sociology." In effect, this was what Ross and Giddings were presenting; later Charles A. Ellwood would express his Quaker concerns in somewhat similar fashion. The theological presuppositions were definitely liberal, but the social concern was a fusion of social science (in its infant stage) with the moral principles of idealistic Protestantism.

One has the impression that Rauschenbusch was more influenced by historical studies – theological, biblical, and patristic – and by writers who focused specifically on economic problems than he was by the social sciences *per se*.

As for organic evolution, it clearly registered in Rauschenbusch's thought in terms of a gradualist, developmental view of history. The *Origin of Species* appeared in 1859 and the *Descent of Man* in 1871; they were available to him. But he had no heart for an impersonal, ruthless social Darwinism; hence his approval of Ross and Giddings and his rejection of Sumner.

To conclude, among the liberal socioeconomic influences acting upon Rauschenbusch we find a unified rejection of orthodoxy and support for Enlightenment rationalism integrated with Christian idealism, a common criticism of capitalist industrialism together with support for varying degrees of socialism (mainly Fabian), the rejection of political orthodoxy in favour of the Bull Moose movement (essentially a left-wing democratic socialist answer akin to the British Labour Party, Swedish Socialist Party, and Co-operative Commonwealth Federation in Canada), and the rejection of static conceptions of society for dynamic concepts of social change in the name of high religion and social science. All this created a remarkable epoch in American history, an epoch that contained more social excitement than any previous time, save for the Puritan theocracy in colonial New England or Penn's utopian dreams for Pennsylvania. In terms of a whole society, emancipated from a theocratic perspective, there is nothing to rival these social hopes, however naive and utopian they may have been. It was a powerful liberal *Zeitgeist*.

In many ways there was a remarkable unity among the theologians, biblical scholars, historians, and socioeconomic thinkers of Rauschenbusch's era. This is not to say that Rauschenbusch was predetermined to follow in their path. But at almost every point he found powerful materials to use in his Kingdom of God ethics.

CHAPTER SIX

The Influence of Christian Socialist Transformationism

Transformationists have a positive and hopeful attitude towards culture, based on the oneness of creation and redemption, incarnation and atonement. From this theological base they pioneered in the development of Christian socialism on the positive side and attacked mammonistic materialism on the other – both prominent factors in the teachings of Walter Rauschenbusch.

The transformationists are difficult to classify. First, there is the basic division between the Catholics and Calvinists. The Catholics are not theological liberals; they are Anglican, trinitarian, and sacramentarian. Ethically they are anticapitalist, but monarchical and conservative in politics and aristocratic in their view of the stratification of society. Yet it is precisely at the point of origins that Catholic transformationists like Frederick Denison Maurice and Charles Kingsley are important. They were pioneers in the use of the term socialist and in affirming essentially socialist principles. Rauschenbusch was impressed by their exposure of the horrors of capitalism and their rejection of ruthless competition.

The Calvinist transformationists Leonhard Ragaz and Herman Kutter could also be classified with the liberals. I have not classified them in this way because their emphasis on transformationism was intense and some of their theological affirmations were not couched in liberal language. Ragaz explicitly identified with left-wing Protestantism; this introduced a sectarian motif into his analysis. In the entire history of Christian ethics it would be difficult to find a more powerful indictment than the one he levelled at wealth, economic exploitation, and the terrible evil of ruthless competition.

It is also possible that part of Rauschenbusch's transformationist origins lay in the American *Zeitgeist* through what Winthrop Hudson calls evangelicalism. He means by this the legacy of early American

Protestantism in the permeation of society with Christian moral sanctions. This side of Protestantism was activist and morally responsible, in contrast to an individualist pietism. Yet in specific documentation, the evidence points in the direction of the four Christian socialist transformationists dealt with in this chapter.

It is not possible to locate any trace of this emphasis in the Rauschenbusch family background. In terms of the *Zeitgeist*, here is a good example of how the American culture was able to mediate a general background of activism and transformationism. Yet it was Rauschenbusch's European background that brought into play the specific influence of the Anglican Catholics and the Swiss Reformed socialists. Without his awareness of thought currents in both America and Europe, he might well have missed the impact of these forces. Rauschenbusch specifically identified himself with Maurice, Kutter, Ragaz, and Kingsley and hailed their outstanding contribution to the new solidarity-based Kingdom of God ethics. In Ragaz and Kutter he found a prophetic fire that moved him. However, while Rauschenbusch was a Christian socialist, it is clear that he was never as completely devoted to economic collectivism as these two were. He reached maturity in a political climate where Bull Moose progressivism was the only live option left of centre. His tension with socialism at the points of personal morality and fanatical dogmatism probably precluded an all-out identification with the then prevailing socialist movements in the United States. But in the sense to be defined here, Rauschenbusch was a Christian socialist.

The evidence in terms of books and authors is rather clear. Rauschenbusch read the transformationists in England and Switzerland with great delight. It is doubtful whether any of these four men moulded his original thinking on social questions to the same extent as Henry George during the early New York days. Yet there is evidence that he discovered Maurice and Kingsley during the New York pastorate.[1] It is possible that he came across Ragaz and Kutter during his last trip to Europe (1907–08). These Swiss leaders were much closer to his own outlook. In any case, all these men moved him towards a closer identification of socialism with the prophetic outpouring of God's mercy and wrath in their time. This socialist *kairos* became another element in the meaning of the Kingdom of God.

Pessimism about capitalism, optimism about socialism, and identification of the kingdom with socialist movements became characteristic themes in Rauschenbusch's conception of the social gospel. It is also possible that here he found theological foundations somewhat superior to certain elements that he had appropriated from the Kantian-Ritschlian orientation. In *A Theology for the Social Gospel* he indicates his awareness that social concern could find expression in the context of high-church Christianity.[2]

MAURICE AND KINGSLEY

The transformationists amplified Rauschenbusch's ethics even though they did not start him in this direction. While Ragaz and Kutter were close to his own background and outlook, it was Maurice and Kingsley – particularly F.D. Maurice, the Catholic-Anglican trans-formationist – who provided a number of themes that fit his system of thought. He had a high opinion of the role of the pioneer Christian socialists of England. In his Yale lectures he attributed the earliest exposition of solidaristic ideas on theology and social questions to Maurice and Kingsley, lauding the fact that other high-church intel-lectual leaders were also beginning to weave "solidaristic ideas into their most sacramental and ecclesiastical doctrines."[3]

It is not clear, however, whether Maurice would recognize himself in terms of solidaristic ideas bathed in Enlightenment theology, although Rauschenbusch was surely correct in ascribing to him a transformationist ethic and a radical attack on individualism and on the vices of industrialism and capitalism. He says Maurice had "one of the finest minds of England in the Victorian Age" and that he was one of the best products of his generation. Obviously, then, the Rochester prophet had a high regard for Maurice as one of the towering originators of a socially concerned Christianity. This is true even though Maurice's main thrust took place in the context of Anglican orthodoxy.[4] Rauschenbusch was attracted by the criticism of mammonism and the alternative of socialism, both understood as solidaristic in the negative as well as positive meanings of that word. Evidence that Maurice built his social ethic on a different foundation than that of free-church Christianity can be found in the polemical character of his book *The Kingdom of God*, which was aimed against Quakerism. In fact, the subtitle of the book is "Hints to a Quaker."

Nevertheless, there were elements in Maurice that spoke to Rau-schenbusch.

A radical attack on materialism   At the heart of England's industrial system Maurice discovered warfare in the form of competition. He candidly labelled as a lie the idea that competition is the law of the universe. The answer was neither Marxism nor patchwork liberal reform, but a radical, revolutionary return to the kingdom and king-ship of Christ.[5] Maurice looked with dismay at the growing cleft between rich and poor, the cynicism of the first matching the brooding discontent of the second. He wrote an article for *Fraser's Magazine* dealing with labour conditions, an article that created great excitement in conjunction with Kingsley's slashing attack on sweatshops entitled "Cheap Clothes and Nasty."

These were characteristic themes in social-gospel criticism: The inherent evils of capitalism and the gravity of the social crisis; the poison spewed by a money-grabbing culture; the exploitation of labour and the suffering of people in general under pathological industrialism. This crimson critique cut across theological lines.

A radical socioethical criticism of the Church   This is a more serious matter coming from an Anglican than from a free-church person reared in the tradition of religious criticism. In any case, Maurice saw that the Church, rather than judging the institutions of society, provided reasons for accepting them. He did not hesitate to refer to "the horrible apostasy of the church." He attacked both the unsocial Christians in the Church and the un-Christian socialists outside it. The unsocial Christians based men's relation to Christ on external rites, he observed, substituting religion for Christ, and took no responsibility for the social life of humanity. The un-Christian socialists, meanwhile, were inclined to base their social tenets on humanity's animal nature and to make common self-interest the ground for social action. Maurice's profoundly Christian criticism called for the Church to be the Church, uniting humanity on the great events of Christ's life, death, resurrection, and ascension. He saw it buried under pseudoreligion and mammonism, yet still visible. He strongly rejected the sectarian approach of the Church and developed a concept of interacting Catholic and Protestant elements.

Use of the term socialism and an affirmation of essentially socialist principles   James Luther Adams points out that the term "Christian socialism" was first used by the Maurice-Kingsley-Ludlow group of Broad Churchmen and that the term denoted "a wide variety of social doctrines and movements which have attempted to give a basic, structural application to the social principles of Christianity ... Christian socialism usually did not demand the common ownership and control of the means of production and exchange."[6]

Maurice apparently did have in mind the bold use of the term. "The socialism I speak of," he wrote in *Tracts on Christian Socialism*, "is that of Owen, Fourier, Louis Blanc – of the Englishmen, Frenchmen, Germans, who have fraternized with them or produced systems of their own."[7] State ownership of the means of production was not the key; the key was the action of working classes associating on their own behalf. Fifty years later Rauschenbusch was ready to go beyond this into a more explicit form of state socialism. Yet he retained Maurice's desire to socialize Christians and to Christianize socialists; he retained it as a rejection of *laissez-faire* and as a call for social and political action. Above all, Rauschenbusch retained the term itself as launched by the pioneer of Anglican social thought.

Use of the Kingdom of God as a major motif   In a letter to John Malcolm Forbes Ludlow, Maurice said that "the Kingdom of Heaven is to me the great practical existing reality which is to renew the earth ... to preach the Gospel of that Kingdom the fact that it is among us, and is not to be set up at all, is my calling and my business."[8] He thus had the same central focus as the later social-gospel advocates. As an orthodox Anglican he rejected the idea of the kingdom as the ultimate consequence of sanctified temporal effort. It had been planted by the mighty acts of God, creation and redemption. The purpose of the social movement was not to change society by some clever suggestion of the social leaders but to find its foundation in the living God.

Use of the kingdom in a transformationist sense   As a transformationist Maurice focused not on sin but on Christ the King and his kingdom. Christ, not the devil, was in control. The accent is on the positive. The time is now. This does not mean accommodation and compromise; it does mean a radical change when Christ becomes king, when Christ, the living word of God, moves forward into unredeemed human life. Maurice repeatedly makes it clear that this is not the Christ of culture (although he makes a large allowance for historical particularities such as nationality) but the Christ who converts and redeems society. His will and reign move forward.

As the social movement progressed after Maurice, it retained the transformationist vision but became considerably less impervious to cultural Protestantism. This is the Johannine vision. It burned brightly from Maurice to William Temple, along with the synoptic Enlightenment Christianity of Rauschenbusch and the dramatic Pauline vision of the Niebuhrs. There is, however, an ominous note lurking around the Isle of Patmos. There John or his namesake exchanged transformation for wrath and judgment. Now every transformationist must look carefully to see if Patmos is his destination.

Closely linked with Maurice in his impact on Rauschenbusch was Charles Kingsley. "If Maurice was the man of vision, the Moses of Christian Socialism," writes Charles Raven, "Kingsley with his power of tongue and pen can claim to be its Aaron."[9] Rauschenbusch invariably places Maurice and Kingsley together in a Moses-Aaron kind of relationship; when he quotes one he means the other as well. D.R. Sharpe notes that Kingsley's novels, *Alton Locke* and *Yeast*, were part of the provocative social-protest literature known to Rauschenbusch. Bodein argues that Kingsley was on the list of his major influences. Rauschenbusch discovered both Maurice and Kingsley during his early New York days.

The opening quotation from Charles Raven properly suggests that the difference between Kingsley and Maurice was functional rather than ideological or theological. Kingsley was a high-church Anglican, a pastor and preacher, a moralist, and a socialist reformer. As a man of letters he was gifted in his abilities: novelist, poet, essayist, and historian. However, his true status as a literary figure is controversial. He was not primarily a writer; authorship was mainly instrumental to his reformist and moralistic concerns. Some critics scorn his literary abilities. While critical, Raven places him with Dickens in bringing about an awakening on grave social issues. Though shrill, his novels of social protest had a power of description that brought home to the English mind and heart the ugly squalor and depressing dullness of the new industrialism. His *Alton Locke* is a "tract writ large," an expansion of *Cheap Clothes and Nasty*, which cried out against the newly enthroned mammonism.

Charles Kingsley was a Christian reformer taught by keen research into prevailing social conditions, with a skill in writing fiction that made these facts vivid and immediate. Theologically and ethically he stood with Maurice: there was the radical attack on materialism, a radical socioethical criticism of the Church, use of the term socialism, the affirmation of essentially socialist principles, and use of the Kingdom of God as a leading motif.

As the Aaron of the movement, Kingsley belongs with Bellamy and George despite the vast theological and ethical chasm between the Americans and himself. American liberals and radicals find it difficult to combine a juggernaut of anticapitalist criticism with conservative politics, monarchical prejudice, and a modified aristocratic view of stratification. In Kingsley's day this combination was possible. Rauschenbusch and the men around him responded particularly to social critics and prophets writing in some recognizable sense as Christians. Hence the influence of Kingsley's novels, which reflected poverty, the futility of almsgiving, the hypocrisy of the poor law (which he described as "an ingenious means for keeping a poor man a slave without starving him into revolution")[10], the right to work and to enjoy the fruits of one's labour, and the necessity for scientific farming, without which the country would be a desert and the city a crowded sty.

It was exactly to this sort of thing that Rauschenbusch responded: the exposure of raw capitalism and the rejection of competition as the law of life. All through the American social-gospel movement ran a radically critical view of the pathological effects of capitalist industrialism, usually known as mammonism. This perspective was based on the cumulative effect of descriptive studies in fiction and nonfiction, pastoral experience with people qua people, and the corporate defeats of the Church in urban industrialism – a legacy still with us today. Kingsley's writings were a part of the mountain of evidence available for social criticism and righteous indignation.

The weakness of both Maurice and Kingsley was, in part, the weakness of Rauschenbusch. All of them lacked a base in mass movements. The Englishmen came on the scene at the end of the Chartist movement. Max Beer described them as "leaders and officers without any army behind them." They had very limited knowledge of the labour and cooperative movements. Kingsley was more oriented to political action than was Maurice but neither had roots in functional or ideological organizations. Rauschenbusch had a much more realistic knowledge of these mass movements and an intention to relate the Church to them. But he, likewise, never got to the inner dynamics of social movements; his role was that of teacher, preacher, writer, and forum leader.

The contribution of the two Anglicans lay, however, primarily in another direction. Henry Vedder has suggested that their role consisted of introducing "socialist ideas among a wide circle of Christians, both clergy and laity" and that the outplaying of their ideas on Christian socialism "destroyed in England [the] hostility between advanced political and social ideas and established religion."[11] Their prophetism was Catholic in its denunciations and negativisms; their transformationism was Catholic in its hopes, however tenuous and inadequately structured. This weakness was to be corrected by Catholic-Anglican transformationists such as Archbishop William Temple.

However, shining through all of Kingsley's works was a rich sense of the solidarity of humanity, a thought central to Rauschenbusch. In an 1855 sermon on public spirit at Bedford, Kingsley used the text from I Corinthians 12:25–6 to preach eloquently about the unity and solidarity of humanity: "You can be happy and prosperous only by acknowledging each other as brothers," he said. "[You are] members of the same body, knit together ... by the external laws according to which the Lord Jesus Christ constituted human society."[12] On this rich sense of social solidarity Kingsley erected a foundation for subsequent generations to build on. Rauschenbusch was in that company of builders. Maurice and Kingsley had prepared the way for his more mature thinking.

EMILE DE LAVELEYE

Reference has already been made in the Anabaptist-sectarian section to Emile de Laveleye, the Belgian economist whose writings greatly influenced Rauschenbusch. In *Protestantism and Catholicism in Their Bearing Upon the Liberty and Prosperity of Nations*, this Roman Catholic author argues that democratic Protestant churches have an affinity for free institutions while despotic Roman churches have an affinity for autocracy. This little book, however, was less famous than de Laveleye's solid volume *De la Propriété et de ses Formes Primitives*.[13] Rauschenbusch refers to the final paragraph of this book in *Christianizing the Social Order*, adding in a footnote that these are "the closing words of a great book" by "the eminent Belgian economist Emile de Laveleye." In *Christianity and the Social Crisis*, he again refers to him as "the eminent Belgian economist," quoting the statement that "if Christianity were taught and understood conformably to the spirit of its Founder, the existing social organism could not last a day."[14]

Despite de Laveleye's anti-Roman Catholicism, his theory of property contributed to Rauschenbusch's transformationist concepts. The book is an anthropological defence of the existence of primitive collectivism from which people fell into individualism. Since collectivism is humanity's natural state, the return to the communal form is both possible and desirable, if not inevitable; hence the transformation of capitalism into its original, communistic *imago deo*.

The fall from collectivism, according to de Laveleye, was threefold: by the time of Tacitus and Caesar some families already had more slaves and power than their neighbours, which led to intensive cultivation of the land; the Roman church was a part of the fall, because it was the sole exception to the rule that individuals could not dispose of land without the consent of the community. Thus more and more people gave their land to the Church. The abbeys became copossessors of the public grounds contrary to the organization of primitive collectivism. By the ninth century, one-third of all lands in Gaul belonged to the clergy. De Laveleye's sturdy anti-Romanism finds expression in his picture of the Church as the agent of individualistic inheritance practices leading to subcommunal ecclesiastical collectivism; and, as common fields became the domain of the sovereigns, the people finally had no power to resist the royal families and feudal lords. All cultivation became servile. The free farmer of the second century became the serf of the ninth.

In addition to affirming an original collectivism and then tracing its fall – for which the Church was partially to blame – de Laveleye espouses a doctrine of natural law. He repeatedly insists that there is a natural instinct of justice and an innate concept of law. Lest one might think that these are autonomous secular ideas, de Laveleye goes on to affirm, with Johann Fichte, that Christianity has within its breast a power of renewal that can become a force in the state even as it has been among individuals. The egalitarian ideas of the gospel must penetrate institutions and laws.

Against this background of primitive collectivism, natural law, and egalitarianism seeking transformation, de Laveleye calls for a retooling of ideas about property. Here we must avoid the Roman theory of property with its excessive protection of individual rights through inheritance and other aristocratic notions leading to inequality. Today younger nations like the United States and Australia have a wonderful opportunity to bypass the influence of the Roman Empire and go back to the founding fathers of more ancient and primitive times. There one finds that only temporary use of property is ever conceded to individuals, since the true basis of property is the community. This view is buttressed by extensive materials from Russia (especially the Russian agrarian *mir* with its native collectivism), India, Java, Germany, Scandinavia, Holland, and Switzerland.

According to de Laveleye, the substratum of this primitive collectivism is seeking to re-express itself, supported by natural law and Christian ethics. Individualism and hereditary approaches must go. Actually this is not an attack on property itself, since its possession is one of the conditions of liberty. In fact, the main object is to make the distribution and use of property widespread and economic. While there is no single final form of property that is flawless, says de Laveleye, some kind of collectivist pattern will come closest to the ideal.

Here, then, is another transformationist influence on Rauschenbusch's tutelage from Catholicism, in a curiously anti-Roman and pre-free-church presentation. From de Laveleye he derived historical and anthropological evidence for an anticapitalist, presocialist credo.

The range of Rauschenbusch's reading in the key modern languages, among a wide variety of books and disciplines, is impressive. No matter what the writer's specialty, the books selected by him were usually set in a religious context. Perhaps the reason for his rejection of the whole Marxist corpus was that secularization was not widespread in his era.

It was natural for Rauschenbusch to have a more profound encounter with the German-speaking Christian socialists of continental Europe, in this case Herman Kutter, the Savonarola of Zurich, and his fellow townsman Leonhard Ragaz. Rauschenbusch calls Ragaz "one of the most brilliant preachers of Switzerland" and declares that "together with Kutter [he is] one of the most eminent leaders of Christian socialism in Switzerland, and all together one of the finest examples of the new type of Social Christianity that I have met."[15] It was Richard Heath, the English nonconformist and author of *The Captive City of God*, who translated and interpreted Kutter for the English-speaking world. Rauschenbusch's own books were translated into German by Leonhard Ragaz. These men had an affinity for one another that they expressed through intercultural exchange by means of translations.

Leonhard Ragaz was Emil Brunner's predecessor in the chair of Theology at Zurich. Like Kutter, he represented the type of liberal theologian against whom Karl Barth directed much of his polemical fire. These men were cultural Christians, seeking the fulfillment of culture in Christ through social change. Barth made a number of references to both men as promoters of cultural Protestantism.[16] Ragaz and Kutter represented what Barth and Brunner rejected; Rauschenbusch's heroes became the scapegoats of Continental theology in the subsequent generation, although the legacy of socialism was not rejected by Barth and Brunner. What was rejected was the older framework for Christian socialism.

Because many of the basic convictions of Kutter and Ragaz were similar, I shall list their common convictions before embarking on a closer look at some of their representative works. The two Swiss theologians both held that the central truth of the Bible is the Kingdom of God – the earthly reign of God embracing all individuals; the Kingdom of God is coming primarily through socialism in spite of its professed antireligious basis – since the atheism of the socialists is a hidden confession of the living God; Christians are called to the creation of community – totalitarian movements represent our scourging as this community seeks to come to fruition; sin is supremely expressed in capitalistic mammonism – a corporate materialism that has penetrated the entire culture; the kingdom comes outside of the Church and in spite of the Church; the Church is apostate and institutionalizes something that cannot be institutionalized, namely, the Kingdom of God.

These convictions resurfaced in Rauschenbusch, who accepted all of them in principle while softening the impact of several, especially the apostasy of the Church and socialism as the bearer of the kingdom. On the latter point, Rufus Weeks interprets Kutter as believing that "the Kingdom of God proclaimed by Jesus and the cooperative commonwealth foreseen and willed by the socialists are one and the same."[17] Surely Rauschenbusch made this identification too, but not quite as boldly as Kutter did. Little did either know that this so-called "great identification" was going to be one of the most vulnerable parts of the socialist belief.[18]

Herman Kutter's election to the ministry of the Neumünster in the city of Zurich in 1898 and his re-election in 1904 seem to have led to his profound interest in the religious meaning of socialism. To Kutter, social democracy (or parliamentary socialism) was something far deeper than a social movement or an economic doctrine. It was the then-current form of the ancient struggle for justice that operates, now in open rebellion, now in the secret chambers of the human heart, but always striving for expression in one of many valid forms. The flag of Marxism and the Socialist party are not the cause and content of socialism, but only the weapons forged to express this deeper passion for justice, which, says Kutter, is essentially religious.

In addition to the five major emphases that Kutter shared with Ragaz, there are some unique Kutter emphases that make their appearance in Rauschenbusch. Kutter was a brilliant stylist, writing a flaming, impassioned prose that was moving and evangelistic in its appeal to the will. In the economic literature of recent times or in the paradoxes of crisis theology, which describe rather than redeem life, there appears to be no equal to the prophetic power of a Herman Kutter crying out in the wilderness of a brash imperialism, raw capitalism, and tribalistic nationalism. There follow examples of the issues that he stressed.

The utter corruption wrought by mammon   In a transparently frank and cynical diatribe, Kutter outlines what he calls the ten commandments of mammon. Among them are these: "Six days shalt thou do Mammon's business, and all the seventh think of him. Thou shalt honor Mammon that thou mayst live long and prosper and that the securities which he puts into thy hand may rise in value ... Ye shall covet no other good but gold."[19] His concept of mammon was a reinterpretation of the biblical term for the all-pervasive idolatry of money, which the Christian socialists felt was the key problem of their time.

It is interesting that this theme was elaborated without any explicit acknowledgment of debt to Marx. Yet it certainly was a radical expression of the economic factor as the clue to all the mainsprings of human action. Nothing was more characteristic of Rauschenbusch and the men of his era than this emotional attack on mammonism. It seems a bit shrill and hysterical to contemporary ears but the question persists: Have we found an authentic Christian criticism of the economic order in the admittedly more complex situation of the twentieth century?

The double standard of modern civilization   In another burst of righteous indignation, Kutter declares that anonymity "is the trump card of modern civilization. A man may be a swindler, but must not be called so; he may visit the brothel and wallow in sensuality, but he must never get the name of *rake* ... Our society makes a parade of morality because it has none; it grows furious over a little scandal to hide its own great scandal. Its morality is the painted shield of its immorality."[20] Perhaps this awareness of a Pharisaical double standard is the reason for the somewhat cynical tone of his radical attacks on conventional morality. Nothing creates bitterness more than the feeling of lofty moral pretensions that conceal inner decay; the outside of the cup is clean, the inside laden with bacteria.

The priority and primacy of concrete historical movements over against their ideological rationalization   Kutter had a strong sense of the creative role of revolutionary movements. He listed five developments as the greatest revolutions of history: the prophecy of Israel, the advent of Jesus, the Reformation, the French Revolution, and social democracy. All of them, he said, "have the characteristics of eternal powers ... They all set themselves in stiffest opposition to their time and thus inaugurate a new era. They have a force in them which will not abide question, an imperative which hardly realizes itself, but which will and must create that to which it impels. *They must!* And all that the following age does to explain this 'must' in wise terms of human philosophy is no explanation."[21]

He further contrasts these movements with their rationalization – including Christianity – in an antitheological, antiphilosophical attack: "The dogmatic of Christianity is altogether a secondary matter to the faith; the deep philosophical systems of Protestantism are not its strength; the metaphysics of Marx do not define Social Democracy. It has ever been the effort of men to make every new revelation conform to their powers of philosophic expression, but the effort has never been crowned with success, and has often been attended with calamity."[22]

This anti-intellectual attitude is characteristic of the Rauschenbusch era, even though Rauschenbusch himself was a superbly educated man with a love of learning. In a sense this is a truly biblical point, devastating when pressed too far. But in proper focus it is a powerful insight. Even H. Richard Niebuhr, in a post-liberal, post-social-gospel mood, declared as the first basic conviction of his book *The Kingdom of God in America*: "Christianity, whether in America or anywhere else but particularly in Protestantism and in America, must be understood as a movement rather than as an institution or series of institutions. It is gospel rather than law; it is more dynamic than static."[23]

A powerful sense of the transformationist character of the gospel for all of the culture   Nothing is more characteristic of Kutter than the belief that the inner drive of the gospel is radically to attack the citadels of sin. He says that "to believe in Jesus means to be ardent for the right against all injustice; to attack evil at its roots without considerations of utility or inability. It means to make the impossible true, the unattainable possible, the unrealized actual."[24]

In Kutter's opinion there was a divinely ordained stirring among the masses in his day. He had a striking sense of God's movement in the very stuff of history. The transformationist dimension of his thinking at times shone forth with great passion:

For there is a great stirring in the masses; there is a light and a glow in the depths. Flames are bursting forth. The lowly are raising themselves from the dust, and the mighty are trembling in their seats ...

Yes, God is speaking today. God is working miracles, but of a different kind from what your traditional Christian formulas and your "inward" piety can understand – mightier, more elemental, more real. For God is a God of reality. His life cannot be woven out of systems of doctrines ...

Is He the God of the Christians alone? Nay, also of the Social Democrats. He gives the Spirit to whomsoever He will. Let not the Church forget that.[25]

The transformationist energies of the faith must be given to the social-democratic movement. God is working in this movement in spite of the Church. But how much better it would be, he laments, if the Church gave its message and motive to the movement: "Why, O church, dost thou not rise to give the Social Democracy its baptism of idealism?"[26]

Kutter speaks as a Christian seeking a socialism that would embody the word of God. To him the gospel comes as a tremendous burst of transformationist energy. Paralysis results when evil is accepted as necessary, ordained by fate. It is the death of civilization to acquiesce to evil. Christianity apparently has an unlimited option on redemption if it will seize upon the socialist *kairos*, shake the foundations of mammon, and erect the socialist society – the Kingdom of God on earth. Such was the message of Herman Kutter, to whom Rauschenbusch owed a great deal.

Leonhard Ragaz, whose beliefs coincided with Kutter's at many points, was inaugurated professor of Systematic Theology at Zurich in 1909, two years after Rauschenbusch published *Christianity and the Social Crisis*. He was succeeded by Emil Brunner. His unique positioning makes him a symbol of the times. Among Ragaz's special characteristics are the following.

An explicit acknowledgment of historical kinship for left-wing Protestants and other nonconformists, both Roman and Protestant   In his 1922 book on the Kingdom of God, Ragaz observes that Christianity is the struggle of the degeneration of the Kingdom of Christ as well as the struggle against this degeneration. The truth of the kingdom none-theless shows through the forms of corruption. God is working through the protesters: Francis of Assisi and John Huss, the Refor-mation of the sixteenth and seventeenth centuries. But God worked there only in part. The hope for an earthly impact from Christianity "revived powerfully in the Anabaptist movement, but it was tempo-rarily crushed again by force and disturbed through its own mis-takes."[27] Even pietism, that oft-discredited and backward movement, put this audacious hope of freedom back into circulation, only to lapse into narrowness. After this came the Blumhardts "and with them a new day of Christ and the Kingdom of God."

A great sense of conflict between Paul and Jesus   Ragaz believed that in the revolution of the Kingdom of God (and this kingdom theme prevails at all times) we must return from Paul to Jesus. We have replaced the kingdom theme with justification, the Sermon on the Mount with the book of Romans, the grandeur and liberty of the gospel with narrowness and Pharisaism. Even Paul is infected with the errors of the Pharisees despite his fame as their enemy. Paul must be understood in the light of Jesus and thus rescued from Paulinism.[28] This theme was, of course, powerfully hammered home by the social-gospel leaders, Rauschenbusch among them.

Judaism and Christianity are the two channels into which the stream called Israel is diverted   Israel is the central stream in which the holiness of the Kingdom of God flows. One of the central problems of history is the contract between Israel and paganism. Paganism is the deification of the world; it is static – fate. Israel, on the other hand, is the living God from whom springs an ever-growing creation. When paganism blocks this creationist power "there is a volcano that is ever prepared to blow up what is petrified or tending toward apostasy; ever preparing for the Day of God and his victory."[29] Creation in this sense is one of the bases of a transformationist hope.

The apostolic community of Christ, founded at Pentecost, still stands on the basis of Israel. But too soon and too often this Kingdom-Israel of Christ is replaced by religion, dogma takes the place of the kingdom message, the credo of orthodoxy takes the place of faith, church replaces community, Caesar merges with Christ, individual salvation replaces redemption, and other-worldliness replaces a this-worldly hope. When this happens a remnant continues to await the day of judgment.

Eschatology is joined to creation as the second foundation to the transformationist hope   Half of Christianity, so-called, believes in God without believing in the Kingdom of God – the new heaven and new earth where justice will dwell; the other half believes in the kingdom without believing in God. The first contingent is responsible for historical tragedy since its proponents do not see the link between faith and the kingdom. The judgment announced by Jesus and the prophets has come, and this is the meaning of the crisis that confronts Christianity. Because of this, God can be found among the atheists since doing the will of God, rather than adhering to a creed, is the criterion. The kingdom will come in this world. Nature will be transformed. Sickness and the last enemy, death, will be conquered. Humanity will help bring in the kingdom; God is totally responsible for the kingdom but people are totally responsible for its coming. The kingdom is not *of* this world but *for* this world. Both Baal (nature and the cosmic order) and Caesar (political order) will thereby be saved.

For all his attacks on dogma, Ragaz used the concept of the second coming for much of his analysis. There is a conflict between the Kingdom of God and the kingdom of this world. The present world must waver because He is coming. In the powerlessness of God, the divine power is being prepared. We must become powerless in order to become victorious – fight the lamb and then the lion. Only the kingdom can vanquish power. Christ comes when the world is over-thrown. There is no fixed date, since he is always ready. He does not come once and for all, since his coming only inaugurates the new age. Antichrist is the principle of the demonic, endowed with extraordinary powers. This principle is embodied in all the dominant social movements. Ragaz's final implication is that individuals must in no way collaborate with the world; we must fight it. The Kingdom of God versus the kingdom of the world – this is our fundamental moral situation.

Discipleship in the building of community is the Christian obligation Ragaz's concept of response has an individual as well as a collective focus. As individuals we are to be disciples of Jesus without imitating him in servility. On the collective side we are called to a community that transcends any ecclesiastical definition. Christian socialism is the most dynamic movement creating community. So strongly did Ragaz believe this that he resigned his position in theology in 1921 in order to join social movements less bound by ecclesiastical and academic restrictions.[30]

This galaxy of Catholic and Calvinist transformationists – Maurice, Kingsley, de Laveleye, Kutter, and Ragaz – influenced Walter Rau-schenbusch towards Christian socialism. All were powerful figures. Their convictions flamed with power and passion and their writings were polemical and evangelistic; their lives, in the main, were nothing short of dramatic. Kingsley and Maurice used the context of theological orthodoxy; de Laveleye was a cryptosectarian in the Roman church; Kutter and Ragaz were Calvinists who retained the transformationist catholicity of Reformed theology while also embracing a liberal and sectarian theology and political socialism. These latter two Christian socialists had a certain firm, definite quality to their convictions that was not always characteristic of later liberals. Rau-schenbusch's prophetic attack on materialistic capitalism, his identification of socialist movements with the Kingdom of God, and his sharp criticism of conservative churches as abetting capitalism all have their roots in the writings of these five men.

One way of expressing the transformationist relation to the other motifs I have examined is to say that pietism and sectarianism provided the form while liberalism poured the content under the motivation of transformationism. There is also an interaction among the motifs whereby content is provided from all three. For example, the transformationists provide the socialist emphasis in a theological context. Sectarianism persists in terms of discipleship and ecclesiology. These issues will be dealt with in the summary to this study on intellectual origins.

Some tensions remain in the formulations provided by transformationism. There is the tension between the prophetic calling for a triumphant social faith and the realistic admission that the faith is often strangled by tradition. There is the conflict between concrete social movements calling for identification and the secluded life of the scholar. There is the lack of understanding between all Christian transformationists and their secular transformationist colleagues. There is the concept of the kingdom as coterminous with socialism and the kingdom as more than any human value. Finally, there is the chasm between Rauschenbusch's transformationist hopes and the tragic moment of his life during the fanatical anti-German hysteria of World War I, when some of his comrades in social action abandoned him.

CHAPTER SEVEN

Summary and Conclusion

This study has revealed the nature of Walter Rauschenbusch's Kingdom of God ethics in terms of his unique appropriation and selection of materials from the basic motifs of pietism, Anabaptist sectarianism, liberalism, and Christian socialist transformationism. The grand theme of the Kingdom of God, constructed from the materials found in the four motifs, runs through the entire structure of his ethics. This contention is supported by evidence from Rauschenbusch's family background in which pietism, sectarianism, and liberalism were all prominent; from the *Zeitgeist*, where pietism and liberalism were given credence; from Rauschenbusch's understanding of himself, first as a pietist and then as a sectarian and a liberal; and from numerous influential writers and their books as they percolated in the life of a well-read man with an excellent educational background obtained in Europe and North America.

The course of development of Rauschenbusch's ethics reflected his conditioning in terms of the four basic motifs used in his Kingdom of God ethics and also displayed originality and creativity in the application of his source materials. Hence this book has not dealt with a brittle determinism or a merely capricious originality. It is rather a study of the manner in which Walter Rauschenbusch exercised his intellectual freedom in a specific historical context. The proof that has been offered is not absolute in character; on the contrary, I have assumed only that research would make my conclusion possible, probable, and permissible.

There follow, in conclusion, some reflections on each of the four motifs that were germane to the development of Rauschenbusch's ethics.

Pietism does not contribute positively to the Kingdom of God master theme, since it came to Rauschenbusch in a subjective and individualistic form. Indeed, it was precisely the breakdown of this

individualistic subjectivism that moved him towards the more corporate Kingdom of God master theme. However, because of the
background of the two Rauschenbusches in the Lutheran and Baptist
traditions, and in view of the nineteenth-century theological *Zeitgeist*
in which pietism was a powerful movement, it is probable that pietism lent a significant contribution to the younger Rauschenbusch's
ethical concepts. A further remarkable fact is the relation of pietism
to sectarianism and liberalism. The affinity contributes much to our
general quest for the interaction among the motifs in relation to the
Kingdom of God master theme.

The study of *sectarianism* reveals the powerful Kingdom of God
materials available to Walter Rauschenbusch. Its impact is seen in his
father's early encounter with left-wing Protestant research on the
Continent. This early encounter made available basic historical materials from C.A. Cornelius of Munich – materials that Walter Rauschenbusch used throughout his career. Hence in terms both of
family background and books there is important evidence in the
direction of sectarian influence. The *Zeitgeist* contributed very little
to the sectarian dimension of his development. On the other hand,
his own self-understanding as a prophet of left-wing Protestantism
is a very important strand of evidence regarding the appropriation
and selection of materials for his Kingdom of God ethics. This is
particularly true given that he classed left-wing Protestantism
together with social movements that were culturally but not theologically liberal (socialism, labour, etc.). More importantly, this evidence
underscores one of the most frequently ignored sources for the origins of his social ethics. Here is a free appropriation of sectarian
motifs in relation to the other three motifs as basic to an understanding of his Kingdom of God ethics.

The study of *liberalism* also reveals the solid Kingdom of God
materials that he obtained from liberal sources. Unlike sectarianism,
which he did not share with all advocates of the social gospel, he
did share liberalism with all of the American and many European
advocates of the new social ethics. His family background presents
evidence of an early relationship with liberal movements in Germany,
followed by a constant interaction of liberal experiences even in the
pietist setting of his early life. The *Zeitgeist* is full of liberal emphases
at work at every level of culture and theology. His own self-image is
consciously liberal. It seems clear that liberal influences were strong
and that they functioned in relation to sectarian and pietistic influences in a two-layered kind of liberalism: cultural and theological.

The *transformationists* also contributed a solid body of Kingdom of
God materials. Although these are not found in his family background or in the *Zeitgeist* (this is not important here unless one

makes allowance for a certain transformationist aspect of American evangelicalism), Rauschenbusch's self-understanding was clearly shaped by the Christian socialists in England and Switzerland, whose books he read with great relish. While these works did not enter his life as early as those of Henry George and Edward Bellamy, they amplified and enriched his thinking by providing a theological context for radical Christian social ethics.

In all of the four motifs, an effort was made to search for the explicit relationship between Rauschenbusch and the proposed sources of intellectual influence. This approach seems more valid than the environmentalist argument that the social gospel was simply the response of middle-class Protestantism to industrialism and urban capitalism.

Rauschenbusch's final synthesis (together with that of other social thinkers) received praise from John A. Hutchison in the *Festschrift* for Reinhold Niebuhr. He said: "It is the enduring achievement of the Social Gospel to have recaptured the social nature of the Christian faith and to have expressed it in new and challenging terms. In such a climate of opinion [individualism and other-worldliness] the Social Gospel reasserted and reclaimed the social nature of the Christian religion. This must be regarded as [an] important religious as well as social achievement. Socially it had the force of challenging if not breaking the close alliance between Protestantism and the American business class."

In these respects – and they are important ones – the Frontier Fellowship continued the Social Gospel tradition.[1]

Coming from one of Reinhold Niebuhr's closest followers, this statement is noteworthy in suggesting the permanent aspects of the work of Walter Rauschenbusch as a leading exponent of the social-gospel movement. On the other hand, Rauschenbusch's synthesis was vulnerable to attack. This suggests the need for evaluation.

The general perspective from which Rauschenbusch approached his intellectual pursuits was that of a church historian with a rich European background. While he acknowledged the resources of the Old and New Testaments, the Apostolic Church, the Reformation, the Enlightenment, the Anabaptists, and the Puritans, he had a tendency to underestimate the validity of all earlier formulations of social concern and hence to fling himself too uncritically upon the dynamic resources operating in his time. His understanding of periodization made him feel that this was an opportunity without parallel in the history of the Church.

While the form and dynamic power of sectarianism and pietism remained with him, he was always tempted to pour in the content of current idealism. This content was particularly vulnerable to attack. He could have drawn more deeply on the tragic sense of history that many sectarians possessed. He could have drawn on Maurice's affirmation of God's great redemptive events as over against sanctified temporal effort. He could have taken Weiss and Schweitzer more seriously than Wellhausen. He could have been more critical of the theological foundations of Mazzini. While we cannot expect him to have all the insights now available to us, these options were available to him.

To be sure, Walter Rauschenbusch lived at a time of great social excitement, a time when the tidal wave of ethical power tended to sweep everything before it. New life was bursting forth everywhere. It is not difficult to assume that this was due to emancipation from stultifying orthodoxies, both theological and ethical. An almost incredible united front of forces existed in his formative and mature years. In theological, biblical, historical, economic, social, and political thought the new liberalism surged forward with much inner confidence and outer impact. It appeared that to dissent from any part of the new idealism was to dissent from it all. This was, of course, not true.

The Anglicans proved it by synthesizing cultural liberalism and Catholic orthodoxy. But this was less clear in the United States, where idealism conquered almost every aspect of main-line Protestantism in an astonishingly short period of time. Not only did important elements of sectarianism and pietism suffer serious losses but other ecclesiastical parties also started to speak with a Kantian-Ritschlian accent. The tactical situation was therefore quite difficult for Rauschenbusch, particularly when social concern was wrenched away from a clear relationship to past traditions.

All of this led to a complex formulation of the social gospel. This study has documented the multiple origins of the normative and classical presentation by Walter Rauschenbusch. There was in his day far less awareness of particular confessional backgrounds than in today's ecumenical climate, where the starting points are first confessional and historical and then ecumenical. At the very least we are obliged to discover what was selected, what was rejected, and on what principle these multiple backgrounds were dealt with. Above all, we must seek to find if one of these backgrounds was regulative of the others.

Rauschenbusch's formulation was not only complex; it was unique. Visser t' Hooft has pointed out that Rauschenbusch was wrong in dating social concern from the nineteenth century but that he was right in assuming that his particular formulation was unique. The bypassing of natural law for an emphasis on the discipleship of love, integrated with transformationist themes in an idealistic-scientific setting – all this was unprecedented in the history of the Church. It is precisely this mixture that requires scrutiny and testing.

In addition, even though the Rauschenbusch presentation was systematically unified around the Kingdom of God motif, there were contradictory elements in his outlook. This synthesis was made against the background of the radical questioning of all traditions and in the climate of freedom and experimentation. For example, he combined the pietist prejudice against mere theory with the contradictory aim of reconstructing Christian thought by creating a theology for the social gospel; again, he emphasized love as pre-eminent and yet made it compatible with self-interest; he stressed the importance of taking Jesus seriously and literally while stressing the importance of institutional analysis and power relationships. It is necessary to identify these conflicts and tensions and then to consider them in formulating a sounder statement of social policy for our own time.

Finally, one must consider some of the more specific values of the approach taken here. First, in this ecumenical era it is significant to observe the interaction of various theological and confessional movements. European and American theologians engage in unceasing discussion of the great issues of faith and life. This conversation is international and interdenominational. Proponents of the rigorously confessional movements would not, perhaps, be blown about by winds of doctrine as Rauschenbusch was. Before he had completed his system he had communicated with the left, centre, and right in the Church. He had been influenced by the whole sweep of church thought and life and, in addition, by movements outside of the Church. His is a *de facto* ecumenicity that antedated the more formal ecumenical contemporary organizations.

Second, in the meeting of motifs and movements, it is the pietistic and sectarian backgrounds mediated by his father that have been most neglected in previous evaluations of Rauschenbusch. Visser t' Hooft has correctly suggested that Rauschenbusch made a bold attempt to integrate basic sectarian themes with a liberal universality. The peculiar emphases of the sectarians on discipleship, the primacy of love, kingdom consciousness, and the role of the Church as a voluntary fellowship are clearly stamped on the social gospel. Yet even if this were merely a formal influence (it is more than that), the important point is the synthesizing of materials from pietism, sectarianism, liberalism, and transformationism. All four are necessary for arriving at a correct understanding of his Kingdom of God ethics. This rules out a single-motif approach. This new pattern of multiple motifs also sheds light on the unusual character of Rauschenbusch's eclectic formulation. It is not merely the liberal consensus of his day; it is a unique formulation based on complex origins in a specific historical situation.

Third, this study raises questions regarding such behaviourist and environmentalist explanations of the social gospel as offered by Henry May and James Dombrowski.[2] Walter Rauschenbusch's reaction to urban-industrial capitalism was highly individual, and the way to it was opened by a particular kind of theological and cultural influence.

Fourth, the Kingdom of God theme can now be understood in a particular sense. Rauschenbusch took materials from many sources to develop his concept. It is remarkable how universally this theme is deployed in pietism, sectarianism, liberalism, as well as transformationism. While Rauschenbusch did not see the meaning of the term in the total history of its biblical and theological interpretation, he found an integrating centre for his position in the more gradualist sense of the kingdom. While vulnerable to later criticism, he used the concept as a prophetic instrument of judgment on moribund, unjust, and even demonic institutions.

Fifth, it is clear that crucial tensions remained in Rauschenbusch's formulation. Perhaps the central tension is between the Kingdom of God as leading to the Christ of culture and the view of the kingdom as bringing conflict, suffering, and crisis. In addition, there was the tension between following Jesus in discipleship and the necessity of dealing with the power structures of society.

Despite its weaknesses, however, Rauschenbusch's formulation of social ethics made a genuine contribution to the Church. His prophetic critique of the economic order was most effective. In formulating this critique he helped to break the union between Christianity and bourgeois values. He brought corporate perspectives back to an individualistic Protestantism and at the same time helped to restore social concern as a permanent aspect of the Church's witness. His formulation of the social gospel was definitive for his time. Today's restatement of Christianity's encounter with culture must take into account what we now know to be a useful presentation whose intellectual origins lie in diverse and sometimes contradictory sources.

Rauschenbusch and
Martin Luther King

The journey to Rauschenbusch's becoming a major mentor of Martin Luther King started in Mt Sterling, Missouri in the middle of the nineteenth century at the Baptist church where his father led the congregation in the decision that "no slaveholder can ever be a member or a communicant of this church," thus making antislavery a test of membership.[1] One hundred years later Dr King found that Rauschenbusch was basic to his thinking.

After the Missouri statement against slavery and after Emancipation in 1863, a spirited debate took place among the leaders of social Christianity, a debate brilliantly set forth in Ralph E. Luker's important new book *The Social Gospel in Black and White American Racial Reform, 1885–1912* (1991).[2] There were many voices: neoabolitionists (Harlan Paul Douglas), genteel cosmopolitan assimilationists (Josiah Royce), and separationists (Edgar Gardner Murphy and Thomas Dixon, Jr).

Rauschenbusch's key books made it clear that Christian love and justice were incompatible with racism. His last and most mature work, *A Theology for the Social Gospel*, cited lynching as evidence of pervasive social sin and criticized Southern writers for trying to show the bestial origins of black people in contrast to the common ancestry in Adam.

There were more detailed articles by the Rochester prophet on racism, for example, "The Belated Races and the Social Problem" (1914).[3] The anti-German hysteria he experienced also permitted him to understand the demeaning view of black people.

In *Stride Toward Freedom*, Martin Luther King's famous chronicle of the Montgomery bus boycott, he observed that "I came early to Walter Rauschenbush's *Christianity and Social Crisis* which left an indelible impression on my thinking by giving me a theological basis for social concern which had already grown up in me as a result of my early experience."[4]

Kenneth Smith, one of King's key professors at the seminary, noted King's growing satisfaction with Rauschenbusch and the social gospel.[5]

Max Stackhouse of Princeton wrote his Harvard dissertation comparing Reinhold Niebuhr and Rauschenbush. In that thesis he observed that "the more one reads of Rauschenbusch the more one sees the social gospel in Martin Luther King, Jr."[6] Stackhouse also said that Rauschenbusch's work was America's indigenous form of liberation theology.[7]

The dynamics of the Rochester reformer touched two great awakenings in the US: the creative *kairos* responding to urban industrialism as the major thrust of his work, roughly 1890–1920; and the continuing, forceful impact of Rauschenbusch as discovered by Martin Luther King during his seminary days at Crozier Theological School in Chester, Pennsylvania from 1948–51, and in subsequent years prior to his assassination in 1968.

This amazing mentorship thirty years after Walter Rauschenbusch's death permitted him to share Martin Luther King's dream, extending the sweep and scope of his work.

No other pioneer of social Christianity could equal this dual participation in two awakenings.

Notes

CHAPTER ONE

1 In 1968 Max Stackhouse of Princeton Theological Seminary rescued *For the Right* from the obscurity of the Baptist Historical Society files and then edited it and added a new introduction. It also had a new title – *The Righteousness of the Kingdom*, edited and introduced by Max Stackhouse in his collection of Rauschenbusch writings entitled *Walter Rauschenbusch: The Righteousness of the Kingdom*, 289–312. The editor pointed to continuities between the earlier social Christianity of this book and the conciliar denominationalism of today. The approach of the rediscovered book (1880–1900) is sturdily historical because the Kingdom of God exegetes history. See the review by Paul Gustafson in the *Journal for the Scientific Study of Religion* 7, no. 1 (Spring 1968):286–7. Stackhouse's book contains three hundred items, including six books (which ran to twenty-eight editions in five languages), 139 articles, seven reviews, many clippings, letters, lecture notes, book outlines, and collections of hymns that Rauschenbusch edited – the definitive bibliography of Walter Rauschenbusch.
2 King, *Stride Toward Freedom*, 91.
3 Rauschenbusch, *Christianity and the Social Crisis*, 8–9.
4 Rauschenbusch, *A Theology for the Social Gospel*, 57.

CHAPTER TWO

1 Schneider, "The Americanization of August Rauschenbusch," 3.
2 Rauschenbusch, *Leben und Wirken von August Rauschenbusch*, 221.
3 Rauschenbusch, "The Zurich Anabaptists and Thomas Müntzer," 9.
4 The author of the essay was Ernst Crous, former state librarian in Berlin.

5 This outline is taken from Hopkins, *The Rise of the Social Gospel in American Protestantism, 1865–1915*, xi-xii.

6 Sharpe, *Walter Rauschenbusch*, 37.

7 Ibid., 41.

8 Ibid., 57.

9 Ibid., 55.

10 Ibid.

11 Ibid., 122.

12 All of his major works in English were written during an eleven-year period of brilliant creativity while holding an appointment at Rochester Theological Seminary. See the bibliography at the end of this book for a complete list of his writings.

CHAPTER THREE

1 Schneider, "The Americanization of August Rauschenbusch," 3

2 Rauschenbusch correspondence in Eden Theological Seminary archives.

3 Ibid.

4 Ibid.

5 The Pin Oak Baptist Church, Gasconade County, Mt Sterling, Missouri, first record book, Eden Seminary archives.

6 Zummach, *These Glorious Years*, 69.

7 Sharpe, *Walter Rauschenbusch*, 43–4.

8 The book was published in 1897, the last year of the New York pastorate.

9 Rauschenbusch, *The Rochester Theological Seminary Bulletin*, 12.

10 Rauschenbusch, *Christianity and the Social Crisis*, xv.

11 Ibid., 242.

12 Rauschenbusch, "Henry George," 30–1. The author is indebted to D.R. Sharpe for lending this handwritten manuscript from his collection, which is now part of the Rauschenbusch Family Papers at Colgate-Rochester Divinity School.

13 Ibid., 17–18.

14 James Hastings Nichols and Sidney Mead, "Puritanism, Precisionism-Pietism-Moravianism-Quietism-Jansenism," The History of Christianity Since 1650, mimeographed lectures for Church History 303, University of Chicago, 1953, 5.

15 Grumberg and Mirbt, "Pietism," 67.

16 Ibid., 67.

17 Friedmann, *Mennonite Piety through the Centuries*. See the chapter in Study One, "Anabaptism and Pietism," 3–85.

18 See personal letters of Walter Rauschenbusch to Max Leuschner, dated 10 April and 23 December 1903, now in the Kaiser-Ramaker library of Sioux Falls College and Seminary in Sioux Falls, South Dakota.

CHAPTER FOUR

1 A term of reproach meaning something like "enthusiastic fanatical dissenters."
2 The materials in English concerning the left-wing groups on the Continent were very small when August Rauschenbusch went abroad in 1869 to collect materials for his book. De Bray's *The Rise, Spring and Foundation of the Anabaptists* (1668) and Brown's *The Life and Times of Menno* (1853) were probably the only books available. Walter Rauschenbusch's English Baptist friend, Richard Heath, published his *Anabaptism from the Rise at Zwickau to its Fall at Münster 1521–1536*, (1895), the first modern book after de Bray. Of course, the Anglo-Saxon left wing is another matter.
3 Rauschenbusch, "The Zurich Anabaptists and Thomas Muenzer," 91.
4 Ibid., 91.
5 Littel, *The Anabaptist View of the Church*, 19.
6 *Rochester Theological Seminary Bulletin* 69, no. 3 (November 1918): 33–4.
7 Rauschenbusch, *The Freedom of Spiritual Religion*, 12.
8 Ibid., 13.
9 Rauschenbusch, "The Revolutionary Ancestry of the Congregationalists and Baptists."
10 Rauschenbusch, "The Influence of Historical Studies on Theology," 125.
11 From *The Watchman*, 1899, quoted in Moehlman, ed., "Rauschenbusch Scrapbook," 41.
12 Hudson, "Baptists are not Anabaptists," 171–8. See also his essay "Who were the Baptists?" 303–12.
13 Troeltsch, *Protestantism and Progress*, 124–6.
14 Payne, *The Anabaptists of the Sixteenth Century*, 5ff; see also Bender, "The Anabaptists and Religious Liberty," 83–100.
15 Jones, *Studies in Mystical Religion*, 369.
16 Quoted in Torbet, *A History of the Baptists*, 7.
17 Ibid., 54. See also Scheffer and de Gijsbert's *History of the Free Churchmen* for important evidence on the relationship between Baptists and Anabaptists. More recent research into this problem was done by the late Irvin Horst at the University of Amsterdam.
18 Rauschenbusch, "The Church and Money Power," *Proceedings of the Baptist Congress* 20 (1894): 10–17.
19 Rauschenbusch, *Christianizing the Social Order*, 49.
20 Rauschenbusch, *A Theology for the Social Gospel*, 142.
21 Ibid., 131.
22 Rauschenbusch, *The Social Principles of Jesus*, 60.
23 Rauschenbusch, *Christianizing the Social Order*, 83.
24 Rauschenbusch, "The Prophetic Character of the Anabaptist Movement."

25 Rauschenbusch's successor at Rochester, C.H. Moehlman, wrote a letter to me on 25 July 1955 in which he said, "He [W.R.] followed the latest German scholars in that regard [Anabaptism] and presented a very sympathetic approach to left-wing movements. He laid stress on their communism. He recommended highly the book by Vedder on Hubmaier." See Vedder, *Balthasar Hubmaier, The Leader of the Anabaptists*.

26 Rauschenbusch, *Christianizing the Social Order*, 93.

27 Rauschenbusch, "The New Apostolate," quoted in Sharpe, *Walter Rauschenbusch*, 343.

28 H. Richard Niebuhr, *The Kingdom of God in America*, x–xi.

29 Rauschenbusch, *A Theology for the Social Gospel*, 151.

30 Ibid., 99.

31 Ibid., 174–5.

32 Weiss, *Jesus' Proclamation of the Kingdom of God*; Schweitzer, *The Quest for the Historical Jesus*.

33 Sharpe, *Walter Rauschenbusch*, 43.

34 Quoted in ibid., 57.

35 Ibid., 57–8.

36 Bodein, *The Social Gospel of Walter Rauschenbusch*, 16.

37 Rauschenbusch, "The Religion of the Passion Play," 21.

38 Rauschenbusch, *Christianizing the Social Order*, 49, and *The Social Principles of Jesus*, 52.

39 Strong, *Systematic Theology*.

40 See Longford's essay affirming the basic agreement between Rauschenbusch and Strong, *The Chronicle*, 3–19.

41 Visser t' Hooft, *The Background of the Social Gospel in America*, 37, 51, 64.

42 Moehlman, ed., "Rauschenbusch Scrapbook", vol. 3, 71.

43 Rauschenbusch, "The Unspoken Thoughts of Jesus," 31.

44 Rauschenbusch, *Christianity and the Social Crisis*, 414.

45 Rauschenbusch, *The Social Principles of Jesus*, 108.

46 Matthew 10: 8–10.

47 Rauschenbusch, *Christianity and the Social Crisis*, 140–1.

48 Rauschenbusch, *Unto Me*, 13–14.

49 Ibid., 28.

50 Rauschenbusch, "The New Evangelism" (1904), in Moehlman, ed., "Rauschenbusch Scrapbook," vol. 2, n.p.

51 Ibid.

52 Rauschenbusch, *Christianity and the Social Crisis*, 341.

53 Ibid.

54 *Rochester Democrat and Chronicle*, 15 September 1903. See also Rauschenbusch, *A Theology for the Social Gospel*, 195–6.

55 Rauschenbusch, *Christianity and the Social Crisis*, 314–15. Rauschenbusch has a long quotation from Tolstoy in *The Social Principles of Jesus*, 50, supporting the kingdom idea.

56 Rauschenbusch, "The Influence of Historical Studies on Theology," 123.

57 Rauschenbusch, *Christianity and the Social Crisis*, 401–2.

58 Ibid., 401.

59 See chapter 5 herein, especially 000–000.

60 Bender, "The Anabaptist Theology of Discipleship," 30.

61 Visser t' Hooft, *The Background of the Social Gospel in America*, 51, 64.

62 Dombrowski, *The Early Days of Christian Socialism*.

63 Rauschenbusch, *Christianizing the Social Order*, 96, 125.

64 Ibid., 96.

65 *Rochester Democrat and Chronicle*, 15 September 1903.

66 *Springfield Daily Republican*, 1 December 1908, 7.

67 Bender, "The Anabaptist Theology of Discipleship," 31–2.

68 McNeill, *Modern Christian Movements*, 68.

69 See Horst, *The Radical Brethren: Anabaptists and the English Reformation*. See also H. Richard Niebuhr and Waldo Beach, "Ethics of Puritanism and Quakerism," ch. 10 in *Christian Ethics, Sources of the Living Tradition*.

70 Rauschenbusch, *Christianity and the Social Crisis*, 8.

71 Ibid., 139–40.

72 Ibid., 65.

73 Ibid., 66–7.

74 Rauschenbusch, "Die Geschichte der Idee des Reiches Gottes," in Moehlman, ed., "Rauschenbusch Scrapbook," vol. 1, 14–15.

75 See Study I, "Anabaptism and Pietism," in his *Mennonite Piety Through the Centuries*, and his essay "Anabaptism and Pietism," 144–69.

76 Rauschenbusch, *Christianizing the Social Order*, 270–1.

77 Rauschenbusch, *Unto Me*, 19.

78 Ibid., 20–1.

79 Rauschenbusch, *A Theology for the Social Gospel*, 48.

80 Rauschenbusch, *The Social Principles of Jesus*, 38.

81 Ibid., 9. See also Rauschenbusch, *Unto Me*, 49.

82 Rauschenbusch, *Dare We Be Christians?*, 44.

83 Rauschenbusch, *Christianizing the Social Order*, 43–4.

84 See Rauschenbusch, *Dare We Be Christians?*, 46, and *Christianizing the Social Order*, 332.

85 *Dare We Be Christians?* was written in 1914, after *Christianity and the Social Crisis* (1907) and *Christianizing the Social Order* (1912), and three years before his Yale lectures, *A Theology for the Social Gospel*, 1917.

86 Rauschenbusch, *Dare We Be Christians?*, 43–4.

87 Stephen Rauschenbusch, the son of Walter, was the chief investigator for the Nye Munitions Investigating Committee of the US Senate in the 1930s.

88 Rauschenbusch, "The Ideals of Social Reformers," 216. The interpretation of this passage as pragmatic pacifism is based on his argument that force is not effective.

89 Ibid., 216.

90 Rauschenbusch, "The Related Races and the Social Problem,"
    Moehlman, ed., "Rauschenbusch Scrapbook", vol. 3, 30. This is part of
    an address to the American Missionary Association.

91 See the *Rochester Democrat and Chronicle*, 15 September 1903.

92 Rauschenbusch, "The Zurich Anabaptists and Thomas Muenzer," 91.

93 Rauschenbusch, "What is a Christian Nation?" Moehlman, ed., "Rau-
    schenbusch Scrapbook", vol. 2.

94 Ibid.

95 Visser t' Hooft, *The Background of the Social Gospel in America*, 53.

96 Ibid., 102.

97 Rauschenbusch's *A Theology for the Social Gospel* develops his sociology
    most completely, especially chapter 8, "The Super-Personal Forces of
    Evil," and chapter 11, "The Salvation of the Super-Personal Forces."

98 Ibid., 96, 110.

99 Ibid.

100 See ibid., 114.

101 Rauschenbusch, *A Theology for the Social Gospel*, 116.

102 Ibid.

103 Rauschenbusch, "The Church and Money Power," *Proceedings of the Bap-
    tist Congress* 11.(1894): 10–17; also quoted in Moehlman, ed., "Rauschen-
    busch Scrapbook," 51.

104 Ibid.

105 Peachey, "Social Background and Social Philosophy of the Swiss Ana-
    baptists," 105, 113.

106 Rauschenbusch, *A Theology for the Social Gospel*, 122.

107 Rauschenbusch, "Why I Am a Baptist," 24.

108 Ibid., 11.

109 For a more precise outline of his views of the division between church
    and state see "The Relation of Church and State," *Proceedings of the Bap-
    tist Congress* 8 (1889): 138–140. Also quoted in Moehlman, ed., "Rauschen-
    busch Scrapbook," 39–43.

110 Rauschenbusch, *Christianity and the Social Crisis*, 192–3.

111 Ibid., 193.

112 Ibid., 116.

113 Ibid., 118.

114 Ibid.

115 Ibid., 119–20.

116 Heath, *The Captive City of God*, 26.

117 Ibid., 48.

118 Ibid., 75–6.

119 Ibid., 90–1.

120 Ibid., 93.

121 Ibid., 145.

122 The final paragraph of Heath's book on Anabaptism contains a moving tribute to the eternal power of these Continental sectarians, a tribute that Rauschenbusch would have supported wholeheartedly. See Heath, *Anabaptism*, 193–4.

123 de Laveleye, *Protestantism and Catholicism*, 27–8.

124 Ibid., 29, 43.

125 Ibid., 46.

126 Rauschenbusch, *Christianizing the Social Order*, 70; Vedder, *Socialism and the Ethics of Jesus*.

127 Vedder was also the author of *Balthasar Hubmaier* and in general reflected the learning in Anabaptist materials of the mid-nineteenth century. His chapter on the Anabaptists in *Socialism and the Ethics of Jesus* recommends the reading of Kautsky, Bax, and Heath. His chapter on the "Social Failure of the Church" recommends Harnack, Wernle, Weizsäcker, Schmidt, Ulhorn, Weiss, Sabatier, Frene, Pfleiderer, Geffcken, Hergenröther, and Stevens.

128 Vedder, *Socialism and the Ethics of Jesus*, 475–6.

129 While Rauschenbusch recommended reading Vedder, the latter also recommended the former, listing *Christianity and the Social Crisis* in the last chapter of his book on socialism (*Socialism and the Ethics of Jesus*, 482) as one of the basic works on the social question. Others listed by Vedder include Peabody, Mathews, Ely, Campbell, Stelze, Brown, Hodges, Reichert, Thompson, and Spargo.

130 By periodization I mean Rauschenbusch's concept that the Kingdom of God breaks through into history with varying degrees of intensity and through changing religious and cultural movements. Each of the latter has its own unique character. The changing eras or periods dominated by one of these kingdom-bearing movements is the essential meaning of periodization.

131 Rauschenbusch, *Christianity and the Social Crisis*, 142.

132 Ibid., chapter 4.

133 Rauschenbusch, *Christianity and the Social Order*, 56.

134 Ibid., 63.

135 Rauschenbusch, *A Theology for the Social Gospel*, 215.

136 Rauschenbusch, *The Freedom of Spiritual Religion*, 13.

137 *Springfield Daily Republican*, 1 December 1908.

CHAPTER FIVE

1 Sheldon, *In His Steps: What Would Jesus Do?*; Gabriel, *The Course of American Democratic Thought*; Denison, "Professor George D. Herron, D.D. – A Sketch of His Life and Character," 18.

2 See Schweitzer, *The Quest for the Historical Jesus*, 11–12.

3 Albert Schweitzer, *ibid.*; Weiss, *Jesus' Proclamation of the Kingdom of God*.

4 Mead and Nichols, "The History of Christianity since 1650."

5 McKelvey, "Walter Rauschenbusch's Rochester," 1.

6 Zucker, ed., *The Forty-Eighters, Political Refugees of the German Revolution of 1848*.

7 McKelvey, "Walter Rauschenbusch's Rochester," 3.

8 Rauschenbusch, *Christianity and the Social Crisis*, 264.

9 Kant, *Religion Within the Limits of Reason Alone*, xxii.

10 See especially *The Christian Faith*.

11 Rauschenbusch, *A Theology for the Social Gospel*, 125.

12 Ibid., 92.

13 Ibid.

14 Ibid., 265.

15 Pinson, *Pietism as a Factor in the Rise of German Nationalism*.

16 Ritschl, *The Christian Doctrine of Justification and Reconciliation*, 252, 288.

17 Swing, *Theology of Albrecht Ritschl*, which includes Ritschl's "Instruction in the Christian Religion," 175, 197–8.

18 Ibid., 175.

19 Ritschl, *Justification and Reconciliation*, 135.

20 Ibid., 273, 282.

21 Ibid., 335.

22 See ibid., 289.

23 Rauschenbusch, *A Theology for the Social Gospel*, 125–7.

24 Royce, *The Problem of Christianity*, vol. 1, 95.

25 Ibid., 122.

26 Ibid., n.p.

27 Ibid., xv-xvi. See also James, *Varieties of Religious Experience*, 518–19.

28 Royce, *The Problem of Christianity*, vol. 1, 116.

29 Rauschenbusch, *Christianizing the Social Order*, 9.

30 Foster, *History of New England Theology*, 412. Horace Bushnell's theology was liberal but his ethics were those of a Tory. He thought it was against the will of God to interfere in any way with the operation of economic law.

31 Rauschenbusch, *Christianity and the Social Crisis*, 46. Karl August Hase (1800–90) belonged to what Schweitzer calls the last phase of rationalism, according to which miracles are explained, the resurrection may have taken place after a return of consciousness, and the birth stories and "legends of childhood" are abandoned. The life of Jesus is divided into two periods: the first, during which he accepted the prevailing messianic ideas; the second, when he formulated his own. John alone avoids the eschatological errors of the first period. See Schweitzer, *The Quest for the Historical Jesus*, 58–62.

32 Rauschenbusch, *Christianity and the Social Crisis*, 53.

33 Schweitzer, *The Quest for the Historical Jesus*, 254–5.

34 Schweitzer called Weiss's *Die Predigt Jesu vom Reiche Gottes* "one of the most important books in historical theology. It seems to break a spell. It closes one epoch and begins another." To explain its comparative lack of impact he points to its brevity (sixty-seven pages) and the fact that major theological shifts take from one to two generations. The latter point suggests why Rauschenbusch simply could not get "inside" the Weiss-Schweitzer position. See Schweitzer, *The Quest for the Historical Jesus*, 238.

35 Moehlman, personal letter to the author, dated 25 July 1955.

36 See Mathews, *New Faith for the Old: An Autobiography*.

37 Ibid., 120.

38 Mathews, *The Social Teachings of Jesus* 54, 62; see also 73, 75. This book was a rewritten version of a series of articles first published in the *American Journal of Sociology*.

39 Peabody, *Jesus Christ and the Social Question*, 285.

40 Particularly important for Rauschenbusch was Harnack's *The Mission and Expansion of Christianity in the First Three Centuries*. This work was originally published in 1906 as *Mission und Ausbreitung des Christentums in den ersten drei Jahrhunderten*. Rauschenbusch's *Christianity and the Social Crisis* contains five major references to it.

41 Rauschenbusch, *A Theology for the Social Gospel*, 25.

42 Harnack, *History of Dogma*, vol. 1, 1–8.

43 Ibid., vol. 1, 107–8.

44 Harnack, *What is Christianity?*

45 Harnack, *History of Dogma*, n.p.

46 Rauschenbusch, *A Theology for the Social Gospel*, 28; Troeltsch, *The Social Teaching of the Christian Churches*, vol. 1, n.p.

47 H.R. Niebuhr, "Ernst Troeltsch," 96.

48 Mackintosh, *Types of Modern Theology*, 193–4.

49 Rauschenbusch, "The Influence of Historical Studies on Theology," 54.

50 Rauschenbusch, "The Value and the Use of History," Moehlman, ed., "Rauschenbusch Scrapbook," vol. 3 (May 1914).

51 Shinn, *Christianity and the Problem of History* 125. See also the critique of Rauschenbusch as church historian by George Hunston Williams in his chapter on church history in Nash, ed., *Protestant Thought in the Twentieth Century*.

52 Rauschenbusch, *Christianizing the Social Order*, 394.

53 Sharpe, *Walter Rauschenbusch*, 80. This manuscript was lent to me by D.R. Sharpe.

54 Ibid., 426.

55 Barker, *Henry George*, 621.

56 Egbert and Persons, eds., *Socialism and American Life*, vol. 1, 241.

57 Geiger, *The Philosophy of Henry George*, 384.

58 Rauschenbusch, "Natural and Artificial Monopolies," in Moehlman, ed., "Rauschenbusch Scrapbook," 36.

59 George, *Progress and Poverty*.

60 Geiger, *The Philosophy of Henry George*, 375.

61 George, *Progress and Poverty*, 523.

62 Geiger, *The Philosophy of Henry George*, 340, quoting George.

63 George, *Progress and Poverty*, 552.

64 Ibid., 405.

65 Rauschenbusch, *Christianity and the Social Crisis*, 229.

66 Sharpe, *Walter Rauschenbusch*, 197, 426; Bodein, *The Social Gospel of Walter Rauschenbusch*, 5; Ward, "Walter Rauschenbusch," vol. 15, 302; Minus, *Walter Rauschenbusch, American Reformer*, 65–6.

67 Bliss, *Encyclopedia of Social Reform*, 107. Bliss says of Bellamy's novels as a whole: "They are dreamy, fantastic novels but with such power that Mr Howells declared that 'the mantle of Hawthorne has fallen upon Mr Bellamy.'"

68 Rauschenbusch, "That Boston Fad," *Christian Inquirer*, August 1889, quoted in Bodein, *The Social Gospel of Walter Rauschenbusch*, 5.

69 See his criticism of socialism in "Christian Socialism," *A Dictionary of Religion and Ethics*, 90–1.

70 Smith, "The Religion of Edward Bellamy," 90–1, quoting from Bellamy's *Equality*.

71 Bellamy, *Looking Backward*, 234–5.

72 Smith, "The Religion of Edward Bellamy," 106–7.

73 Morgan, *Edward Bellamy*, 203.

74 Bellamy, "Equality" (1897), quoted in Morgan, *Edward Bellamy*, 303–4.

75 Bellamy, *Looking Backward*, 238–9.

76 Quoted in Morgan, *Edward Bellamy*, 304.

77 Sharpe, *Walter Rauschenbusch*, 426.

78 Troeltsch, *The Social Teachings of the Christian Churches*, vol. 2, 795.

79 Ibid., 728–9.

80 Rauschenbusch, *Christianizing the Social Order*, 310.

81 Ibid., 309–10.

82 Sharpe, *Walter Rauschenbusch*, 84.

83 Rauschenbusch, *Christianizing the Social Order*, 41.

84 Gangulee, ed., *Giuseppe Mazzini, Selected Writings*, part 6, "Religious and Moral Outlook," 189–213; Minus, *Walter Rauschenbusch*, 66.

85 Quoted in Silone, *The Living Thoughts of Mazzini*, 20–1.

86 Quoted in ibid., 40–1.

87 Laidler, *Social-Economic Movements*, 185.

88 Rauschenbusch, *Christianity and the Social Crisis*, 386.

89 In Rauschenbusch, *Christianizing the Social Order*, 395.
90 Rauschenbusch, *The Social Principles of Jesus*, 196.

CHAPTER SIX

1 Sharpe, *Walter Rauschenbusch*, 197. Both Maurice and Kingsley are mentioned in his first book, the original draft of which was prepared in Europe in 1891, although it was not published until 1907.
2 Rauschenbusch, *A Theology for the Social Gospel*, 29.
3 Ibid.
4 H. Richard Niebuhr and Waldo Beach, eds., *Christian Ethics*. They stress the theological distance between Maurice and the early formulations of the American social gospel.
5 See Maurice, *The Kingdom of Christ*. See also Reckitt, *Maurice to Temple*, 97.
6 Adams, "Christian Socialism," vol. 20, 639.
7 Quoted in Reckitt, *Maurice to Temple*, 84.
8 Quoted in Binyon, *The Christian Socialist Movement in England*, 88.
9 Raven, *Christian Socialism 1848–1854*, 93–4.
10 Kingsley, *Sermons for the Times*, 310.
11 Vedder, *Socialism and the Ethics of Jesus*, 201–2.
12 Kingsley, *Sermons for the Times*, 301–2.
13 de Laveleye, *De la Propriété et de ses Formes Primitives*.
14 In *Christianity and the Social Crisis*, 89.
15 Quoted in Laidler, *Social-Economic Movements*, 117.
16 Barth, *Die Protestantische Theologie im 19. Jahrhundert*.
17 See the translator's introduction in Kutter, *They Must*.
18 The American edition of Kutter's *They Must* contains an advertisement for the book and for Rauschenbusch's *Christianity and the Social Crisis*. Of Kutter's volume it is said, "This is the most startling, thrilling and inspiring contribution to the literature of Christian socialism – truly the voice of a prophet of God." Of Rauschenbusch's book: "The latest and best American book on Christian Socialism."
19 Kutter, *They Must*, 120–1.
20 Ibid., 176.
21 Ibid., 109.
22 Ibid.
23 Niebuhr, *The Kingdom of God in America*, xi-xii.
24 Kutter, *They Must*, 87.
25 Ibid., 88–9.
26 Ibid., 133.
27 Ragaz, *Der Kampf um das Reich Gottes in Blumhardt Vater und Sohn – und Weiter!*, 25.

28 Ragaz, *Le Message revolutionaire*, 230.
29 Ragaz, *Israel, Judaism and Christianity*, 60.
30 He expressed great love for the Quakers. One of the leading German Quakers, Emil Fuchs, reciprocated in his book *Leonhard Ragaz! Prophet Unserer Zeit*.

CHAPTER SEVEN

1 Hutchison, ed., *Christian Faith and Social Action*, 8–9.
2 May, *Protestant Churches and Industrial America*; Dombrowski, *The Early Days of Christian Socialism in America*.

APPENDIX

1 The Pin Oak Baptist Church, Gasconade County, Mt Sterling, Missouri, first record book, Eden Seminary archives.
2 Luker, *The Social Gospel in Black and White American Racial Reform, 1885–1912* (Chapel Hill: University of North Carolina Press, 1991).
3 Quoted in Luker, 416.
4 King, *Stride Toward Freedom*, 91.
5 Lewis, *King, A Critical Biography*, (New York: Praeger, 1978), 29.
6 Stackhouse, "Eschatology and Ethical Method," 1965.
7 Stackhouse, *Christian Century*, 25 January 1989.

Bibliography

COLLECTIONS OF RAUSCHENBUSCH PAPERS

COLGATE-ROCHESTER DIVINITY SCHOOL, Rochester, New York 14620 holds the definitive collection of Rauschenbusch materials, the Rauschenbusch Family Papers. This collection acquired its distinction when the monumental library of D.R. Sharpe came to Colgate-Rochester. Sharpe was Rauschenbusch's first secretary and his first biographer. C.W. Moehlman, Rauschenbusch's successor in Church History, also aided the collection with his "Rauschenbusch Scrapbook."

SIOUX FALLS COLLEGE, South Dakota, is the main college and seminary of the North American Baptists, formerly the German Baptist Church, to which August and Walter Rauschenbusch belonged. The college's Kaiser-Ramaker Library has an extensive file of materials.

EDEN THEOLOGICAL SEMINARY in St Louis has a collection of letters written by August Rauschenbusch to individuals in Germany and America.

ELMHURST COLLEGE near Chicago has papers collected by Rudolph Schaade, former pastor of the Second Baptist Church of Hell's Kitchen in New York City, where Walter served for eleven years. Schaade was on the Elmhurst faculty.

SECONDARY SOURCES

Adams, James Luther. "Christian Socialism." *Encyclopedia Britannica*. fourteenth ed. Vol. 20. Chicago: Encyclopedia Britannica, 1950.

Allen, Jimmy R. "A Comparative Study of the Concept of the Kingdom of God in the Writings of Walter Rauschenbusch and Reinhold Niebuhr." Ph.D dissertation. Southwestern Baptist Theological Seminary, 1958.

Altschuler, Glenn C. "Walter Rauschenbusch: Theology, the Church, and the Social Gospel." *Foundations* 39 (April-June 1979): 140–51.

Ashmall, Donald H. "Spiritual Development and the Free Church Tradition: The Inner Pilgrimage." *Andover-Newton Quarterly* 21 (January 1980): 141–52.

Bainton, Roland. *Christian Attitudes toward War and Peace*. New York: Abingdon Press, 1960.

– "The Left Wing of the Reformation." *Journal of Religion* 21 (April 1941): 125–34.

– *The Reformation of the Sixteenth Century*. Boston: Beacon Press, 1952.

Barker, Charles Albro. *Henry George*. New York: Oxford University Press, 1955.

Barnett, Henlee Hulix. "The Ethical Thought of Walter Rauschenbusch." Ph.D dissertation. Southern Baptist Theological Seminary, 1948.

Baillie, John, et al., eds. *The Library of Christian Classics*. 26 vols. Philadelphia: The Westminster Press, 1953–66.

Barth, Karl. *Die Protestantische Theologie im 19. Jahrhundert*. Zurich: Evangelischer Verlag Ag., 1947.

Bell, Aaron Ignatius. *The Urban Impact on American Protestantism*. Cambridge: Harvard University Press, 1943.

Bellamy, Edward. *Looking Backward*. New York: Modern Library, 1951.

Bender, Harold S. "The Anabaptist Theology of Discipleship." *Mennonite Quarterly Review* 24 (1950): 25–32.

– "The Anabaptists and Religious Liberty." *Mennonite Quarterly Review* 29 (1955): 83–100.

– *Conrad Grebel*. Goshen, IN: Mennonite Historical Society, 1950.

Binyon, Gilbert Clive. *The Christian Socialist Movement in England*. London: Society for Promotion of Christian Knowledge, 1931.

Bliss, W.D.P. *Encyclopedia of Social Reform*. New York: Funk and Wagnalls, 1908.

Bodein, Vernon Parker. *The Social Gospel of Walter Rauschenbusch and Its Relation to Religious Education*. New Haven: Yale University Press, 1944.

Bond, Richard Ellison, Jr. "A Critical Analysis of the Concept of Justice in Paul Tillich, Heinrich Rommen, and Walter Rauschenbusch." Ph.D dissertation. Yale University, 1972.

Brackney, William Henry. *The Baptists*. Westport, CT: Greenwood Press, 1988.

Brackney, William Henry, and Susan Fischer. *A Guide to Manuscript Collections in the American Baptist Historical Society*. Valley Forge, PA: 1986.

Brown, J. Newton. *The Life and Times of Menno*. Philadelphia, 1853.

Brunson, Drexel Timothy. "The Quest for Social Justice: A Study of Walter Rauschenbusch and His Influence on Reinhold Niebuhr and Martin Luther King, Jr." Ph.D dissertation. Florida State University, 1980.

Bryant, M. Darrol. "Sin and Society." In *Society and Original Sin*, edited by D. Foster and P. Mojzes. Weaverville, CA: New Era Books, 1985.

Burckhardt, Abel E. "Walter Rauschenbusch as a Representative of American Humanism." Th.M dissertation. Union Theological Seminary, 1925.

Burkholder, J.R., and Calvin W. Redekop, eds. *Kingdom, Cross and Community*. Scottdale: Herald Press, 1976.

Clipshaw, Ernest F. "An Englishman Looks at Rauschenbusch." *Southern Baptist Quarterly* 16 (July 1981): 113–21.

Collingwood, R.G. *The Idea of History*. Oxford: Oxford University Press, 1946.

Cornelius, C.A. *Geschichte des Münsterischen Aufruhrs in drei Büchern*. Leipzig: T.O. Weigle, 1860.

Dahlberg, Edwin. "Edwin Dahlberg in Conversation: Memories of Walter Rauschenbusch." Transcribed by John E. Skoglund. *Foundations* 35 (July-September 1975): 209–18.

David, William Edward. "A Comparative Study of the Social Ethics of Walter Rauschenbusch and Reinhold Niebuhr." Ph.D dissertation. Vanderbilt University, 1958.

Davis, Dennis R. "Impact of Evoluntary Thought on Walter Rauschenbusch." *Foundations* 38 (July-September 1978): 254–71.

de Bray, Guido. *The Rise, Spring and Foundation of the Anabaptists*. Cambridge, 1668.

de Laveleye, Emile. *De la Propriété et de ses Formes Primitives*. Paris: Felix Alcan, 1901.

– *Protestantism and Catholicism in Their Bearing upon the Liberty and Prosperity of Nations*. London: John Murray, 1875.

Denison, W.H. "Professor George D. Herron, D.D. – A Sketch of His Life and Character." *Social Gospel* 1, no. 6 (July 1898), 6.

Dickinson, Richard Donald Nye. "The Church's Responsibility for Society – Rauschenbusch and Niebuhr: Brothers Under the Skin." *Religion in Life* 26 (Spring 1958): 163–71.

Dombrowski, James. *The Early Days of Christian Socialism*. New York: Columbia University Press, 1936.

Durant, J., ed. *Darwinism and Divinity*. London: Basil Blackwell, 1985.

Eberts, Harry William. "The Legacy of Walter Rauschenbusch." *Religion in Life* 36 (Fall 1968): 382–400.

Ede, Alfred J. "Social Theologies of Walter Rauschenbusch and Vatican II in Dialogue." *Foundations* 35 (July-September 1975): 198–208.

Egbert, Donald Drew, and Stow Persons, eds. *Socialism and American Life*. Princeton: Princeton University Press, 1952.

Erb, Peter, ed. *On Being the Church. Essays in Honor of John W. Snyder*. Waterloo, Ontario: Conrad Press, 1992.

Ferm, Vergilius, ed. *An Encyclopedia of Religion*. New York: The Philosophical Library, 1945.

Fishburn, Janet Forsythe. "Church and Family: The Conflict Between Civil Religion and Sacramental Christianity." *Quarterly Review* 5 (Summer 1985): 54–67.

Foster, D., and P. Mojzes, eds. *Society and Original Sin*. Weaverville, CA: New Era Books, 1985.

Foster, Frank Hugh. *History of New England Theology*. Chicago: University of Chicago Press, 1907.

French, Henry Frank. "The Concept of the Church in the Theology of Walter Rauschenbusch." Ph.D dissertation. Drew University, 1986.

Friedmann, Robert. "Anabaptism and Pietism." *Mennonite Quarterly Review* 14, no. 2 (April 1945): 90–128, and 14, no. 3 (July 1945): 144–69.

– *Mennonite Piety through the Centuries*. Goshen, IN: The Mennonite Historical Society, 1949.

– "Recent Interpretations of Anabaptism." *Church History* 24 (June 1955): 132–49.

Fuchs, Emil. *Leonhard Ragaz! Prophet Unserer Zeit*. Oberursel/Ts.: Kompass Verlag, n.d.

Gabriel, Ralph Henry. *The Course of American Democratic Thought*. New York: Ronald Press, 1940.

Gangulee, N. *Giuseppe Mazzini, Selected Writings*. London: Lindsay Drummond, 1944.

Garrow, David J. "The Intellectual Development of Martin Luther King, Jr: Influence and Commentaries." *Union Seminary Review* 42 (1986): 5–20.

Geiger, George R. *The Philosophy of Henry George*. New York: Macmillan, 1933.

George, Henry. *Progress and Poverty*. New York: Random House, 1879.

Gottschalk, Louis. *Understanding History: A Primer on Historical Method*. New York: Alfred A. Knopf, 1950.

Grumberg, Paul, and Carl Mirbt. "Pietism." *Schaff-Herzog Encyclopedia of Religious Knowledge*. Vol. 9. New York: Funk and Wagnalls, 1911.

Handy, Robert T. "Christianity and Socialism in America, 1900–1920." *Church History* 8 (March 1952): 39–54.

Harnack, Adolph von. *Outline of the History of Dogma*. Translated by Edwin Knox Mitchell. Boston: Starr King Press, 1957.

– *The Mission and Expansion of Christianity in the First Three Centuries*. New York: Putnam and Co., 1908.

– *What is Christianity?* London: Headley Bros., 1901.

Hauerwas, Stanley M. "The Pastor as Prophet: Ethical Reflections on an Improbable Mission." In *The Pastor as Prophet*, edited by E. Shelp and R. Sunderland. New York: Pilgrim Press, 1985.

Hauerwas, Stanley M., and Mark Sherwindt. "The Kingdom of God: An Ecclesial Space for Peace." *Word and World* 2 (Spring 1982): 127–36.

Heath, Richard. *Anabaptism from Its Rise at Zwickau to Its Fall at Münster, 1525–1536*. London: Alexander and Shepherd, 1895.

– *The Captive City of God*. London: Headley Bros., 1905.

Hege, Christian, and Christian Neff, eds. *Mennonitisches Lexikon*. Vol. 3. Frankfurtam Main unter Weierhof: Pfalz, 1913.

Hershberger, Guy F. "The Modern Social Gospel and the Way of the Cross." *Mennonite Quarterly Review* 23 (April 1956): 83–103.

Hershberger, Guy F., ed. *The Recovery of the Anabaptist Vision*. Scottdale: Herald Press, 1957.

Hopkins, Charles Howard. *The Rise of the Social Gospel in American Protestantism, 1865–1915*. New Haven: Yale University Press, 1940.

Horne, Cleveland R., Jr. "Christian Economic Ethics: A Study of Contemporary Thought in the Light of the Works of Walter Rauschenbusch." Ph.D dissertation. Southwestern Baptist Theological Seminary, 1956.

Horst, Irvin B. *The Radical Brethren: Anabaptists and the English Reformation*. Nieuwkopp: DeGraaf, 1972.

Hudson, Winthrop S. "Baptists are not Anabaptists." *The Chronicle* (journal of the American Baptist Historical Society) 16 (October 1953): 171–8.

– "Walter Rauschenbusch and the New Evangelicalism." *Religion in Life* 29 (Summer 1961): 412–30.

– "Who were the Baptists?" *Baptist Quarterly* 16, no. 7 (July 1956): 303–12.

Hutchison, John A., ed. *Christian Faith and Social Action*. New York: Charles Scribner's Sons, 1953.

James, William. *Varieties of Religious Experience*. London: Longmans Green and Co., 1914.

Johnson, Carl Elbert. "Walter Rauschenbusch as Historian." Ph.D dissertation. Duke University, 1976.

Johnson, J., ed. *The Bible in American Law*. Philadelphia: Fortress Press, 1985.

Jones, Rufus. *Studies in Mystical Religion*. London: Macmillan, 1923.

Kant, Immanuel. *Religion within the Limits of Reason Alone*. Translated and introduced by Theodore M. Greene and Hoyt H. Hudson. Chicago: The Open Court Publishing Co., 1934.

King, Jr, Martin Luther. *Stride Toward Freedom*. New York: Harper & Brothers, 1958.

King, William M. "The Biblical Base of the Social Gospel." In *The Bible and Social Reform*, edited by E. Sandeen. Philadelphia: Fortress Press, 1982.

Kingsley, Charles. *Sermons for the Times*. London: Macmillan, 1884.

Kutter, Herman. *Social Democracy: Does it Mean Darkness or Light?* Letchworth: Garden City Press, 1910.

– *They Must; or, God and the Social Democracy*. Chicago: Co-operative Printing Co., 1906.

Laidler, Harry W. *Social-Economic Movements*. New York: Thomas Y. Crowell, 1948.

Latourette, Kenneth Scott. "Foreword." In Robert G. Torbet. *A History of the Baptists*. Philadelphia: Judson Press, 1950.

Lewis, David L. *King: A Critical Biography*. New York: Praeger, 1979.

Littel, Franklin H. *The Anabaptist View of the Church*. Philadelphia: American Society of Church History, 1952.

Longford, S. Fraser. *The Chronicle* 25 (1962).

Luker, Ralph E. *The Social Gospel In Black and White*. Chapel Hill: University of North Carolina Press, 1991.

McClintock, David Alan. "Walter Rauschenbusch: The Kingdom of God and the American Experience." Ph.D dissertation. Case Western Reserve University, 1975.

McGiffert, Jr, A.C. "Rauschenbusch After Twenty Years." *Christendom* 3 (Autumn 1938): 98–109.

McInerny, Jr, William Francis. "Scripture and Christian Ethics: An Evaluative Analysis of the Uses of Scripture in the Works of Walter Rauschenbusch." Ph.D dissertation. Marquette University, 1984.

McKelvey, Blake. "Walter Rauschenbusch's Rochester." *Rochester History* 14, no. 4 (October 1952): 1–16.

Mackintosh, H.R. *Types of Modern Theology*. New York: Charles Scribner's Sons, 1937.

McNab, John Ingram. "Towards a Theology of Social Concern: A Comparative Study of the Elements for Social Concern in the Writings of Frederick D. Maurice and Walter Rauschenbusch." Ph.D dissertation. McGill University, 1972.

McNeill, John T. *Modern Christian Movements*. New York: Harper and Row, 1968.

Magill, Sherry Patricia. "The Political Thought of Walter Rauschenbusch: Toward a Religious Theory of the Positive State." Ph.D dissertation. Syracuse University, 1984.

Marney, Carlyle. "The Significance of Walter Rauschenbusch for Today." *Foundations* 19 (1959): 13–26.

Massanari, Ronald Lee. "The Sacred Workshop of God: Reflections on the Historical Perspective of Walter Rauschenbusch." *Religion in Life* 39 (Summer 1971): 257–66.

Mathews, Shailer. *New Faith for the Old. An Autobiography*. Macmillan, 1907. Reprint. New York: Macmillan, 1936.

– *The Social Teachings of Jesus*. New York: Macmillan, 1897.

Mathews, Shailer, and Gerald Birney Smith, eds. *A Dictionary of Religion and Ethics*. Macmillan, 1923. Reprint. Detroit: Gale Research Company, 1973.

Maurice, F.D. *The Kingdom of Christ. Hints to a Quaker*. 1864. Reprint. London: J. Clarke, 1959.

May, Henry F. *Protestant Churches and Industrial America*. New York: Harper and Bros., 1941.

Mead, Sidney Earl, and James Hastings Nichols. "The History of Christianity since 1650." Unpublished lecture notes. University of Chicago, n.d.

Meriwether, David Peck. "An Exercise in Ethical Method: An Analysis of the Ethics of Walter Rauschenbusch with Reference to his Views on Economic Morality." Ph.D dissertation. Duke University, 1986.

Minus, Paul. *Walter Rauschenbusch, American Reformer*. New York: Macmillan, 1988.

Moehlman, Conrad H., ed. "Rauschenbusch Scrapbook." 3 vols. Unpublished. Los Angeles, 1953.

– "Who is Walter Rauschenbusch?" *Crozer Quarterly* 23 (January 1946): 34–8.

Moellering, Ralph L. "Rauschenbusch in Retrospect." *Concordia* 26 (August 1956): 613–33.

Moore, James R. "Walter Rauschenbusch and the Religious Education of Youth." *Trinity Studies* 1 (Fall 1971):12–29.

Moore, Jim. "Herbert Spencer's Henchmen: The Evolution of Protestant Liberals in Late Nineteenth Century America." In *Darwinism and Divinity*, edited by J. Durant. London: Basil Blackwell, 1985.

Morgan, Arthur E. *Edward Bellamy*. New York: Columbia University Press, 1944.

– *The Philosophy of Edward Bellamy*. New York: King's Crown Press, 1944.

Nash, Arnold S., ed. *Protestant Thought in the Twentieth Century*. New York: Macmillan, 1951.

Niebuhr, H. Richard. *Christ and Culture*. New York: Harper and Bros., 1951.

– "Ernst Troeltsch." In *An Encyclopedia of Religion*, edited by Vergilius Ferm. New York: The Philosophical Library, 1945.

– *The Kingdom of God in America*. Chicago: Willet, Clark and Co., 1937.

Niebuhr, Reinhold. *An Interpretation of Christian Ethics*. New York: Harper and Bros., 1935.

– *The Kingdom of God in America*. Chicago: Willet, Clark and Co., 1937.

– "Walter Rauschenbusch in Historical Perspective." *Religion in Life* 26 (Fall 1958): 527–36.

Niebuhr, Reinhold, and Waldo Beach, eds. *Christian Ethics: Sources of the Living Tradition*. New York: Ronald Press, 1955.

Payne, Ernest A. *The Anabaptists of the Sixteenth Century*. London: Carey Kingsgate Press, 1949.

Peabody, Francis G. *Jesus Christ and the Social Question*. New York: Macmillan, 1900.

Peachey, Paul. "Social Background and Social Philosophy of the Swiss Anabaptists." *Mennonite Quarterly Review* 28 (1955): 105–13.

Pinson, Koppel Schub. *Pietism as a Factor in the Rise of German Nationalism*. 1934. Reprint. New York: Octagon Books, 1968.

Ragaz, Leonhard. *Der Kampf um das Reich Gottes in Blumhardt Vater und Sohn— und Weiter!* Erlenbach-Zurich: Rotapfel Verlag, 1922.
– *Israel, Judaism and Christianity*. London: Victor Gollanez, 1947.
– *Le Message revolutionaire*. Zurich: Neuchatel, 1941.
Ramsey, Paul. "A Theology for Social Action." *Social Action* 12 (15 October 1946): 10.
Randall, Jr, John Herman. "The Churches and Liberal Tradition." *Social Science* 256 (March 1948): 162–3.
Rauschenbusch, Walter. *Christianity and the Social Crisis*. New York: Macmillan, 1907.
– "Christian Socialism." In *A Dictionary of Religion and Ethics*, edited by Shailer Mathews and Gerald Birney Smith. Detroit: Gale Research Company, 1973.
– *Christianizing the Social Order*. New York: Macmillan, 1912.
– *Dare We Be Christians?* Boston: Pilgrim Press, 1914.
– *Die Geschichte der Idee des Reiches Gottes*. Rochester: Rochester Theological Seminary, 1902.
– *For God and the People: Prayers of the Social Awakening*. Boston: Pilgrim Press, 1910.
– *For the Right* (1889–1891). A complete file of this journal, for which Walter Rauschenbusch did much of the writing, is available in microfilm from Yale University. In 1968, Abingdon published the hitherto unpublished edition of *For the Right* edited by Max Stackhouse.
– *The Freedom of Spiritual Religion*. Philadelphia: American Baptist Publication Society, 1910.
– "The Ideals of Social Reformers." *American Journal of Sociology* 2 (September 1896): 202–19.
– "The Influence of Historical Studies on Theology." *American Journal of Theology* 2 (January 1907).
– *Leben und Wirken von August Rauschenbusch*. Kassel: J.G. Oncken, 1901.
– "The New Evangelism." *The Independent* 56 (12 May 1904): 1056–61.
– "The Pulpit in Relation to Social and Political Reform." *Proceedings of the Baptist Congress* 10 (1891): 127–9.
– "The Church and Money Power," *Proceedings of the Baptist Congress* 20 (1892): 10–17.
– "Relations of Church to State." *Proceedings of the Baptist Congress* 18 (1899): 138–40.
– "Does the New Testament Provide a Definite and Permanent Church Policy?" *Proceedings of the Baptist Congress* 22 (1903): 108–15.
– "The Prophetic Character of the Anabaptist Movement." *Rochester Democrat and Chronicle*, 15 September 1903.
– "The Related Races and the Social Problem." In "Rauschenbusch Scrapbook," edited by Conrad H. Moehlman, vol. 3. Unpublished. Los Angeles, 1953.

- "The Religion of the Passion Play." In "Rauschenbusch Scrapbook," edited by Conrad H. Moehlman, vol. 3. Unpublished. Los Angeles, 1953.
- "The Revolutionary Ancestry of the Congregationalists and Baptists." *The Springfield Daily Republican*, 1 December 1908.
- *The Social Principles of Jesus.* New York: Association Press, 1914.
- *A Theology for the Social Gospel.* New York: Macmillan, 1917.
- "The Unspoken Thoughts of Jesus." In *Modern Sermons by World Scholars*, edited by Robert Scott and W.C. Stiles, vol. 8, 22–3. New York: Funk and Wagnall's, 1909.
- "The Zürich Anabaptists and Thomas Müntzer." *American Journal of Theology* 9 (January 1905): 91–106. Portions republished in Harold S. Bender. *Conrad Grebel*, 282–7. Goshen, IN: 1950; and in *Spiritual and Anabaptist Writers*, edited by George H. Williams, 73–85. Vol. 25 of *The Library of Christian Classics*, edited by John Baillie et al. 26 vols. Philadelphia: The Westminster Press, 1953- 66.
- *Unto Me.* Boston: Pilgrim Press, 1912.
- "The Value and Use of History." In "Rauschenbusch Scrapbook," edited by Conrad H. Moehlman, vol. 3. Unpublished. Los Angeles, 1953.
- "What is a Christian Nation?" In "Rauschenbusch Scrapbook," edited by Conrad H. Moehlman, vol. 2. Unpublished. Los Angeles, 1953.
- "Why I Am a Baptist." *Rochester Baptist Monthly* 20 (1905–6): 106–8. Reprinted in *Colgate-Rochester Divinity School Bulletin* 20 (December 1938): 134–6.
- "The Zurich Anabaptists and Thomas Muenzer." *American Journal of Theology* 9 (January 1905): 91–106.
Rauschenbusch, Walter, and Ira Sankey, eds. *Evangeliums Lieder 1. und 2.* New York: Biglow and Main, 1893.
Raven, Charles E. *Christian Socialism 1848–1854.* London: Macmillan, 1920.
Reckitt, Maurice B. *Maurice to Temple.* London: Faber and Faber, 1950.
Ritschl, Albrecht. *The Christian Doctrine of Justification and Reconciliation.* Scribener's, 1900. Reprint. Clifton, NJ: Reference Book Publishers, 1966.
- *Geschichte des Pietismus in der lutheranischen Kirche des 17. und 18. Jahrhunderts.* Bonn: A. Marcus, 1880.
- *Instruction in the Christian Religion.* New York: Longmans, Green, and Co., 1901.
- "Rauschenbusch Number." *Rochester Theological Seminary Bulletin* 69 (November 1918).
Robertson, D.B., ed. *Voluntary Associations.* Richmond: Knox Press, 1966.
Royce, Josiah. *The Problem of Christianity.* 2 vols. New York: Macmillan, 1913.
Sandeen, E., ed. *The Bible and Social Reform.* Philadelphia: Fortress Press, 1982.
Sanks, T. Howland. "Liberation Theology and the Social Gospel: Variations on a Theme." *Theological Studies* 40 (December 1980): 668–82.

Scheffer, Hopp, and Jacob de Gijsbert. *History of the Free Churchmen Called Brownists, Pilgrim Fathers, and Baptists in the Dutch Republic 1578–1701.* Ithaca: Andrus and Church, 1922.

Schirmer, Carolyn Best. "Theological Method in Walter Rauschenbusch: An Analysis and Critique of His Use of the Bible." MA thesis. The American University, 1968.

Schleiermacher, Friedrich Daniel Ernst. *The Christian Faith.* Translated by H.R. Mackintosh and J.S. Stewart. Edinburgh: T. and T. Clark, 1928.

Schneider, Carl E. "The Americanization of August Rauschenbusch." *Church History* 24 (September 1955): 3–14.

– "The German Church on the American Frontier." *Church History* 24 (March 1955): 3–9.

Schweitzer, Albert. *The Quest for the Historical Jesus: a Critical Study of Its Progress from Reimarus to Wrede.* London: Adam and Charles Black, 1963. German ed. 1906.

Scott, Robert, and W.C. Stiles, eds. *Modern Sermons by World Scholars.* 10 vols. New York: Funk and Wagnalls, 1900.

Sharpe, Dores Robinson. *Walter Rauschenbusch.* New York: Macmillan, 1942.

Sheldon, Charles M. *In His Steps: What Would Jesus Do?* Chicago, 1898.

Shelp, E., and R. Sunderland, eds. *The Pastor as Prophet.* New York: Pilgrim Press, 1985.

Shinn, Roger Lincoln. *Christianity and the Problem of History.* New York: Charles Scribner's Sons, 1953.

Silone, Ignazio. *The Living Thoughts of Mazzini.* New York: Longmans, Green and Co., 1939.

Smith, Walter A. "The Religion of Edward Bellamy." MA thesis. Columbia University, 1937.

Smucker, Donovan E. "Anabaptist Historiography in the Scholarship of Today." *Mennonite Quarterly Review* 22 (April 1949): 116–27.

– "The Ethics of Rauschenbusch." In *On Being the Church. Essays in Honor of John W. Snyder,* edited by Peter Erb. Waterloo, Ontario: Conrad Press, 1992.

– "Gelassenheit, Entrepreneurs, and Remnants." In *Kingdom, Cross and Community,* edited by J.R. Burkholder and Calvin W. Redekop. Scottdale: Herald Press, 1976.

– "Multiple Motifs in the Thought of Rauschenbusch: A Study in the Origins of the Social Gospel." *Encounter* 18 (Winter 1958): 14–20.

– "The Origins of Walter Rauschenbusch's Social Ethics." Ph.D dissertation. University of Chicago, 1957.

– "Rauschenbusch's View of the Church as a Dynamic Voluntary Association." In *Voluntary Associations,* edited by D.B. Robertson. Richmond: Knox Press, 1966.

– "Walter Rauschenbusch: Anabaptist, Pietist and Social Prophet." *Mennonite Life* 36 (June 1981): 21–3.

- "Walter Rauschenbusch and Anabaptist Historiography." In *The Recovery of the Anabaptist Vision*, edited by Guy F. Hershberger. Scottdale: Herald Press, 1957.

Stackhouse, Max. "Eschatology and Ethical Method: A Structural Analysis of Contemporary Christian Social Ethics in America with Primary Reference to Walter Rauschenbusch and Reinhold Niebuhr." Ph.D dissertation. Harvard University, 1965.

- "Jesus and Economics: A Century of Reflection." In *The Bible in American Law*, edited by J. Johnson. Philadelphia: Fortress Press, 1985.

- "Rauschenbusch Today: The Legacy of a Loving Prophet." *Christian Century* 87 (25 January 1989).

Stackhouse, Max, ed. *Walter Rauschenbusch: The Righteousness of the Kingdom.* Nashville: Abingdon Press, 1968.

Strain, Charles R. "Toward a Generic Analysis of a Classic of the Social Gospel: An Essay-Review of Walter Rauschenbusch, *Christianity and the Social Crisis.*" *Journal of the American Academy of Religion* 46 (December 1978): 525–41.

- "Walter Rauschenbusch: A Resource for Public Theology." *Union Seminary Quarterly Review* 33 (Fall 1978): 23–34.

Strong, Augustus H. *Systematic Theology.* 3 vols. Philadelphia: Judson Press, 1907–09.

Sweet, William Warren. *Makers of Christianity.* New York: Henry Holt, 1937.
- *The Story of Religion in America.* New York: Charles Scribner's Sons, 1950.

Swing, A.T. *Theology of Albrecht Ritschl.* New York: Longmans, Green and Co., 1901.

Thompson, James J. *Tried by Fire: Southern Baptists and Religious Controversy.* Macon: Mercer, 1982.

Torbet, Robert. *A History of the Baptists.* Philadelphia: Judson Press, 1950.

Trench, William Crowell. "The Social Gospel and the City: Implications for Theological Reconstruction in the Work of Washington Gladden, Josiah Strong, and Walter Rauschenbusch." Ph.D dissertation. Boston University, 1986.

Troeltsch, Ernst. *Protestantism and Progress.* New York: G.P. Putnam's Sons, 1912.

- *The Social Teaching of the Christian Churches.* 3 vols. London: George Allen and Unwin, 1949.

Vedder, Henry C. *Balthasar Hubmaier, The Leader of the Anabaptists.* 1905. Reprint. New York: AMS Press, 1971.

- *Socialism and the Ethics of Jesus.* New York: Macmillan, 1914.

Verhey, Allen Dale. "The Use of Scripture in Moral Discourse: A Case Study of Walter Rauschenbusch." Ph.D dissertation. Yale University, 1975.

Visser t' Hooft, W.A. *The Background of the Social Gospel in America.* Haarlem: H.D. Tjeenk Willink and Zoon, 1928.

Vulgamore, Melvin L. "The Social Gospel Old and New; Walter Rauschenbusch and Harvey Cox." *Religion in Life* 35 (Winter 1967): 516–33.

Ward, Harry. "Walter Rauschenbusch." In *Dictionary of American Biography*, Vol. 8. New York: Charles Scribner's Sons, 1908.

Watley, William Donnel. "Against Principalities: An Examination of Martin Luther King Jr's Nonviolent Ethic." Ph.D dissertation. Columbia University, 1980.

Weatherly, Owen. "A Comparative Study of the Social Ethics of Walter Rauschenbusch and Reinhold Niebuhr." MA thesis. University of Chicago, 1950.

Weeks, Rufus. "Translator's Introduction." In Herman Kutter. *They Must; or, God and the Social Democracy*. Chicago: Co-operative Publishing Co., 1906.

Weiss, Johannes. *Jesus' Proclamation of the Kingdom of God*. Translated by Richard Hyde Hiers and David Laurence. Philadelphia: Fortress Press, 1971.

Wellhausen, Julius. *Israelitische und Judische Geschicte*. Berlin: G. Reimer, 1883.

– *Sketch of the History of Israel and Judah*. Translated by Jay Sutherland Black. Edinburgh: Adam and Charles Black, 1891.

White, Ronald C. "The Social Ministry of the Church: Precedents amd Possibilities." *Covenant Quarterly* 7 (November 1979): 3–12.

Williams, Claude J. "Walter Rauschenbusch: A Prophet of Social Righteousness." Ph.D dissertation. Southern Baptist Theological Seminary, 1952.

Williams, George H. "Church History." In *Protestant Thought in the Twentieth Century*, edited by Arnold S. Nash. New York: Macmillan, 1951.

Williams, George H., ed. *Spiritual and Anabaptist Writers*. Vol. 25 of *The Library of Christian Classics*, edited by John Baillie et al. Philadelphia: The Westminster Press, 1964.

Wray, Frank J. "History in the Eyes of the Sixteenth-Century Anabaptists." Ph.D dissertation. Yale University, 1953.

Zucker, A.S., ed. *The Forty-Eighters, Political Refugees of the German Revolution of 1848*. New York: Columbia University Press, 1950.

Zummach, Charles F. *These Glorious Years: The Centenary History of the German Baptists of North America, 1843–1943*. Cleveland: Roger Williams Press, 1943.

Index